13-593 / > 85

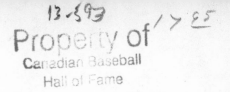

D0124353

WQ - AKE - 914

THE HISTORY OF
NATIONAL LEAGUE
BASEBALL

THE HISTORY OF
NATIONAL
LEAGUE
BASEBALL

SINCE 1876

Glenn Dickey

STEIN AND DAY / *Publishers* / New York

Library of Congress Cataloging in Publication Data

Dickey, Glenn.
    The history of National League baseball.

    Bibliography: p. 301
    Includes index.
    1. National League of Professional Baseball Clubs—
History.   I. Title.
GV875.A3D5   796.357′64′09   78-24076
ISBN 0-8128-2577-2

As always, to Nancy and Scott.

ACKNOWLEDGMENTS

With sorrow, I acknowledge my debt to Garry Schumacher, whose information and anecdotes gave me a feeling for National League baseball in the earlier years of this century. Garry died before he could see this book in print.

Though I have seen many of the events and players described here and have interviewed many of those people prominent in the league's history, I naturally had to rely on other published sources as well. I have included a complete bibliography, and it should be noted here that no baseball historian can be without *The Baseball Encyclopedia* and *The Sports Encyclopedia: Baseball.*

National League clubs were very helpful in providing information and access to their picture files.

My editor, Benton Arnovitz, conceived this project.

Finally, a word of thanks to my friend, Walter Corder, who supplied me with a book of information and records from before the turn of the century, and whose enthusiasm and verve are a constant inspiration.

Contents

THE BLACK REVOLUTION

THE EXPANSION ERA

Introduction

by PETE ROSE

I have been a National League fan for as long as I can remember. I was born in Cincinnati, and I grew up watching the Reds. I never dreamed I'd be playing for them some day, but I was prepared when I got my chance; I'd been switch-hitting since I was nine years old.

As far as I was concerned, the National League WAS major league baseball. Television wasn't the big thing then that it is now, so the only time I saw the American League was at World Series time. I just never thought of baseball as anything but the National League.

I believe consistency is the most important thing in life, and especially in baseball. If you can play well game after game, year after year, then you can call yourself a good player. To me, that's one of the great things about the National League. It has always had a lot of consistent players, guys like Hank Aaron and Stan Musial. Or, if you go back far enough, Rogers Hornsby and Honus Wagner and Wee Willie Keeler.

I remember some of the players on the Reds that I watched as I was growing up, guys like Ted Kluszewski, whom I got to know as the Reds' batting coach when I was with the club, and others such as Johnny Temple and Gus Bell. I never patterned myself after any player, though, because I didn't stay at one position long enough.

When I was playing Knothole Gang ball in Cincinnati, the equivalent of Little League, I was a catcher. I didn't play second base, my first major league position, until I was in high school. Actually, counting my minor league experience, I had only played a little more than four years as a second baseman when I came up to the Reds.

The Dodgers are the team I remember best from my years as a youngster. I don't remember Jackie Robinson much, but I sure remember players like Pee Wee Reese, Gil Hodges, Duke Snider, Carl Furillo. They were great players. Every time the Dodgers came to town, it would be a big day.

It was a great thrill when I got a chance to sign with the Reds. Maybe I could have gotten an offer from somebody else, but I didn't wait. I wanted to play in the National League.

I remember when I was growing up, we'd go out to old Crosley Field. My dad worked for a bank, so sometimes we'd get the bank's box seats, right behind the dugout. When we didn't, we sat way up at the top.

Crosley Field was small, only seating about 28,000, and it was one of the great old ball parks. We were really close to the players, like Wrigley Field in Chicago is. The old parks were fun that way. I remember at Connie Mack Stadium, the old home of the Phillies, some of the fans were hanging over the field. The old parks were great for watching a game, if you didn't get behind a light pole, that is.

But the progress made in building new ball parks in the National League has been good for everyone. The new stadiums are more comfortable for the fans because the seats are wider and the rest room facilities are cleaner.

I played in Crosley Field from 1963 through the first half of the 1970 season, when we moved to Riverfront Stadium, and I'd have to say that Riverfront is much better for the players.

I like the artificial turf. Cincinnati gets a lot of rain, but the Reds didn't have a rained-out game until 1978. As soon as the rain stops, they get out those Zamboni machines and scoop up the water, so the game can go on. That's important in Cincinnati, because some of the fans come in from 50-100 miles away, and you don't want to disappoint them by sending them home without seeing a game.

Playing on artificial turf is much better for me as a fielder because I can always count on getting a good bounce. On dirt infields, you never know when you're going to get a bad bounce. People say that's part of the game, but I don't agree. I don't like to see a game decided on a bad bounce.

I've always been interested in numbers and history, and I've had a lot of goals for myself. I wanted to get 3000 hits, and now that I have, I'd like to get the National League record for hits. That was one reason I stayed in the National League, signing with Philadelphia after I'd played out my option with Cincinnati.

I think it's great that I'm in the National League record book for my 44-game hitting streak. And there's one thing nobody ever talks about: I hold the record for best fielding percentage for an outfielder. That's important to me, because I've always worked very hard on my fielding.

When I was on my hitting streak, I became even more interested in the history of the league because people kept bringing up the old names, like Keeler.

I'm fascinated by baseball history. I think it's great, what some of the old-timers did. That's why I think you'll enjoy this book by Glenn Dickey; it's got all the information in it. Don't miss the last chapter, about the Big Red Machine. Even though I'm with the Phillies now, I'm proud to have been a part of that team, one of the great teams in National League history.

Pete Rose, the spirit behind the Big Red Machine, aroused the baseball world in 1978 by hitting in 44 straight games at age 37. *(Copyright Cincinnati Reds, Inc., 1976)*

Preface

There is obviously more than one way to write the history of a league. Mine was to divide that history into five clearly discernible eras, varying from 14 to 27 years in length and shaped by events. Some men overlapped eras—John McGraw, for instance, was a player in one period, a manager in another—but for the most part, the eras are naturally divided.

Within that framework, I concentrated on the most significant players, teams and events. Inevitably, this led to some slighting of individual efforts; two examples which come readily to mind are the 12-inning no-hitter by Harvey Haddix in 1959 and the double no-hitter by Jim "Hippo" Vaughan and Fred Toney in 1917. So, I have inserted a list of special historical moments, by years, in the back of the book.

There are also statistical tables in the back, because baseball fans are the most statistics conscious sports enthusiasts. These records should settle some arguments. I make no such claim for my occasional value judgments in the book itself.

G.D.

IN THE BEGINNING

1. Abner Who? Cartwright's Rules

On February 2, 1876, five men sat down in a New York hotel room to discuss the future of baseball. At that time, Ulysses S. Grant was president of the country, which was still recovering from the ravages of the Civil War. There were only 37 states in the Union. Gen. George A. Custer still had nearly five months to live before he would discover all those Indians at Little Big Horn.

The National League was about to be born.

There had been baseball before, and even an organized league, but the National League would become the first lasting league and the longest-lived league in American sports history.

The origins of baseball are murky. In their more fanciful moments, the Russians even claim to have invented it. For years, Gen. Abner Doubleday was credited with inventing the game, and many people still believe he did.

Baseball historians, however, generally credit Alexander Cartwright with the invention, or modification, of baseball, and Cartwright has a place in the Baseball Hall of Fame at Cooperstown, New York.

In his mid-20s, Cartwright played sports with a group of young men in the Murray Hill section of Manhattan. The popular game of the time was town ball, in which runners were declared out when hit by a thrown ball.

Cartwright and his friends informally changed the rules of the game as they played, and Cartwright suggested that they form their own club and post their own rules. On September 23, 1845, they formed the Knicker-bocker Base Ball Club and adopted 20 rules for their game. There have been many changes in baseball since then, but this was its rough beginning.

These are the 20 rules:

1. Members must strictly observe the time agreed upon for exercise, and be punctual in their attendance.

2. When assembled for practice, the President, or Vice-President in his absence, shall appoint an Umpire, who shall keep the game in a book provided for that purpose, and note all violations of the By-Laws and Rules during the time of exercise.

3. The presiding officer shall designate two members as Captains, who shall retire and make the match to be played, observing at the same time the players put opposite each other should be as nearly equal as possible; the choice of sides to be then tossed for, and the first in hand to be decided in a like manner.

4. The bases shall be from "home" to second base, forty-two paces; from first to third base, forty-two paces, equidistant.

5. No stump match shall be played on a regular day of exercise.

6. If there should not be a sufficient number of members of the Club present at the time agreed upon to commence exercises, gentlemen not members may be chosen in to make up the match, which shall not be broken up to take in members that may afterwards appear; but in all cases, members shall have the preference, when present, at the making of a match.

7. If members appear after the game is commenced they may be chosen in if mutually agreed upon.

8. The game to consist of twenty-one counts, or aces; but at the conclusion an equal number of hands must be played.

9. The ball must be pitched, and not thrown, for the bat.

10. A ball knocked out of the field, or outside the range of the first or third base, is foul.

11. Three balls being struck at and missed and the last one caught is a hand out; if not caught is considered fair, and the striker is bound to run.

12. A ball being struck or tipped and caught either flying or on the first bound is a hand out.

13. A player running the base shall be out, if the ball is in the hands of an adversary on the base, or the runner is touched with it before he makes his base; it being understood, however, that in no instance is a ball to be thrown at him.

14. A player running who shall prevent an adversary from catching or getting the ball before making his base, is a hand out.

15. Three hands out, all out.

16. Players must take their strike in regular turn.

17. All disputes and differences relative to the game, to be determined by the Umpire, from which there is no appeal.

18. No ace or base can be made on a foul strike.

19. A runner cannot be put out in making one base, when a balk is made by the pitcher.

20. But one base allowed when a ball bounds out of the field when struck.

The most significant of the rules was No. 13, which provided that a player could be tagged out or forced out and that the ball could not be thrown at him. That differentiated the game from town ball and also no doubt lengthened the careers of the players.

But the rules that provided for three outs in an inning, three strikes to a batter, and a precisely laid-out diamond (although the distances have changed since) all gave form to the game we know as baseball. So did the rule that the umpire has the final word. Leo Durocher could tell you about that.

The Knickerbockers occasionally played against other teams, as well as in games among themselves, and there were other teams and other games on a less organized basis. But it wasn't until 1871 that the first league was formed, the National Association of Professional Baseball Players.

The National Association lasted five years, but attendance went down each year, for several reasons.

1) The league was dominated by the Boston Red Stockings, who won the championship the last four years of the league. In the league's final year, 1875, the Red Stockings were 71–8 and didn't lose a home game.

2) The league had no central leadership and scheduling was chaotic; that last year, for instance, the Red Stockings played 79 games and Keokuk, Iowa played only 13, losing 12 of them.

3) Many of the players were hard drinkers and were frequently in no condition to play.

4) Fixed games were commonplace. Gamblers sold pools on the grounds before games, and players in uniform sometimes made bets.

5) In a forerunner of the problems that were to plague baseball and other professional sports more than a century later, players continually jumped teams. The only rule was that they had to stay with a team for one season, and it was common for good players to jump from team to team.

Obviously, something had to be done or organized baseball was doomed. William A. Hulbert, an executive with the Chicago club in the National Association, decided the only way to save the game was to form a new league with different rules.

Hulbert planned carefully. He first approached the dominant player of the day, pitcher Albert G. Spalding of the Boston Red Stockings. Spalding had been born in Illinois, and Hulbert reportedly tried first to convince the star pitcher that he should return to his home state. He also promised Spalding that he would be captain and manager, and that he would get $4000, a hefty salary in those days. It is reasonable to assume that the money and position were more compelling arguments than pride of state.

Spalding was a superb pitcher and a multifaceted personality. He was accustomed to the best: As a child, his mother said, he had a habit of eating the inside of a slice of bread and hiding the crusts under his plate.

In five seasons in the National Association, he won 206 games and lost only 56; his final year was his best, 56–5. He pitched one full year with the Chicago team in the new National League in 1876, compiling a 46–12 mark. After that, he retired to the executive offices.

In 1877, Spalding also formed a sporting goods company that supplied the baseball used in the National League, and the company named after him is still a respected name in the sports world.

Spalding showed his executive ability as soon as he agreed to terms with Hulbert. He went back to Boston and convinced three other stars—Ross Barnes, Jim "Deacon" White and Cal McVey—to sign with Chicago for the 1876 season. Barnes hit .372, White .355, and McVey .352 in the final National Association season. With Spalding, they became known as the Big Four.

Then, Spalding and Hulbert went to Philadelphia and signed two other outstanding players, Adrian "Cap" Anson and Ezra Sutton. Anson was to become the outstanding player in the National League in its first quarter century.

William Hulbert was the guiding force behind the formation of the National League. *(George Brace photo)*

What Hulbert had done was illegal under the National Association bylaws—players were not supposed to negotiate with other clubs during a season, though they had complete freedom once the season was completed— but he was unconcerned because he knew the Association was breaking up.

Nor was he concerned when news of the signings leaked out. The Big Four players were called "seceders," the worst epithet that could be used in an era in which Civil War memories were still so fresh, but their play obviously didn't suffer. There was talk that the Association might suspend the players, but it was no more than talk. "In the eyes of the public," Hulbert told Spalding, "you players are bigger than the Association."

At the conclusion of the season, Hulbert and Spalding went to work. They spent a month at Hulbert's home drawing up a new league constitution with the following provisions: 1) Alcohol would not be sold on the grounds; 2) no gambling would be allowed; 3) teams would be obligated to play a complete schedule; and 4) each franchise would represent a city of at least 75,000.

The most important provision, though, was one that gave control to the owners, rather than to the players. From the beginning, Hulbert had wanted a league that would be run on a businesslike basis, so he could make a profit.

Hulbert and Spalding did their work well. With some changes (allowing the sale of alcohol in parks is perhaps the most conspicuous), the document they drew up has provided the basis of the National League for more than a century.

Next, Hulbert called a meeting of the western teams of the Association— his own, St. Louis, Cincinnati, and Louisville. At the time, the Association was dominated by the eastern teams, and Hulbert had no trouble in convincing his fellow western club owners that they must stand together. His plans for a new league were enthusiastically endorsed.

Surprisingly, when Hulbert contacted the owners of the eastern teams— Philadelphia, Brooklyn, Boston, and Hartford—he learned that they, too, were ready to start a new league.

So, on February 2, 1876, on a New York day during which gale-force winds blew, Hulbert met with owners G. W. Thompson of Philadelphia, Nathaniel T. Apollonio of Boston, William H. Cammeyer of Brooklyn, and Morgan G. Bulkeley of Hartford.

Hulbert reviewed the problems and corruption of the National Association with the owners, concluding that the Association must be abandoned. He then showed them the constitution he and Spalding had produced and secured their agreement to abide by the rules.

For the president of the league, Hulbert nominated Bulkeley, the Hartford owner. It was a smart move by Hulbert, who thus appeased the eastern club owners, but it cost him historic recognition. As the first president of the National League, Bulkeley has a place in the Baseball Hall of Fame. Hulbert, who organized the league and ascended to the presidency in its second year, is not represented.

Now the National League was ready for business, here are the presidents and managers of the teams during that first season:

TEAM	PRESIDENT	MANAGER
Philadelphia	Thomas J. Smith	Alfred H. Wright
Boston	Nathaniel T. Apollonio	Harry Wright
Chicago	William A. Hulbert	Albert G. Spalding
Cincinnati	Josiah L. Keck	Charles H. Gould
Hartford	Morgan G. Bulkeley	Robert V. Ferguson
Louisville	Walter N. Haldeman	John C. Chapman
Brooklyn	William H. Cammeyer	William H. Cammeyer
St. Louis	John R. Lucas	S. Mason Graffen

Note that Bulkeley was the president of both the Hartford club and the league, and that Cammeyer was both president and manager of his team, the Mutuals of Brooklyn. Cammeyer thus accomplished directly what other owners have tried to do in more subtle fashion in later years.

Chicago is the only one of the eight charter members of the National League which has had continuous membership. Cincinnati, St. Louis and Philadelphia were all out of the league part of the time in the first quarter-century, though they returned; the Boston and Brooklyn teams have moved; and Louisville and Hartford no longer have major league franchises.

Interestingly, no team nickname has remained in the league continuously. Cincinnati started as the Redlegs and later became the Reds, and the franchise was out of the league from 1881 to 1890.

Chicago started as the White Stockings but became the Cubs in 1901 because of the conflict between the National and American leagues. Player raids on its roster forced the National League club to sign young players, called "cubs" in the newspapers. The nickname stuck, and the Chicago American League team became the White Sox.

The St. Louis team started as the Brown Stockings or Browns, from the players' uniforms; a change in uniforms in 1889 forced a change in nickname to the Cardinals, and the St. Louis American League club later adopted the Browns nickname.

Similarly, Philadelphia started as the Athletics and became the Phillies in 1883; later, the Philadelphia American League club assumed the nickname of Athletics. The American League assumed one other nickname that started in the National League: Red Sox, for the Boston team.

In that first season, each team played ten games against each other team. The season ran from April 22 until October 21, and three games were scheduled each week. Games started in late afternoon and, particularly late in the season, were often ended by darkness.

The first National League game was played in Philadelphia, at a diamond at Twenty-fifth and Jefferson streets, with the Athletics hosting the Boston Red Stockings. Boston won the game, 6–5, before a crowd estimated at three thousand.

The game provided innumerable firsts. Boston shortstop George Wright was the first National League player to go to bat. Philadelphia shortstop Davy Force had the first assist and first-baseman Wes Fisler the first putout.

Jim O'Rourke of Boston got the first hit, a single, and Boston's Tim McGinley scored the first run, on a long fly by Jack Manning in the second inning. (Technically, Manning thus got the league's first RBI, though runs-batted-in were not recorded for many years after that.)

The Athletics got a first when second baseman Levi Meyerle hit a double in the bottom half of the first. Meyerle also got the first triple in the National League two days later in the same park.

The first home run wasn't hit until May 2, when in a game in Cincinnati, Ross Barnes of Chicago hit an inside-the-park home run.

Neither the time it took for the first home run to be hit nor the type of homer it was is any surprise, in retrospect. There were only 40 home runs hit in the entire 1876 season, and most of them were inside-the-park hits. Pitching dominated the game in its early days. The baseball was poorly constructed and much less lively than it is today, and pitchers stood only 45 feet away, instead of the present 60 feet, 6 inches.

The first no-hitter of the National League is officially credited to the aptly named George Washington Bradley. He threw his on July 15, 1876, at St. Louis, pitching for the home team against Hartford.

It may be that Joe Borden, who'd earlier pitched a no-hitter in the National Association, should be credited with the National League's first, too. On May 23, 1876, he threw an 8–0 win for Boston over Cincinnati that, properly scored, may have been a no-hitter.

The game was scored by Oliver Perry Caylor, a writer for the *Cincinnati Enquirer,* who showed two hits for Cincinnati. But the late Lee Allen, former historian for the Baseball Hall of Fame, wrote in *100 Years of Baseball* that Caylor had recorded two Borden walks as hits. Allen never received any support for his position, and the Hall of Fame does not list a no-hitter for Borden.

The rules of the day provided that pitchers could not raise their arms above their waists, so pitching was more like that in softball today. That made it relatively easy for pitchers to pitch complete games, and the star pitchers pitched virtually every game. Bradley, for instance, started 64 games, completed 63, and hurled 573 innings!

Chicago won the championship by six games in that first season, with 52 wins (46 by Spalding) and only 14 defeats, for a .788 percentage. Trailing, in order, were Hartford, St. Louis, Boston, Louisville, Brooklyn, Philadelphia and Cincinnati.

Ross Barnes of Chicago was the batting champion at .404. Barnes' average, however, came largely because he was very adept at a practice known as fair-foul hitting. In that first year, a ball that hit in fair territory was considered fair even if it rolled foul before it reached first or third base. Barnes often bunted balls that rolled foul, giving him extra time to run to first. For the 1877 season, the rule was changed to its modern form—the ball must remain in fair territory until it passes first or third base to be considered fair—and Barnes' average shrank to .272.

The Brooklyn and Philadelphia teams refused to make their last western trips because of financial hardships, and they were expelled from the league for the 1877 season. Chicago and Boston were the only clubs to make money, with approximate home attendances of 82,000 and 64,550 respectively.

Statistics derived from newspaper accounts of the games that year place the total league attendance at about 343,750, an average crowd of just over 1,300. One newspaperman thought he had the solution to the league's money problems: Lower the admission price, then at 50 cents.

"Say what you will, gentlemen of the league," wrote Henry Chadwick, baseball editor of the *New York Clipper,* "you must come down in your price; you must come down to the twenty-five cent admission fee; and you must proportionately lower your salaries. One thousand dollars for seven months of such services as a professional ballplayer is called upon to perform, even when he is not indisposed, is amply sufficient."

2. Improving the Odds: Gamblers and the Game

Despite the views of Henry Chadwick, baseball players in the early days of the National League were hardly a spoiled lot. Nothing tells what it was like better than Cincinnati writer Oliver Perry Caylor's interview of John O'Rourke, a Boston player expelled by the team in 1880 because of his complaints.

"Our troubles began in Chicago while on our last trip West," O'Rourke told Caylor. "We were put up at the Tremont House and huddled together like sheep in a room, 25 by 13 feet. There were 12 of us to occupy two double beds and several cots which lay so close together that some of them had to be removed to enable the boys to get into the places allotted them. The mosquitoes were thick and, to add to our torment, the room was over a boiler. Harry Wright slept in the room one night. The next night, Harry got a room to himself while Trott, Burdock and myself walked the streets all night rather than sleep in such a place."

Part of the players' problems were caused by the stinginess of some of the owners, but in truth, the owners had serious problems themselves. The idea of professional sports was still new, and gate receipts were low.

Best estimates indicate that it cost a club only about $20,000 to play a full season in those long-ago times, but even so, many clubs couldn't make expenses.

The Philadelphia club, for instance, had receipts of only $11,643 in 1876, which is why the Athletics didn't make their last scheduled western swing. One afternoon in Hartford, the visiting Cincinnati team received only $12.75 as its share of the gate receipts—and it cost $13 just for the players' transportation to and from the park!

Given these circumstances, it is to the credit of the National League team owners that they did not compromise their principles. They remained true to the constitution drawn up by William Hulbert and Albert Spalding, and they set the league firmly on the road to success.

Two examples show clearly how firm the owners were in their resolve to put the league on a business-like basis. The first challenge arose when

Philadelphia and Brooklyn failed to make their final road trips. That kind of transgression was winked at in the National Association, but when the National League owners met in December, 1876, they voted to expel the two franchises even though that left them with an unbalanced league of only six clubs for the 1877 season, two eastern and four western franchises.

(At the same meeting, Hulbert was named the league's president. Morgan Bulkeley left baseball to pursue his chief interests, banking, insurance, and politics. In his busy lifetime, he was mayor of Hartford, governor of Connecticut, and a U.S. senator.)

A potentially even more damaging problem cropped up at Louisville in the 1877 season. On August 13, the Grays were comfortably in first place with a 27–13 record. The Grays' chief strength was in pitcher Jim Devlin, considered second only to Boston's Tommy Bond, with Albert Spalding retired.

Then, the Grays lost eight games in a row, under mysterious circumstances. Eventually, they finished second, behind Boston.

The losing streak began when third baseman Bill Hague developed a painful boil in his left armpit. At the urging of George Hall, the team's best hitter, the club acquired Al Nichols, who had played the previous season with the now defunct Brooklyn club and had since been picked up by an independent club, Pittsburgh. Both Hall and Nichols were to play an important role in future developments.

Louisville started its last eastern trip by opening in Brooklyn (the Hartford club that year played its games in Brooklyn). In Louisville, club president Charles E. Chase got an anonymous telegram telling him that the gamblers were betting heavily on Louisville to lose. And the Grays lost the game, 5–1, though Devlin was pitching.

Chase had regarded the telegram as a hoax, but when the Grays lost, he was no longer so skeptical. He noticed that the game had been lost because of errors by Nichols, Hall and shortstop Bill Craver. Since Hague was recovered from his boil and ready to play, Chase was surprised that Nichols was still in the lineup. He immediately wired manager Jack Chapman to ask why. Chapman said it was Hall's suggestion, because Nichols was a Brooklyn boy and could be expected to try harder before his home-town fans.

The pattern reasserted itself for the next game, again against Hartford in Brooklyn. Once more Chase got a telegram before the game warning him that gamblers were betting heavily against his team. Again his players lost, this time by 7–0. Again, Devlin was the pitcher, and Devlin, Nichols, and Hall all made errors that contributed to the Louisville loss. This time, Chase wired Chapman to keep Nichols out of subsequent games, but the team continued to lose.

The next move was made by John Haldeman, son of Louisville owner Walter N. Haldeman. The younger Haldeman was covering the team for the *Louisville Courier-Journal.* In an exhibition game against Indianapolis, Haldeman realized that Devlin and Hall were trying to throw the game (which did not count in the league standings), and he accused them of that after the game. They both denied it, but Haldeman reported the incident to Chase and thus started a chain of circumstances that uncovered the whole story.

In 1890, Chase recalled the entire story for the *Sporting Times,* a baseball weekly. The series of events had made such a deep impression on him that he could still recall the conversations, though they had taken place 13 years before.

He first confronted Devlin, who denied ever throwing a league game but admitted being "careless" in the exhibition games that teams often scheduled between regular season games.

"I want a full confession," Chase remembered telling Devlin. "I'll give you until 8:00 P.M. to tell me the whole story."

When Chase returned to the hotel at which he lived, he found Hall waiting. Apparently, Hall thought that Devlin had told Chase the story, and he told Chase of the games he had thrown. He also implicated Nichols, who served as the go-between with the gamblers. Chase then went back and questioned Devlin again, and he finally forced the pitcher to admit his part in the scheme.

The next night, Chase called a meeting of the team in his office and asked them to give permission for the club's board of directors to examine all telegrams sent to or received by them during the season. One player, shortstop Craver, refused and he was immediately expelled from the team.

The telegrams implicated Hall, Nichols, and Devlin because they often contained the word "sash," which was code for a fixed game. No other players were implicated by the telegrams.

After all this, it was still not clear who had been the instigator. Hall claimed it was Nichols, but Chase later contended that it was Hall, because he was the one who had suggested the club obtain Nichols. Chase believed Hall had planned to use Nichols to approach other players.

Both Hall and Nichols approached Devlin, suggesting the pitcher help them throw an exhibition game, for which he would receive $100. Since the exhibition game didn't count in the league standings, Hall and Nichols convinced Devlin that the Louisville loss would be meaningless.

It was not meaningless to Devlin, however. He never got another cent, but was forced to help throw league games because of his fear that his play in the exhibition game would be exposed. Hall and Nichols never admitted how much they received, but it was considerably more than Devlin's $100.

Craver's part in the scheme was never explained. No evidence was ever uncovered that he had thrown a game, but his refusal to allow the directors to examine his telegrams—even when he learned that the price of refusal was expulsion—is suspect.

As soon as the Louisville directors learned of the duplicity of the players, they expelled them. At the league's annual meeting in December, the other team owners seconded the Louisville action and banned the players from the league forever.

There was one dissenter from that action, St. Louis, which had signed the four banished players for the 1878 season. Rather than try to find other players, St. Louis dropped out of the league, as did Hartford. But teams were added in Milwaukee, Indianapolis and Providence, and the league actually had one team more for 1878 than it had in 1877.

One irony of the situation was that Devlin was a friend of Hulbert, the league president. Devlin, who was more a victim than a beneficiary of the scheme, applied frequently for clemency in future years, but the ban held.

Public interest in baseball declined when the betting scheme was exposed, but the long-term effect was positive. The public realized that the owners would no longer tolerate the throwing of games, and the sport was on a more solid footing.

●

An indication of the progress the National League was making in selling professional baseball to the public was the formation in 1882 of a new league, the American Association, to compete with the National League.

Part of the blame for the formation of the new league could be laid at the feet of National League president Hulbert. Then as now, Cincinnati was a big beer-drinking community, and the Cincinnati fans wanted to drink their beer while watching baseball games on Sunday, both of which were forbidden by the National League constitution. When Cincinnati scheduled Sunday games and allowed beer to be sold, Hulbert expelled the Reds from the league after the 1880 season.

There was another reason for the expulsion. The National League, in a September 29, 1879 meeting, had adopted the reserve clause, which was to remain a staple in baseball contracts for almost a century, but Cincinnati opposed it.

Fittingly, plans for the American Association were laid in a saloon in Pittsburgh. Denny McKnight was named president of the league. The new league allowed Sunday games, and it cut ticket prices from 50 cents to 25 cents.

Meanwhile, the National League was going through changes of its own. Hulbert had suffered heart trouble and when, in December 1881, he was again elected president of the league, it was against his will. When the owners met to adopt the 1882 schedule, just three months later, Hulbert was too ill to attend. Arthur Soden, who had first proposed the reserve clause, was named president pro tem. On April 10, Hulbert died at his Chicago home, and Soden served the year as league president.

After the 1882 season, the National League owners gathered and selected A. G. Mills as the new league president. Mills had an extensive baseball background, having formed one team, the Olympics, which became part of the National Association, and then having worked with Hulbert with the Chicago team in the National League.

Mills realized the importance of organization in baseball, and he proposed the Tripartite Agreement, to be signed by the National League, the American Association, and the Northwestern League, a minor league of the time. The agreement included the reserve clause.

Among other things, the agreement made possible the first postseason play between champions of major baseball leagues. It could have happened in 1883, when Boston (National League) challenged Philadelphia (American Association). But Philadelphia, which had played poorly toward the end of the season, declined.

The next season, 1884, there finally was a postseason competition, though a short one. It was set up as a best-of-five series between the New York Metropolitans (American Association) and the Providence Grays (National League); it lasted only three. The incredible Charles ("Old Hoss") Radbourne, whose exploits are detailed later, won all three games pitching for the Grays, 6–0, 3–1 and 12–2.

●

The American Association was both the longest-lived (ten years) and the only cooperative league of those that sprung up in the first quarter-century to challenge the National League's supremacy.

The next challenge came from the Union Association, but that would-be challenge was virtually stillborn. Henry V. Lucas, a St. Louis millionaire, founded the league, but the National League and American Association raided so many of the Union Association's players that it was reduced to 5 of its original 12 franchises by the end of the year and folded after that season.

A much more serious challenge was mounted by the Brotherhood, a group originally started in 1885 to protect players. Each player joining was to contribute $5 a month to a fund to carry ill or indigent players over the winter.

By 1889, the Brotherhood had become a strong organization and when Indianapolis owner John T. Brush managed to obtain approval for a salary classification, grading players from A to E, with salaries ranging from $1,500 to $2,500, the players were ready to fight. They laid plans to establish a new league, generally referred to as the Players League, for 1890. The Brotherhood fielded eight teams, in Boston, Brooklyn, New York, Chicago, Philadelphia, Pittsburgh, Cleveland, and Buffalo.

It was a ruinous season for all three leagues—National, American Association, and Players. The National League changed its schedule to create direct conflicts with the Players League and the tactic cut badly into attendance for both leagues.

By the end of the season, the American Association was forced to fold. The Players League clearly could not continue under the existing circumstances, and the Brotherhood asked the National League for a truce. Albert Spalding, president of the Chicago club in the National League and head of the league's "war committee," pulled a gigantic bluff, saying his league would only consider unconditional surrender by the Brotherhood. Had the players refused, it is possible that the National League would have had to disband; certainly, at the very least, Spalding would have had to compromise. But the players agreed, and the war was over.

In the aftermath, the National League acquired four clubs from the Players League and expanded to an unwieldy 12 teams for the remainder of the decade: Boston, New York, Philadelphia, Brooklyn, Baltimore, and Washington in the east; and Chicago, Pittsburgh, Cincinnati, St. Louis, Cleveland and Louisville in the west.

The Brotherhood's attempt to field a third league had been disastrous for everybody. The competition very nearly ended major league baseball right there, because the owners suffered such great losses.

But it was the players who eventually suffered the most. When the National League again became a monopoly in 1892, the vengeful owners returned to the practices that had caused the players' rebellion. Club rosters were reduced to 13, and those players who were signed had to take great salary cuts, sometimes as much as 40 percent. They grumbled, but they had no choice.

●

The first quarter-century was a time of great change for the National League. Because the game was still so new, playing and scoring rules were constantly altered.

Some of the early rules seem funny today. Before 1887, for instance, a batter could call for a high or low pitch. Other regulations made baseball very different from today's game, so that it is impossible to make meaningful comparisons between players of that era and those of later days.

In 1876 the distance from pitcher to batter was 45 feet. In 1881 it was lengthened to 50 feet, and in 1893 to the present 60 feet, 6 inches. Not until 1883 was the pitcher allowed to pitch overhanded.

In 1879, it took nine balls for a batter to get a walk. By 1887, that had been reduced to five. In 1889, it became the present four.

When the National League started, a hitter got five strikes; the three-strike rule was adopted in 1888. But foul tips did not count as strikes until 1895, and foul balls not until 1901. In 1903, a foul tip caught after two strikes was ruled an out.

Not until 1891 did baseball adopt a substitution rule. Before that, substitutions had been allowed only in case of injury or with the permission of the other team.

In 1887, a walk counted as a hit, and Tip O'Neill batted .492. Stolen base statistics, started in 1886, originally credited a runner for each base advanced on another player's hit; that was changed in 1898.

There was little continuity to the league beyond its name. The number of teams in the league fluctuated from a low of 6 to a high of 12. Teams came and went and if fans doubted that the league would last, who could blame them?

At one time or another during the first quarter-century, 24 teams played in the league: Chicago, Boston, St. Louis, Cincinnati, Louisville, Hartford, New York (Mutuals), New York (Giants), Philadelphia (Athletics), Philadelphia (Phillies), Providence, Indianapolis, Milwaukee, Buffalo, Cleveland, Troy (N.Y.), Syracuse, Worcester, Detroit, Kansas City, Washington, Pittsburgh, Brooklyn, and Baltimore.

From 1891 to 1899, the league operated with an unwieldy 12 teams. But on the eve of the twentieth century, a transformation occurred: The league trimmed down to 8 teams for the 1900 season: Chicago, St. Louis, Cincinnati, Boston, New York, Brooklyn, Philadelphia, and Pittsburgh.

That was to be the makeup of the league for the next 53 years. Never again would the permanency of the league be seriously questioned.

3. Birds and Beaneaters: The Orioles Show the Way

["What are your rules for hitting?" Abe Yager of the *Brooklyn Eagle,* 1898.]

["Keep your eye clear and hit 'em where they ain't." Wee Willie Keeler, Baltimore Orioles.]

The last decade of the nineteenth century was dominated by two teams, the Boston Beaneaters and the Baltimore Orioles. Of the two, the Beaneaters were the more successful, winning five pennants, 1891–93 and 1897–98. The Orioles won three, 1894–96. But of the two teams the Orioles had the more lasting effect on the game. Their style of play dominated in the National League until the lively ball altered the basic offensive concepts of baseball in the 1920s.

Boston's success was no surprise, then or now. The Beaneaters were a successful team during most of the National League's first quarter-century, winning eight pennants, and their manager in the '90s, Frank Selee, was one of the smartest baseball men of all time.

Frank Selee managed the Boston
Beaneaters to five pennants,
three of them consecutive,
in the 1890s. *(George Brace photo)*

Selee's great ability was in judging talent. By his own admission, he didn't bother much with strategy during the game, but he was a master at building a team. After he left Boston, Selee went to Chicago, where he formed the Cubs team that was to dominate the National League from 1906 to 1910, although he had left the club by then.

Selee's best move was in recommending the purchase of pitcher Charles ("Kid") Nichols from Omaha of the Western (minor) League. From the time pitchers started throwing overhand, not one of them has ever had the fantastic decade Nichols had from 1890 to 1899; not Cy Young, not Christy Mathewson, not Walter Johnson, not Grover Cleveland Alexander.

In that stretch, Nichols' win totals, in order, were as follows: 27, 30, 35, 33, 32, 30, 30, 30, 29 and 21; for the first nine years of that stretch, he averaged more than 30 wins a season! Equally remarkable by today's standards, he almost always pitched a complete game. He had as many as 50 complete games in a season, three times completing every game he started in a season, and had only 22 games in ten years in which he did not finish.

Nichols virtually pitched himself out in that stretch, and won only 63 games in the remaining five years of his career. But his career total of 360 wins is the seventh best of all time and was good enough to get him elected to the Hall of Fame in 1949.

From the accounts of the day, Nichols was not a pitcher of great guile. He relied on an excellent fast ball and good control. Obviously, that was enough.

Boston was by no means a one-man team, though, and Nichols had plenty of support. In Hugh Duffy and Bobby Lowe, the Beaneaters had hitters who accomplished what nobody else had done before and, in Duffy's case, since.

Duffy had bounced around for three years before joining Boston in 1891. His lack of size (five foot seven, 168 pounds) caused some people to question his overall ability, but he could always hit. He hit over .300 in each of his first ten full seasons in the majors.

But nobody—not even Duffy himself—was prepared for what happened in 1894, when he hit .438, still the highest batting average ever posted under modern rules.

Duffy was not merely a singles hitter, either. Eighty-four of his 236 hits that year were for extra bases; 51 were doubles, 15 triples, and 18 home runs—which also led the league. His slugging average of .688 and his 145 RBIs were the league's best.

Duffy was so good that year it seemed he must have, like Joe Hardy in *Damn Yankees,* made a deal with the devil. In every hitting category but triples he set a personal high. His batting average was 75 points better than his second-best mark in his 17-year career and 111 points higher than his lifetime average. His slugging average never reached .500, before or after that season.

For many fans, he was too good to be believed. The reaction of baseball fans who didn't see Duffy play that year has always been: "Oh, that was the year they counted walks as hits." It wasn't, of course, but he gave up explaining that to people in his later years.

Lowe's achievement came in a single game, when he became the first to hit four home runs in a game. He hit the first two in the third inning, as the Beaneaters batted around, and he followed with homers in the fifth and sixth.

After the fourth home run, the game was stopped as the fans showered Lowe with silver, reportedly $160 worth. He had one more time at bat, in the eighth, but could manage only a single. The silver in his pockets may have slowed him down.

Lowe's mark has been matched since, but only six times in a nine-inning game. Nobody has done better.

●

The Baltimore team that entered the National League when it expanded to 12 teams in 1892 was a hopelessly bad team, its few good players surrounded by players who were minor league in action if not in name.

In just two years, the Orioles became the best team in baseball, largely because of the efforts of manager Ned Hanlon whose trades changed the team and whose strategy revolutionized the game.

Hanlon wasn't with the team when it entered the National League. The Orioles' manager then was veteran outfielder George Van Haltren. He lasted for only the first 11 games, 10 of which the Orioles lost. Van Haltren was replaced by Jack Waltz, a salesman at the brewery owned by Orioles' owner Harry Von Der Horst. Waltz's managerial career was short, too: eight games, of which the Orioles lost six.

While Waltz was manager, Von Der Horst was negotiating with Hanlon, and Hanlon joined the team in Cincinnati as manager on May 9, 1892. Nobody thought much about the move at the time, because Hanlon's managerial career had not been a success: fifth, sixth, and eighth place finishes with Pittsburgh, 1889–91. Nobody will ever know whether Von Der Horst spotted something or just got lucky.

Hanlon was no more successful at Baltimore in the beginning that he had been in Pittsburgh. The Orioles finished 12th in the first half of the split 1892 season, crawled up to 10th for the second half, and finished 8th in the '93 season.

But during this time, Hanlon was making the moves that would turn the Orioles into the most feared team in baseball. By 1894, only three players remained from the team he had inherited—pitcher Sadie McMahon, catcher Wilbert Robinson, and a reserve infielder named John McGraw.

Hanlon's first move was to trade Van Haltren to Pittsburgh for Joe Kelley, a 20-year-old outfielder. Then he dealt shortstop Tim O'Rourke to Louisville for Hugh Jennings. That deal was not a popular one at first, because O'Rourke had hit .310 for Baltimore, while Jennings was hitting only .222 (and followed that with .182 in 1893, a season he split between Louisville and Pittsburgh). But Jennings was a better fielder than O'Rourke; he later blossomed into a good hitter, too, and is in the Hall of Fame now.

The new manager's best trade, though, came after the 1893 season when he was able to trade two mediocre players, infielder Bill Shindle and outfielder George Treadway, to Brooklyn for Willie Keeler and Dan Brouthers, both of whom are now in the Hall of Fame. By 1894, the Orioles included six future Hall of Famers in their lineup: Keeler, Brouthers, Jennings, McGraw, Robinson and Kelley.

Before the 1894 season, Hanlon took the team south to Macon, Georgia to prepare for the season. Spring training has so long been an important part of baseball that it is hard to realize how unusual Hanlon's move was. As usual, he knew what he was doing. He wanted to work his team on the strategy of play that became known as "inside baseball."

To understand what Hanlon did, it is necessary to recognize that the game of baseball was played quite differently then than it is now. It consisted almost entirely of individual effort.

Consider, for instance, what happened when a batter hit a long fly ball. While an outfielder chased down the ball, the other members of his team stood and watched. When he threw the ball in, the infielder closest to the base would take the throw. There was no such thing as a cutoff man.

Hanlon made the Orioles play team ball, in the strictest interpretation of that phrase. When a ball was hit to the outfield against the Orioles, there would be an outfielder moving to back up the one chasing the ball, and there would be infielders—and sometimes even the pitcher—moving into position to take cutoff throws or to back up a base. Everybody was involved.

The Orioles were the first team to have a catcher fake a throw to one base and then throw to another, for instance, or to work cutoff plays with the catcher; Wilbert Robinson would throw to second base in an apparent attempt to get a runner advancing there, and the ball would be cut off by Jennings, who would throw another runner out at third or home.

Hanlon taught a hitting technique that became known as the "Baltimore Chop." The Baltimore infield was kept very dry and hard, and the swift Orioles would chop down on a pitch, causing it to bounce high in the air. By the time it came down, the hitter was safe at first.

But perhaps the cleverest play of all was that perfected by Keeler and McGraw. Time after time, with McGraw on first base, Keeler would hit a ground ball through the infield, catching the shortstop or second baseman floundering in the opposite direction. It seemed almost as if Keeler had the opposing infielders mesmerized, or that he could read their minds and know exactly where they would be.

The truth was more prosaic. When McGraw reached first, he would fake a move toward second base on the first pitch. Thinking McGraw was coming down, the shortstop or second baseman would break to cover the base. That would show Keeler who was covering the base. On a subsequent pitch, McGraw would again break for second and Keeler would hit the ball through the hole left by the infielder rushing to cover second.

The Orioles were not the first to use this play, now known as the hit-and-run; Cap Anson had used it with Chicago in the 1880s. But the Orioles were the first to make it an important part of their game. Today, teams defense the play by alternating coverage at second base throughout a game, but at that time, nobody else realized what the Orioles were doing.

Those techniques were within the rules of baseball. Other tricks that the Orioles used to win games were not. An Oriole baserunner who noticed that the umpire's back was turned to him would cut across the diamond from first to third, for instance.

Hitters used to complain that it was impossible to get an extra base hit in the Orioles' park. A line drive that seemed to be between the outfielders would miraculously be cut off, and the ball would be thrown back in. It was some time before other teams realized that the Orioles hid extra balls in the tall outfield grass and would grab one of those extra balls and throw it in when a ball was hit beyond the outfielders.

Sometimes, an opposing hitter would foul a ball into the stands. The ball would be thrown back in and the hitter would connect solidly, but the ball would become a weak infield pop fly. Later it was discovered that the Orioles hired men to sit in the stands and grab those foul balls, and then make a switch and throw in a mushy ball to be used. Eventually, that brought on the current practice of umpires checking each ball put into play.

When an opposing runner tagged up at third on a fly ball, McGraw would loop his hand inside the player's belt and hold him for a short time, often long enough so that the runner could be thrown out at home. That practice ended when Pete Browning surreptitiously unfastened his belt one day and left McGraw holding it as he (Browning) raced home to score.

Opposing runners took a terrible beating even to get as far as McGraw's territory at third. When the umpire's back was turned, the Orioles would kick, trip, and bump baserunners, which often slowed their progress enough to turn them into outs at the next base. Baserunners would be tagged hard enough to cause welts or split lips.

Umpire intimidation was another important part of the Orioles' strategy. When a decision went against them, the Orioles would often explode off the bench en masse, screaming at the umpire and threatening him. The threats were not empty ones. Umpires had their uniforms torn, and one report of the day said that one umpire had his buttoned coat yanked up over his head.

Particularly at home, the close decisions seldom went against the Orioles.

The Orioles enlisted everybody they could in their support. Their fans were just as rowdy as the players.

The groundkeeper played an important role, too. As previously mentioned, he kept the infield hard, so the Orioles could reach base on a "Baltimore chop." In 1893, the distance from the pitcher's mound was changed from 50 feet to the present 60 feet, six inches. Hanlon realized immediately that the change would make it easier to bunt, because a pitcher would have further to go to make the play.

Accordingly, Hanlon told his groundskeeper to let the grass along the foul lines grow high and to slope the ground around the foul lines so that balls would remain in fair territory. It was almost impossible to bunt foul at Baltimore.

The Orioles, though they added some tricks that nobody else had thought of, were operating well within the context of the times. Baseball was not an honorable sport, and players would have scoffed at the thought popularized in later years by Grantland Rice: that it was not whether you won or lost that was important, but how you played the game. They played to win.

The example of Connie Mack is pertinent. Mack is thought of now in almost saintlike terms, but he was willing to use illegal tricks to win games. As a catcher for Pittsburgh in the 1890s, Mack developed a technique of simulating the sound of a foul tip by skipping his hands together. Later, he would touch the bat with his hand as the hitter started his swing, just enough to throw the swing off. That practice ended when one hitter swung at Mack's hand instead of the ball, mashing Mack's fingers.

The Orioles showed in the first series of 1894 just how good they were going to be, as they swept four games from the Giants, who had been the preseason favorites to win the pennant. It wasn't just that they won, but how they won: They stole 14 bases and successfully executed the hit-and-run play 13 times.

"That's not baseball they're playing," protested Giants' manager John Montgomery Ward. He threatened to take the matter up with the league president, Ned Young, but it's not clear on what basis he could have protested.

From there, the Orioles went on to Boston for a series with the defending champion Beaneaters. In the first game, Boston's ace pitcher, Kid Nichols, went into the ninth with a 3–1 lead. Nichols always had good success against the Orioles—as well as against the rest of the league—and it seemed the Beaneaters had the game wrapped up.

But in the ninth, McGraw and Keeler worked the hit-and-run play, and it upset Nichols, who completely lost his effectiveness. Baltimore scored 14 runs in the inning and, naturally, won the game. That was an indication of what was to come; McGraw and Keeler worked the hit-and-run 13 straight times against Boston before being stopped.

Probably never in the history of baseball has a team turned around so dramatically as the Orioles did. In 1893, they had been 10 games under .500 (60–70); in 1894, they were 50 games over .500 (89–39).

As a team, the Orioles batted .343, stole 343 bases and led the league in fielding. Jennings made the most dramatic improvement at bat, from .182 to .335—and he was below the team's average! The outfield of Kelley, Keeler, and Steve Brodie batted .393, .371, and .366, respectively. Other averages include Brouthers, .347, and McGraw, .340.

The pitching staff was the team's one weakness; and this remained true throughout the decade. McMahon (25–8) was the team's only consistent pitcher. But with the quality of hitting the Orioles had, they didn't need great pitching.

Baseball men generally agree with Connie Mack's dictum that a team can be considered a dynasty only when it wins three consecutive pennants. By that rule, the Orioles qualify, because they won the National League pennant, 1894–96, before slipping back to second the next two years behind Boston.

After that, Hanlon took some of his key players and moved to Brooklyn, where he won two more pennants, 1899 and 1900. But more than for his pennants, he is remembered today for introducing a style of play that dominated the game until the introduction of the lively ball. Even now, his influence is felt because of his emphasis on team play.

●

The Orioles were more than just Ned Hanlon, of course. McGraw, of whom more will be written in a subsequent chapter, was an outstanding player and became perhaps the most dominant manager the game has known.

Robinson is remembered best for his years as manager of the "Daffiness Boys," the Brooklyn Dodgers of the mid-twenties and early thirties, but he was a star player, too. On June 10, 1892, against St. Louis, he had perhaps the most productive day a hitter has ever had, going seven-for-seven and knocking in 11 runs. Not until 1975 did another player (Rennie Stennett of Pittsburgh) match Robinson's hit total, and Robinson's RBI total is only one under the major league record.

Wee Willie Keeler became famous as the man who "hit them where they ain't." *(George Brace photo)*

But it is Keeler who is best remembered from that team, because of his engaging nickname of "Wee Willie" and his "hit 'em where they ain't" motto.

Keeler came by his nickname legitimately; he was only five-four-and-a-half and weighed 142 pounds, small even by the standards of his time. He is the smallest member of the Hall of Fame.

His size worked against him in his early years, and he was traded by both New York and Brooklyn, the second time to Baltimore. Hanlon wasn't worried about Keeler's lack of size because he recognized his ability.

Keeler collected 200 or more hits in eight consecutive seasons at Baltimore, starting in 1894. His highest batting average was a phenomenal .432 in 1897. It is claimed that he went an entire season, 1898, without striking out. No strikeout statistics were kept on hitters that year, but in years in which they were kept, he had two full seasons in which he struck out only six and nine times.

In 19 big league seasons, he averaged .345. He hit safely in the first 44 games of the 1897 season, which no hitter had done before and no National Leaguer would do again until Pete Rose equaled that mark in 1978.

Size isn't everything.

4. In the Days of the Waxed Moustache: Greats of an Early Era

The beauty of baseball lies in its traditions. Except for the advent of the lively ball, which altered the entire pattern of the game, the game's changes have been evolutionary, rather than revolutionary. The game's rules and dimensions—except for some minor tinkering with the size of the pitcher's mounds—have remained the same since 1901.

In other sports, changes have been much more drastic. It is impossible to compare Red Grange with O. J. Simpson, for instance, because football has changed so much in a half-century, and statistics are kept differently. In basketball, the change has been even more startling; it is impossible to compare George Mikan with Bill Russell, although Russell's career started in the same decade Mikan's ended. But baseball fans can cheerfully, and sometimes not so cheerfully, debate the merits of Rogers Hornsby and Hank Aaron, with proponents of each using a multitude of statistics to prove a point.

That is not true of the era before the twentieth century. Rules and dimensions of the game were changed so frequently that it is impossible to compare players of that era with those who followed. Amos Rusie, for instance, struck out 345 batters in 1890, but he was pitching from only 50 feet away. Billy Hamilton stole 111, 102, and 111 bases, 1889–91, but that was at a time when a runner got credit for a stolen base if he took an extra base on somebody else's hit. Tip O'Neill batted .492 in 1887, when walks were counted as hits. Obviously, none of these statistics can be compared realistically to statistics compiled after 1901.

Nevertheless, there were some significant players in that era, some of them mentioned in the preceding chapter, and some spectacular deeds.

The most spectacular season, without question, was that credited to Charles ("Old Hoss") Radbourn in 1884. That year, he won an incredible 60 games, losing only 12, with an earned run average of 1.38. He pitched 678 ⅔ innings. He started 73 games and finished all 73, and he even pitched two games in relief!

At that time, pitchers threw underhanded (Radbourn continued to pitch that way even when the rules were changed to permit overhand pitching), which was less of a strain on his arm. Even so, nobody else approached Radbourn's statistics, even in that era.

There was a double irony connected with Radbourn's great season and career. The first is that his career was almost over before it began. Radbourn played one year, 1879, in the Northwest League, a minor league of the time, as a combination pitcher-outfielder. He was impressive enough to be signed by Buffalo of the National League in 1880—but as an outfielder, not as a pitcher.

Radbourn played only six games before developing a sore arm, and he retired to Bloomington, Illinois, all thoughts of baseball behind him, to become an apprentice butcher.

In 1881, the Providence Grays decided that Radbourn could help them as an outfielder who could occasionally pitch and after a series of persuasive telegrams, he agreed to give baseball another chance.

In his first start, Radbourn outpitched Tommy Bond of Boston, then the league's best, and went on to a 25–11 record that year. He also played 25 games in the outfield and another 13 at shortstop that year. Surprisingly, he continued to play in the outfield and infield on occasion throughout his career, despite his great pitching success. Players were not pampered in those days.

Radbourn was never a great hitter—his high mark for a season was .283—but he was good enough to be a factor. In one famous game in 1882, he was locked in a scoreless duel for 17 innings with Stump Weidman of Detroit until he hit a home run leading off the 18th to win the game, 1–0. The fans were as excited, according to a newspaper account, as if they had been "awaiting the outcome of a presidential election."

In 1883, Providence had two pitchers, Radbourn and Charlie Sweeney, who alternated. The two were extremely jealous of each other, and Radbourn's jealousy increased when Sweeney struck out 19 batters in a June 7 game at Buffalo.

Radbourn, obviously trying to match or better Sweeney's mark, began throwing as hard as he could on every pitch in subsequent games. He had good speed, but that was not the greatest reason for his success. He was perhaps the first pitcher to use a curve with consistent results, and he had great control. In his anger, he was forsaking the best elements of his game.

When Radbourn continued to ignore the signals of his catcher, Barney Gilligan, and the advice of manager Frank Bancroft, he was first warned and then suspended. The suspension did not last long because it was soon Sweeney's turn for a temperamental outburst.

In a game against the Phillies, Sweeney was ahead, 6–2, after seven innings, even though he had been drinking before the game. Bancroft suggested that he change places with right fielder Joe Miller for the rest of the game. The suggestion ired Sweeney, who charged off the field, changed into street clothes, and disappeared. He soon showed up pitching for the St. Louis team of the Union Association.

With Sweeney gone, Bancroft had no choice but to reinstate Radbourn, and Radbourn more than compensated for his loss of pitching time, pitching 36 of the last 39 games the Grays played that year. Not coincidentally, the Grays won the pennant.

But Radbourn's year wasn't through. The New York Metropolitans, champions in the American Association, had challenged the Grays to a best-of-five championship series.

The series lasted only three games, all of which Radbourn pitched and won, 6–0, 3–1 and 12–2.

There were times during that season-ending stretch when Radbourn's arm was so sore in the morning that he couldn't raise it to comb his hair. Fortunately for the Grays, his arm loosened up enough to pitch by the afternoon.

Radbourn also played in 15 games in the outfield and infield in 1884 when he wasn't pitching. He got $3,000 for the season, a good salary for the time, and the Providence management was obviously determined to get its money's worth.

Curiously, despite his willingness to work so hard on the diamond, Radbourn was not an ambitious man. He ignored the first telegrams Providence sent him because he was content to remain in Bloomington where he could pursue his main interests—hunting and fishing. A boyhood friend, Bill Hunter, finally convinced him to report. (One story has it that Hunter signed Radbourn's name to a telegram to the Grays.)

Although he never again had a season approaching that one, Radbourn had five more 20-win seasons and finished his career with 310 wins. It is largely because of that great 1884 season, however, that he is in the Hall of Fame, where he is described as the "greatest of the 19th century pitchers." He never lived to see that plaque. Radbourn lost an eye in a hunting accident in 1895, four years after his retirement, and developed partial paresis. He died on February 5, 1897, alone in a dark room in the back of the billiards parlor he owned.

Ballplayers were a colorful bunch in that era, and none more so than Mike ("King") Kelly, whose life was as spectacular as it was short. Baseball was Kelly's stage, and when the season was over, he toured the vaudeville houses, to full crowds.

He was immensely popular with fans, young and old. The youngsters would follow him down the street, and the older fans would join him in the bars, where Kelly was often the first to buy a round.

He drank heavily and also spent much of his salary on clothes, and what little he had left over often went to the race tracks. Once he was discovered at the race track when his teammates were playing a game. "Mike's only enemy is himself," said his Chicago manager, Cap Anson.

Nevertheless, Kelly could play. He averaged .307 in 16 National League seasons, twice led the league in batting, and was elected to the Hall of Fame in 1945.

He is credited with a number of innovations, including the hit-and-run, later popularized by the Baltimore Orioles. He was one of the first catchers to use finger signals to his pitchers. As an outfielder, he was one of the first to back up infielders on plays.

His most famous play, however, was the hook slide, which he originated. He was a very successful base stealer, though he lacked great speed, because of his skill in taking a lead and the nature of his slide.

The slide inspired a song, "Slide, Kelly, Slide!" which became popular despite spectacularly banal lyrics, and also a painting, by Frank O. Small—though the painting shows Kelly sliding headfirst.

As with all charismatic sports figures, a number of stories sprung up around Kelly, and some of them may even be true. In one such story, he was

Michael "King" Kelly was the most colorful player in the National League's first quarter-century. *(George Brace photo)*

on the bench because he was too hung over to play. When a foul ball was hit in the air near the Chicago bench, he leaped up and announced "Kelly now catching for Chicago," and caught the ball.

In another story, Kelly was playing the outfield. With two outs in the ninth inning and Chicago ahead, the ball was almost impossible to follow in the darkening twilight. A batter drove a ball over Kelly's head, but he pounded his glove to simulate the catch and fooled the umpire into declaring the game over.

Kelly also became the focal point of the strife between players and owners in the 1880s because his sale by Chicago to Boston in 1887 taught the players how much they were really worth.

The background was this: Kelly had just come off his most successful season, hitting .388 to lead the league, and the Chicago White Sox had won their second straight pennant, and fifth in the seven years in which Kelly had played for Chicago.

James Billings, treasurer and part owner of the Boston team, wrote to Albert Spalding of Chicago, offering $5,000 for Kelly. Spalding said the White Sox wouldn't consider selling Kelly for that figure but might be willing to consider it for twice that.

Boston finally agreed to the $10,000 figure, if Kelly's salary demands could also be met. The owners had just established a limit of $2,000 on player salaries, but Boston got around that by offering Kelly a bonus of $3,000 for the use of his picture in advertisements. The $5000 figure was twice what Kelly had received in Chicago the previous year and naturally pleased him.

The sale amazed fans everywhere and depressed those in Chicago. Players had been sold before, but for much lower figures. Because $10,000 was considered an unbelievable amount of money for a player, even one of Kelly's stature, the Boston club reproduced the sales agreement for use in newspapers, to prove it.

The Chicago management was not that straightforward. Spalding told the White Sox fans that Kelly had been sold because his drinking had been a bad influence on the younger players.

That hardly placated the fans. When Boston made its first trip to Chicago, an enormous crowd filled the streets around the hotel where the Beaneaters were staying, waiting for the appearance of Kelly. As was his custom, Kelly had spent most of the previous night drinking, and he was catching up on his sleep when the team carriage arrived at the hotel. He was awakened, a band played, and a poem was read in his honor.

After that, a crowd of 10,000 showed up to watch the game, won by Chicago despite a triple and two singles by Kelly.

Kelly was just as popular with the Boston fans as he was with those in Chicago. In his first season with the Beaneaters, he hit an inflated .394 (walks were counted as hits that year; recomputed without walks, his average was .322), and he stole 84 bases (an extra base on a hit was counted as a stolen base then). His grateful fans provided him with a house and a carriage drawn by two white horses to get him to the park.

Although he remained in the majors until 1893, Kelly's best years were behind him. His drinking became more and more of a problem, both to himself and to his teammates; he finally became the bad influence that Spalding had said he was earlier. But none of this seemed to affect his appeal to the fans, either at the games or in the theater during the off-season.

In 1894, he became a minor league manager at Allentown. In November after that season, he developed a cold that turned into pneumonia as he was on his way to Boston for a theater engagement. He never fulfilled that engagement. He was put to bed as soon as he arrived in Boston, but his condition worsened rapidly and he died on November 8.

Throughout his life, Kelly was a profligate, but he was as generous to others as he was to himself. Even in death, that trait showed through. On his last boat trip, the one from New York to Boston on which he had caught his ultimately fatal cold, Kelly learned that a young man had been arrested for boarding without paying. Kelly offered his dress suit to the steamship company as security for the young man, and Kelly's widow had to retrieve the suit from the company so Kelly could be buried in the style with which he had lived.

Kelly was not the only player of his era who was a hard drinker. Drinking probably shortened both his career and his life, but there were at least two other players who were even more tragically affected.

The first player was Louis Sockalexis, a Penobscot Indian, who was signed by the Cleveland Spiders in 1897. In half a season, Sockalexis hit .338 and his manager, Patsy Tebeau, insisted later that he could have been one of the great players in history.

But Sockalexis discovered whiskey after that half-season, and his career ended abruptly. The Spiders gave him several chances to reform, but he played only sporadically and poorly the next two seasons and was soon released.

Tebeau later told a story that dramatically illustrated Sockalexis's dependency on the bottle. The season Sockalexis joined the club, he was celebrating the Fourth of July when he fell out of a second-story window, breaking his right foot. He was sent back to Cleveland, where the doctor put his foot in a plaster cast and ordered him to remain in bed.

"But do you know," said Tebeau, "that he would get up during the night and walk a block on his plaster foot to get a drink?"

Sockalexis died at the age of 42 in 1913, long after his career was over. Ed Delahanty died while his career was still active, in a weird accident that was directly attributable to his drinking.

Delahanty was one of the greatest hitters of the National League's first quarter-century, and his career extended into the twentieth century. He had twice hit .400 or better, an even .400 in 1894 and .408 in 1899, and he had a lifetime average of .346.

By 1903, Delahanty was in the American League, with Washington. He was still a good hitter; he had hit .376 the previous year and was averaging .333 in June of that year. But he had been drinking heavily, apparently trying to drown the memories of a bad year at the track between seasons, and he was suspended by manager Tom Lofton.

Delahanty left the team in Detroit to head home to Washington. Drinking heavily, he got into a fight on the train to Buffalo and was put off just as the train was about to cross the International Bridge at Fort Erie, Ontario.

The enraged Delahanty tried to run up the tracks and board the train again. In the darkness he didn't notice that the drawbridge had been opened, and he fell into the river and was carried over Niagara Falls. His body wasn't found until a week later. A leg and arm were mangled, presumably by a tourist excursion boat that traveled in the water under the falls.

●

Because the Hall of Fame wasn't established until 1939, few of the nineteenth century stars were alive to witness their induction, even those who reached old age. Amos Rusie is an example.

Unlike many of his contemporaries, Rusie lived a long life, dying at the age of 71 in 1942. Even so, it was another 35 years before he was finally inducted into the Hall of Fame. He probably deserved it much earlier because he was responsible for one of the key rules changes—putting the pitching mound at 60 feet, 6 inches—and was one of the big stars of the 1890s.

Writers who saw Rusie pitch insisted that he was in a class with Rube

Waddell and Walter Johnson for speed. Certainly, he was the fastest of his era, leading the league in strikeouts for six straight seasons.

He was a classic speed pitcher, seldom bothering with curves and off-speed pitches. He simply threw as hard as he could for as long as he could. Measured by other careers, that was not long at all. His last big year came in 1898 when he was only 27. He was through at 30, but he was overwhelming while he had his fast ball. He had a streak of eight seasons in which he won at least 20 games, three times going over the 30-win mark, and he won 243 games in just ten years.

It didn't hurt Rusie that his control was shaky enough to keep hitters from becoming anchored at the plate. He led the league in walks for five straight years, and his career total of 1716 is fourth in baseball history.

Rusie quit school at 16 to go to work, and he played amateur baseball in his spare time. Word of his ability got around, and he was signed to play for the Indianapolis team in the National League when he was only 18.

After that season, in which Rusie had a 13–10 record and acquired the nickname of "the Hoosier Thunderbolt" because of his speed, the Indianapolis club folded. He was then sent to the New York Giants.

Rusie was actually a game below .500—at 29–30—in his first year with the Giants, but he led the league with 345 strikeouts. He was 32–19 with 321 strikeouts the next year and 31–28 with 303 strikeouts in 1892.

The pitching distance at that time was only 50 feet, and it was obvious that it was unfair to the batters to allow Amos Rusie to throw from that distance. In 1893, the pitching distance was moved back to the present 60 feet, 6 inches, to give the batters a fighting chance.

Moving Rusie back greatly cut into his strikeout totals, which fell to 208, 195, and 201 in the next three seasons, but he was still the league leader. In evaluating those strikeout statistics, it should be remembered that this was an era when hitters used thick-handled bats and usually just tried to make contact; thus, strikeouts were considerably less frequent than they are in today's game. Had the same conditions prevailed then as do today, Rusie's strikeout totals would probably have been half again as great.

Despite his great ability, Rusie was constantly involved in controversy. The first such example came in his first 30-win season, 1891, when he was not used in a critical five-game September series against Boston. Boston won all five, enabling the Beaneaters to edge out Chicago for the championship. As always in that type of situation, there was talk that the gamblers were behind Rusie's lack of action, but nothing was ever substantiated.

In 1892, National League owners tried to cut everybody's salary at mid-

Ed Delahanty, one of the greatest hitters in the National League's first quarter-century, died in a tragic train accident in 1903. *(George Brace photo)*

Amos Rusie so terrified National League hitters with his fast ball that the mound was moved back ten feet. *(George Brace photo)*

season. Rusie refused to take a cut and he was released at season's end, along with Mike Tiernan and Shorty Fuller, who had also refused the pay cut. Their independence did the three no good, however. No other club would sign them, and they were forced to return to New York—at a cut in pay.

That was nothing, though, compared to the salary struggle Rusie had following the 1895 season. The Giants had finished ninth in a 12-team league that year, but Rusie had had another productive year, 22–21 with a league-leading 201 strikeouts. After the season, though, Rusie's pay was docked $200, for "breaking training rules and indifferent work in the final game."

This appeared to be nothing more than a typical move by Giants' owner Andrew Freedman, a contentious man who was constantly embroiled in disputes with players, fans, umpires, and other owners. He was a vulgar man, given to exchanging insults with players, and his operation of the New York club was so slipshod that fans became disgusted and stopped coming to games.

Rusie was enraged at the "fine," contending with apparent accuracy that it was just a way of cutting his pay, and he refused to sign for the 1896 season until the money was restored to his salary.

Freedman refused to budge, and Rusie sat out the entire 1896 season. That further disgusted the Giants' fans because Rusie was a very popular figure in New York. A big (six foot one, 210 pounds) and handsome man, he was frequently seen out at night in New York, though he objected to his reputation as a carouser, and his popularity went beyond his ability as a pitcher.

With John Montgomery Ward as his lawyer, Rusie appealed to the league board, but the board ruled in Freedman's favor. Rusie then sued Freedman, and the case dragged into the 1897 season. By that time, the other league owners were greatly concerned, because Rusie was a drawing card around the league. They finally chipped in $5,000 to pay for Rusie's lost season, and he returned to the Giants.

The 1897 season was Rusie's best in two regards: His win-loss percentage of .784, based on 29–8, and his earned run average of 2.54 were both the best marks he had ever posted. But the great fast ball was starting to go, and he had only one more good year left, 1898, when he was 20–11 but with only 114 strikeouts.

Rusie was simply pitched out. For the six seasons from 1890–95, he had pitched at least 400 innings in each of five seasons, and in the sixth he had pitched 391 innings. Three times, he had pitched more than 500 innings, going as high as 548 in 1890. That's a lot of fastballs, especially considering the fact that Rusie was not a control pitcher and thus threw a lot of pitches in every game.

Rusie had one last service to contribute to the Giants, though inadvertently. In 1901, he was traded to Cincinnati for a young pitcher named Christy Mathewson. Rusie pitched only 22 innings for the Reds, with an 0–1 record. Mathewson went on to win 373 games in his remarkable career, all but one of them for the Giants.

On the surface, it seems perhaps the most stupid trade of all time, but it wasn't at all. John T. Brush made the trade at Cincinnati, but he knew at the time that he was going to take over the ownership of the Giants soon. He knew how good Mathewson was going to be, and he wanted Christy with the Giants.

●

There were players whose careers started in the nineteenth century and extended into the twentieth, and players who started in the National League and finished in the American League, but none ever amassed the record of Denton True ("Cy") Young.

Young started in the National League and won 289 games, which might have been enough to get him elected to the Hall of Fame; there are pitchers in the hall with fewer victories than that. Young, though, was only warming up. He went on to win another 222 in the American League, for a career total of 511, almost 100 more than the second-place total of 416 by Walter Johnson. All baseball records are made to be broken, but not that one.

Young's nickname apparently stemmed from his fastball. He started his career with Canton of the Tri-State (minor) League in 1890, and he got a tryout with Cleveland of the National League before the next season. Cleveland owner George Moreland was watching.

"I thought I had to show all my stuff," Young said later. "I threw the ball so hard I tore a couple of boards off the grandstand. One of the fellows said the stand looked like a cyclone struck it. That's how I got the name that was shortened to Cy."

Young was never in the class of Rusie as a fastball pitcher but he didn't have to be, because he had a good curve and excellent control. His control was both the secret to his success and his longevity.

He was a wonder. Starting with his first season with Cleveland, he won 20 or more games for 14 straight seasons. He pitched for five different teams and won for them all. He won 36 games the last year he threw from 50 feet and won 32 the first year he threw from 60 feet, 6 inches. He won before the turn of the century and after it.

Young is the career leader in games won and games lost, in complete games and innings pitched. He was the first pitcher to throw three no-hitters, a record that stood until Sandy Koufax pitched four, more than half a century later.

For most of his career, Young was a pitching machine: Just crank him up and send him out there. His managers never had to worry about him. He never had a sore arm, never had a fit of temper, never pitched well one time and poorly the next. For 15 straight years, he pitched in at least 300 innings; usually, he pitched far more.

Young had his own ideas about preparing to pitch. He believed strongly in conditioning. When he went to spring training, he would run for three weeks before he'd try to throw a pitch. He didn't believe in unnecessary throwing. He only warmed up for three or four minutes before a game; when he came in as a relief pitcher, he would only take a few warm-up pitches on the mound. "I figured the old arm just had so many throws in it," he said after his career was over, "and there wasn't any use wasting them."

Who could quarrel with him?

Young was as durable in life as he was in his pitching career; he lived until the age of 88. When he died in 1955, he had been enshrined in the Hall of Fame for 18 years. Fittingly, Ford Frick, then commissioner of baseball, initiated a pitching award in his honor after Young's death, an award which remains to this day as the symbol of pitching excellence.

●

Adrian Constantine ("Cap") Anson is a shadowy figure out of baseball's history for today's fans, but in his time he was a charismatic, influential figure. He was as popular as any player until Babe Ruth, and he was known as the "Grand Old Man of Baseball" when he died in 1922.

Not all of his influence was good. He played a large part, for instance, in keeping blacks out of baseball. Two incidents stand out. In 1883, Anson refused to take the field in an exhibition game at Toledo because the opposing team had a black catcher, Fleetwood Walker; Anson backed down when it seemed the gate receipts would be forfeited. In 1887, when John Montgomery Ward tried to sign a black, George Stovey, for the Giants, Anson was so vehement in his opposition that Ward finally decided not to do it. Anson's actions thus precipitated an unofficial policy that prevailed until Jackie Robinson played for the Dodgers in 1947.

Anson did not regret his actions later, either. In his autobiography, *A Ball Player's Career,* published in 1900 (the first autobiography of a player), he referred to a black who had accompanied an American team on a world tour in 1874 as a "no account nigger."

Anson's career spanned 27 years, counting five in the National Association, and is the longest of any player. Little is known of his National Association career, beyond the fact that he was a star; it was with Chicago in the National League that he made his reputation. He also got his nickname in Chicago, when he was named captain for the 1879 season, and others shortened that to "Cap."

As a fielder, Anson was only slightly more mobile than a lamppost. He was shifted around in the lineup but generally played at first base, where he could do the least harm. At that, he set a record for most errors by a first-baseman (58) in a season in 1884, a mark that has never been equaled or even approached, and he is co-holder of the record for most years leading the league in errors (5).

But when Anson came to bat, his fielding deficiencies were soon forgiven. He was a fearsome hitter, using a split grip and concentrating on making contact. He was a high average hitter—batting over .300 for 20 of his 22 seasons in Chicago—with occasional flashes of power. In 1884, he hit five home runs in two consecutive games, a mark that has since been tied but never surpassed.

Just how good a hitter Anson really was we will never know because scorekeeping in those days was less than an exact science. At one time, for instance, Anson was credited with a .407 average for 1879, until it was discovered that the league statistician, Nick Young (later the league president), sometimes added hits to the totals of his favorites, of whom Anson was one. The *Baseball Encylopedia* now credits Anson with a .396 average for that year. The late Lee Allen, former historian for the Hall of Fame, went through old newspaper clippings and claimed Anson actually hit .317 that year. Take your pick.

Anson became co-manager with Bob Ferguson in 1879 and sole manager in 1880, and he made his mark in that role. He won five pennants in his first seven years as manager of the White Sox, and he was responsible for many changes in the game.

He is generally thought to be the first to take a team south for spring training; he took the White Sox to Hot Springs, Arkansas in 1885. Later,

Cy Young, the winningest pitcher
in major league history
with 511 victories, got 289 of his
wins in the National League.
(George Brace photo)

Adrian "Cap" Anson was the
leading player in the
National League in the first
quarter-century. His bigotry
established a tradition that
kept blacks out of the majors
for decades. *(George Brace photo)*

however, he became skeptical about that, worrying that the players would be hurt upon returning to a cold climate.

Anson was perhaps the first to use the hit-and-run, when he had Mike Kelly. He taught outfielders to back up infielders (a move that was, like the hit-and-run, later popularized by the Baltimore Orioles). He used signals on the field and also sometimes platooned his players.

As a person, Anson was nearly as inflexible as he was as a fielder. He had sworn off alcohol and smoking (apparently after spending a night in jail for drunkenness) and instituted a $100 fine in his club for drinking beer. That did not set well with the players of the time, especially Mike ("King") Kelly; Anson and his famous star had constant disputes.

Anson simply did not believe that an injury should keep a player out of the lineup. A player trying to get a day off for anything less substantial than a broken leg would be accused of not being "manly."

He was a tactless, direct man. One day after a loss to Brooklyn, a Chicago fan sent him a telegram asking him if the game was "on the level." Anson replied in another telegram: "I would not disgrace my players by showing them your telegram, nor degrade myself by answering your question." Since his reputation for honesty was unquestioned, he could get away with that kind of answer.

Both as player and manager, Anson was highly competitive, and his competitiveness often got him into running word battles with players, umpires, and even fans. Around the league, he was sometimes known as "Crybaby Anson" because he so often questioned umpiring decisions, but he was respected despite that nickname.

Though he never won another pennant after 1886, Anson stayed as manager of the White Sox until he was fired after the 1897 season. He tried to raise $150,000 to buy the team but failed. He then signed to manage the Giants but lasted less than a month before being fired by Andrew Freedman, fully as intractable a man as Anson.

Anson was 46 when his baseball career ended, and his postbaseball life was a complex one of business, vaudeville, and politics. He even took one last fling at baseball in his 50s, organizing a semipro team called "Anson's Colts," which toured the country; Anson played first base in his customary style.

Until the year before he died, Anson was in vaudeville. His funeral was one of the largest ever given an American athlete, and he was elected to the Hall of Fame in 1939.

5. The Game Was Different Back Then

By 1901, the rules and dimensions of baseball were the same as they are today, and the teams in the National League were the ones that would remain unchanged until 1953, but that doesn't mean the game was the same one we watch today. In many ways, there were significant differences.

Pitchers had much more freedom because of the widespread use of trick pitches. Some pitchers used spitters; some roughed the ball up with an emory board or piece of sandpaper; still others applied licorice or tobacco to the ball, to make one side darker than the other and thus more difficult to hit. All of these tactics were outlawed in 1920, but the spitter is still used by some pitchers, as Preacher Roe and Gaylord Perry have admitted after the fact.

Even when the pitchers did nothing to the ball—a rare occasion indeed—the hitters still had a problem, because the ball was dead. It was not wound as tightly as it is today, so it was not as lively when the game started. By game's end, it was even deader, because balls that did not go into the stands were generally kept in play; an umpire could not throw out a ball just because it had a nick in it, as he would today.

Home runs were happy accidents. Few were hit, and even fewer were the result of a ball hit over a fence. Home-run hitters were likely to be fast men who hit line drives between the outfielders and made it home ahead of the throw. Tommy Leache of the Pittsburgh Pirates led the National League in home runs with six in 1902, and not one of his homers went over the fence.

Teams played for one run at a time. The ability to bunt well and exercise the hit-and-run were important. Hitters used thick-handled bats and concentrated on making contact, avoiding a strikeout.

Stolen bases were very important because a stolen base could save an out; a runner would not have to be sacrificed to second. In the early 1900s, the Pirates had Honus Wagner, Fred Clarke, and Leache, who had career stolen-base totals of 722, 506, and 361, respectively. In 1911, the New York Giants stole 347 bases.

Because there was so much emphasis on getting one run at a time, as opposed to the "big inning" concept that dominates the game today, there is a tendency to think that games were much lower-scoring in those days, a succession of 1–0 and 2–1 affairs. That just isn't so. Teams of that era scored just about as often as modern teams do; they just did it differently.

Take this example, for instance. In the years 1901–03, the Pirates led the league in scoring with 776, 775, and 792 runs. In the years 1971–73, the leaders were Pittsburgh (788 in '71), Houston (708 in '72), and Atlanta (799 in '73) and by the 1970s the season was considerably longer.

The style of play put all the pressure on the hitters, not the pitchers. The hitters had to take advantage of every opportunity. When a runner got to second or third, it was imperative to get him home, because there might not be another one there for a long time.

Conversely, pitchers could pace themselves. Since there was little danger of the ball being hit out of the park, they could throw easily until a runner got on base; only then would they have to bear down.

Nobody was ever better at this style of pitching than Christy Mathewson. Fred Lieb, the old-time baseball writer, once told of seeing Mathewson pitch a shutout in which he gave up 14 hits in the first seven innings! Mathewson allowed 2 hits in each of those innings but gave up no walks. In the eighth and ninth, perhaps tiring of that nonsense, he retired Cincinnati 1-2-3.

Being able to conserve their energy and arms, pitchers could throw more innings than they do today. More important, they finished what they started. Look at the difference sixty years made.

In 1901, every club in the league had at least 111 complete games, out of 137–142 games (because of tie games and canceled ones, some teams played fewer or more than the scheduled 140 games that season). The Chicago pitching staff completed 131 of its 140 games to lead the league.

By 1961, the number of games had gone up to 154, but the number of complete games had gone down drastically. Only the Milwaukee Braves, with 57, had more than 50 complete games; Philadelphia had only 29.

One 1961 manager, Alvin Dark of the San Francisco Giants, became so disgusted with his pitchers' inability to complete a game that he announced before the start of one game that he wouldn't put in a relief pitcher, no matter how high the score mounted.

Dark knew how to pick his spots. He started Juan Marichal, a throwback to the old-time pitchers, who usually finished what he started. Marichal finished and won the game.

There was little money in baseball at the turn of the century, and it may well be that some players who could have become stars chose instead to stay with other jobs and play baseball on the many semiprofessional teams that existed in towns and cities around the country. Rube Marquard, who later set a record with 19 straight wins for the New York Giants, refused his first major league offer, by Cleveland, because he could make more money selling ice cream in his home town.

Because there was little money in the game, players were very independent. Fines and suspensions weren't the weapons they are now for club managements; a player who knew he could make as much or more at another job wasn't likely to be cowed by a manager telling him he had better shape up or lose his position.

Drunkenness was a continuing problem. In fact, in the early days of the game, there was a strong connection between baseball and liquor, with teams in St. Louis, Baltimore, Brooklyn, Cincinnati, and Louisville owned by brewers, saloon keepers, or whisky distillers. By the turn of the century, that connection was diminishing (the St. Louis Cardinals are the only National League team now owned by a brewery), but the players' drunkenness was not.

Players, managers, and even umpires often showed up for games drunk. Fans heard stories of players being dragged out of saloons so they could make a game. Owners bought steam baths, and writers and fans believed the baths were used to sweat the alcohol out of players' systems.

Players were traded because of "rheumatism" or "dizzy spells," euphemisms for alcoholism. The chief duty of team captains was to try to keep at least some of the players sober.

It was a rough time. Players slid into bases with spikes high; if the infielder dodged the spikes, he tagged the runner in the mouth. In the 1909 World Series, Tommy Leach of Pittsburgh reached third base in one game and Detroit third baseman George Moriarty came over and kicked Leach, punched him and hit him on top of the head, all for no apparent reason other than that Leach had gotten that far. Soon, Leach was punching back.

Such occurrences were common at the turn of the century. Quite often, the fans were involved, too. Most fans were content to yell from the stands, but some came out on the field to assault players or umpires, particularly the latter.

Cursing among the players was so common that some owners became upset, supposedly fearing the example set for the younger players. In 1899, John T. Brush of Cincinnati wrote what became known as the "Brush Purification Rule," which provided severe penalties for any player who cursed other players or the umpire. The rule had one failing: It required other players to report on those who were cursing. No reports were ever made, and the rule was dropped after a year.

Turn of the century baseball was much different for the writers then, too. The baseball beat was long considered the choicest position in the sports department—maybe even the entire newspaper—and no wonder. The hours were short and pleasurable, and the requirements of the job were much less demanding than they are now. There was no competition from radio and television, no night games, no need to wheedle quotes out of uncooperative players.

Games of that era started in the late afternoon, usually about three o'clock, because owners hoped to get businessmen to leave their jobs early and come to the park. The late start was feasible despite the lack of lights in the parks because games were played so much more quickly than they are today. A game that lasted two hours was a rarity.

Writers would sometimes show up at games as late as the sixth inning. After the game, they would write their stories; the current practice of interviewing players after the game did not start until the advent of radio and television. Then, they would go home for a leisurely dinner and after dinner, go to the office to check their stories.

The hardest part of the job for some writers was preparing the box score at the end of the game. Some never learned it; Fred Lieb tells of letting Damon Runyon copy his box score. The box scores varied from paper to paper. In one account, a player might get credit for two hits; in another account, only one. Statistics had not yet become as vital to the game as they would be.

Travel was much different, for players and writers. Though the National League was spread across only half the country, teams spent more time traveling than they do now; an airplane goes across the country faster than a train goes from New York to Chicago.

The trains of those days were not the most comfortable, either, and they were not air-conditioned, an important factor in the muggy eastern and midwestern summers. Players often faced the choice of sweltering in a hot coach or opening a window and getting hit by cinders from the rail bed.

Yet, the players had some traveling advantages. They never crossed more than one time zone, so their schedules remained relatively unchanged. It was more relaxing on the train than on a plane, because they could move around much more easily. Train travel encouraged a closeness among teammates that is largely absent today. Because they were on the trains for long periods of time, players spent more time talking to each other, or playing cards. When they talked, they talked baseball, instead of debentures and two-for-one stock splits.

●

One thing that did change at the turn of the century was the attitude toward the baseball umpire. That change probably did as much as anything else to make the game respectable.

From the time Alexander Cartwright drew up his rules for the game, the umpire was supposed to have the last word. He often had trouble imposing that last word, however, because players, managers and owners thought they should be able to overrule him. Their attitude was understandable, given the way umpires were chosen and the quality of men who took the job.

Before the National League started, umpires were chosen from among the spectators. Traveling clubs carried their own umpires. The forming of the National League didn't improve matters much. Umpires were paid $5 a day, which meant that they were for the most part ex-ballplayers who couldn't get another job.

There were other problems. Umpires were allowed to bet on the games, for instance. One umpire, Richard Higham, was fired in 1882 when it was discovered that he was advising gamblers which way to bet when he was umpiring. It would be naive to think that Higham was the only crooked umpire of the time.

Umpires traveled with teams, ate with the players, and sometimes even played catch with them before the game. Obviously, these men would not be impartial arbiters when the game began.

Newspapers were unsparing in their criticism of umpires. An editorial in the *Chicago Tribune* in the 1880s, for instance, said, "The average league umpire is a worthless loafer." No minced words there.

Other writers were more specific in assessing blame. "How long," asked the *Cincinnati Enquirer,* "will the public put up with Bradley's umpiring?"

"We have had a bellyful of O'Rourke and Stage," announced the *Philadelphia Press.*

One of the chief complaints about umpires was their reluctance to call games because of darkness. Though nobody ever admitted it, that was probably because the National League owners didn't want games postponed until the next day, when they would have to schedule two games for the price of one.

One of the worst examples of this practice came in a game at Washington in the 1890s between Washington and the Baltimore Orioles. The game had not been started until 4:30, apparently because a government official could not get there earlier, and it soon grew dark. Umpire Jack Kerin was determined to get in 4½ innings, so the game would be official.

Finally, Baltimore pitcher John Clarkson took a lemon with him to the mound and fired it to catcher Wilbert Robinson. Kerin called a strike—and then Robinson handed him the lemon.

The game was called.

The status of the umpire in those days was probably no more graphically illustrated than when Albert G. Spalding announced with some pride that it was no longer considered part of the game to hit the umpire! Verbal abuse, of course, was still part of the game.

But at the turn of the century, the National League owners, reluctantly following the example of American League president Ban Johnson, finally stiffened the rules. Players and managers who abused umpires were fined and suspended, and an umpire's decision became the final word Cartwright had proclaimed it to be more than half a century earlier.

Probably nothing shows more clearly how drastically the status of umpires was changed in the early twentieth century than the double forfeit game on August 7, 1906 at New York's Polo Grounds, instigated by John J. McGraw, who had carried his umpire-baiting tactics from his Baltimore playing days to his managerial days with the Giants.

The previous day, Josh Devlin of the Giants had been called out on a close play by umpire James Johnstone. When the Giants subsequently lost the game, fans came out of the stands to attack Johnstone, who was rescued by the police.

On August 7, Johnstone was barred from the park by the gatekeeper, ostensibly because the police could not guarantee his safety, but actually because McGraw thought he had found a way to win the day's game more easily. In fact, New York police inspector Sweeney, at the game that day, had told McGraw that he felt his officers were certainly able to protect Johnstone.

Johnstone did not come into the park and McGraw, feigning surprise, announced that Sammy Strang, a Giant reserve, would be the umpire. The visiting Chicago team said they would not play, and Strang announced that the game was forfeited to the Giants.

Outside the park, Johnstone announced the game was forfeited to Chicago. League president Harry Pulliam, who had already had several run-ins with McGraw, backed up Johnstone and assigned him to the next New York-Chicago game.

Johnstone could not have been terribly eager to umpire that game. Accounts of the day refer to his nervousness, and to his difficulty in walking to the park. But when he appeared on the field, the New York fans cheered him!

That was the first step in making umpiring a respectable profession. Now, umpires are adequately paid, travel apart from the teams, and do not fraternize with players on the field.

The officials are the backbone of any sport, and it is worth noting that, though officiating in other sports (notably basketball and football) has been sharply criticized in recent years, serious disputes with umpires are now exceedingly rare. When fans yell "Kill the umpire!", umpires no longer have to take it literally.

6. NL vs. AL:
A Lasting Rivalry Begins

Just one year into the twentieth century, the National League's position as the only major professional baseball league was successfully challenged by the American League; and though the National League owners fought to ruin the new league, the American League's survival led to a stronger game and the creation of one of the most remarkable competitions in professional sports, the World Series.

The origins of the American League date back to 1893, when Charles Comiskey, then manager of the Cincinnati Reds, and Cincinnati baseball writer Byron Bancroft ("Ban") Johnson first met to discuss the project. Both men had ambitions that reached far beyond their jobs, and a new league would become the vehicle for each to reach his goal.

It was strange the two men were friends, because Johnson hated the man Comiskey worked for, Cincinnati owner John T. Brush—a fact which was to become important more than a decade later. Johnson continually criticized Brush in print. Comiskey was loyal to Brush, but that didn't stop him from helping his friend, Johnson.

In 1893, the presidency of the Western League, a minor league situated in the Midwest, became open. Comiskey pushed Johnson for the job. Brush had split emotions. On the one hand, he hated to see Johnson advance himself; on the other, if Johnson became president of the Western League, he would no longer be in a position to criticize Brush.

So, the Cincinnati owner allowed Comiskey to plead Johnson's case with the Western League owners, and Comiskey managed to imply that it was Brush's idea. Johnson got the job and with Comiskey's help, began to build the league to major status. A year later, Comiskey quit his job at Cincinnati and bought the Sioux City team in the Western League, transferring it to St. Paul.

Within two years, Johnson had made his league the strongest of the minor leagues, with sound financial backing for each team. The league made money each year, and, by 1896, Johnson had decided that if the National League dropped any franchises, he would pick them up and try to make his league a major one.

In 1900, Johnson made his first move, establishing a franchise in Cleveland after that city was dropped by the National League. He also changed the name of his league to the American League, trying to make it sound more national in scope. In reality, however, it was the same league, regionally based and not yet going after the best baseball talent.

It might have remained that way for a while, but the National League owners, now that they had a monopoly, reverted to their old practice of cutting back on salaries, which made the players unhappy and made it possible for another league to move in.

Johnson was ready. In 1901, he established American League franchises in four eastern cities—Baltimore, Washington, Boston and Philadelphia—so the league was no longer merely a regional one. The first two franchises were established in cities abandoned by the National League, but the latter two were in direct competition with the National League franchises, as was the new American League franchise in Chicago.

Johnson's move made the American League almost as stable as the National. Six of the eight teams—Boston, Chicago, Cleveland, Detroit, Philadelphia, and Washington—were to remain intact until the franchise shifting started in the 1950s; the first four teams, of course, are still there. Only Baltimore and Milwaukee later dropped out; Baltimore got back into the league in 1953, and Milwaukee in 1970.

At the same time, Johnson withdrew his league from the National Agreement (which had stipulated that the American League would be a minor league) and announced that it was now to be considered a major league. Because his owners had the necessary financial resources, they declared war on the National League and went after established players. About 30 National League regulars jumped to the American League, among them future Hall-of-Famers Nap Lajoie, John McGraw, Jimmy Collins, Joe McGinnity, Clark Griffith and Cy Young.

The American League faced formidable problems. But Johnson had planned well, and the league survived.

The biggest problem, naturally, centered around McGraw, in the middle of controversy throughout his career. McGraw and Johnson continually battled over McGraw's umpire-baiting tactics, and Johnson finally suspended McGraw in July of 1902.

There are two conflicting theories on what happened next. One is that McGraw started negotiations to sell the club to Brush, who then released McGraw, McGinnity, Roger Bresnahan, Dan McGann, Cy Seymour, Joe Kelley and Jack Cronin to sign with National League clubs, wrecking the Baltimore club.

At the time, McGraw claimed that he had bought his release from Baltimore. Years later, though, he told baseball historian Fred Lieb that he had learned that Johnson planned to move the Baltimore club to New York in 1903—but without McGraw. "I acted fast," boasted McGraw. "He planned to run out on me; so I ran out on him, and beat him to New York by nearly a year."

Johnson reacted to the gutting of the Baltimore club by taking players from other teams to restock the Orioles. Baltimore finished last and, at the end of the season, the franchise was shifted to New York, as part of the agreement with the National League that ended the war between the leagues. That franchise, first known as the Highlanders, eventually became the Yankees.

It had taken the American League only two years to become recognized as a true major league. As soon as the two leagues reached an agreement that ended player raids, fans started pressure for the start of a competition between the league champions.

Barney Dreyfuss, owner of the National League champion Pittsburgh Pirates, was willing to play the Boston Pilgrims (now Red Sox), the American League champions, because Dreyfuss had one of the best National League teams of all time.

The Pirates had changed from an also-ran to a strong team in 1900, when the league reduced from 12 to 8 teams. Dreyfuss had been president of the Louisville club, one of the four that was disbanded. He bought half of the Pittsburgh club and switched his best players from Louisville to Pittsburgh, among them Honus Wagner, left-fielder/manager Fred Clark, second baseman Claude Ritchey, third baseman Tommy Leach, and pitchers Charles ("Deacon") Phillippe, Rube Waddell and Patsy Flaherty.

The partnership between Dreyfuss and William Kerr was neither a happy nor a long-lived one. That first year, Kerr agreed to sell his half to Dreyfuss for $70,000—in cash.

With Wagner hitting .381 to win the first of his record eight National

League batting titles, the Pirates finished second in 1900, only three games behind Brooklyn. Aided by the fact that the American League player raids didn't hit them—probably because Dreyfuss was more generous than other league owners—the Pirates won the next three National League pennants. They were a well-balanced club, with strong hitting, excellent baserunners, good defense and, above all, a sound pitching staff. In 1902 the pitchers failed to complete what they started in only eight of 139 games, and the Pirates won a then-record 103 games.

Dreyfuss was so confident his team could beat the American League champion that he approached Henry Killilea, the Boston owner, in early September. It was obvious by then that Pittsburgh and Boston would be the league champions; the Pirates eventually won by 6½ games, the Pilgrims by a whopping 14½.

The plan was that the World Series would be a best-of-nine series, with the first three games at Boston, the next four at Pittsburgh, and the final two, if necessary, at Boston. Though the Series is now seven games instead of nine, the format remains the same.

Before he agreed to those terms, Killilea asked the advice of Johnson. "If you think you can beat them," said Johnson, "play them."

Killilea decided to take the challenge. He, too, had a fine team, with the incomparable Cy Young—a 28-game winner that year—as the bulwark of a strong pitching staff and Jimmy Collins, perhaps the finest fielding third baseman of all time, the key to the defense. The Pilgrims also had a most unusual slugger in Buck Freeman. Only five foot nine and 150 pounds, Freeman had established the National League home run record with 25 for Washington in 1899, and he had led the American League with 13 in 1903.

Boston also got two unexpected breaks entering the Series. Pittsburgh lost the services of Ed Doheny, a 16-game winner in the regular season, who had a nervous breakdown; and the Pirates' leading winner, 25-game winner Sam Leever, had a sore arm and could pitch only briefly (10 innings) and ineffectively (two losses) in the Series.

The Series started badly for Dreyfuss, too, when he had to pay to get into the park at Boston. "Imagine paying to see my own team play!" he said.

His pain was assuaged when Deacon Phillippe won the first game for Pittsburgh, not to mention the third and—after two days of rain had given him some rest—the fourth. At that point, the Pirates had a 3–1 lead, but they never won another game. The Pilgrims took four straight and the first World Series championship was theirs.

What happened? One theory, advanced by Tommy Leach, was that the Boston fans had done them in. The fans were more a part of the game in those days than they are now, often coming onto the field to cow umpires and players.

The Boston fans were particularly raucous. They had a group known as the "Royal Rooters," led by a Boston saloon keeper named Mike McGreevey. McGreevey was known as "Nuff Ced" because he settled baseball arguments in his bar by announcing the verdict and adding, "Enough said."

The Boston fans took a popular song of the day, "Tessie," and formed their own lyrics, favorable for the Pilgrims, unfavorable for the Pirates. They sang the song incessantly. "It was driving us nuts," said Leach.

A more persuasive argument could be made for the fact that, with Doheny out and Leever ineffective, the Pirates had only one reliable pitcher, Phillippe. As good as he was, Phillippe couldn't do it alone.

Phillippe got a lot of help, from the weather and from Dreyfuss. Before the seventh game, the last at Pittsburgh, Dreyfuss announced that it was too cold to play and postponed the game. The next day it was just as cold, but Phillippe had his extra day of rest and the game was played. But the Pirates lost, 7–3, with Young besting Phillippe.

Two days of rain in Boston delayed the eighth game long enough so that Phillippe could start his fifth game of the Series. But the arm-weary right-hander couldn't match Bill Dineen, who shut out the Pirates, 3–0.

Dreyfuss was heartbroken at the loss, but he did not blame his players. Indeed, he let them split up all the net proceeds from the game, so the losing Pirates actually got more than the winning Red Sox.

Killilea was not afflicted by a comparable attack of generosity. He literally took the money and ran, selling the club immediately.

●

The World Series was an immediate hit with the fans, but a personality clash that dated back more than a decade prevented it from being resumed in 1904.

John T. Brush had bought the New York Giants, who won the pennant in 1904. Brush, of course, hated American League president Ban Johnson, and he refused to let his team meet the AL champions, once again the Boston Pilgrims.

"There is nothing in the constitution or playing rules of the National

League which requires its victorious club to submit its championship honors to a contest with a victorious club in a minor league," said Brush, trying to justify his actions.

White Sox owner Charles Comiskey pointed out that the American League was a recognized major league and had, indeed, won the first World Series. "If the Giants do not want to play the champions of the American League," said Comiskey, "the followers of the game can draw their own conclusions."

The next season, the Giants won again, but Brush's anger at Johnson had apparently receded. He not only permitted his club to play in the Series but also devised a code that made the World Series compulsory.

As it happened, the 1905 Series was one of the true classics. Won by the Giants, 4–1 over the Philadelphia Athletics, every game was a shutout. Christy Mathewson pitched three for the Giants, Joe McGinnity added the fourth, and Chief Bender pitched one for the Athletics. The three runs the A's got backing up Bender in the second game of the Series were the only ones they scored.

Those first five years of dual existence for the National and American leagues have set the tone for everything that has followed. There has always been an uneasy truce between the two leagues. In other sports, leagues work together, but the baseball tradition has always been two separate leagues, going their own ways.

Other sports have interleague or interconference play; baseball teams play entirely within their own league, except for exhibition games and, of course, the World Series.

Other sports adopt rules that apply to every team, but the National and American leagues often have different rules. The American League, for instance, adopted the designated hitter rule but the National League did not. American League expansion started a year before the National League. In 1977, the American League expanded further to 14 teams while the National stayed at 12. Even the umpiring is different; it is widely believed that National League umpires will call a low strike much more frequently than their colleagues in the American League.

This independence causes some serious problems, but it has at least one positive result: the World Series is a seriously contested competition. Teams know they are playing not only for themselves but for their leagues. A comparison to football is pertinent here. Football's showcase, the Super Bowl, has become more of a spectacle than a game. The World Series remains the finest example of baseball.

7. Muggsy and His Tricks

John J. McGraw is just a name in baseball history books to most fans, but to his peers, he was a colossus, a man who dominated the game for nearly a third of a century by the sheer force of his personality.

He was magnanimous, brave and resourceful, said his friends. He was petty, cowardly and vicious, said his enemies. At one time or another, all the adjectives applied.

He battled umpires, cursed fans, and defied league presidents, often successfully. His style of managing was copied by others, but never with as much success; in 31 years of managing, McGraw won 10 pennants and finished second 11 times, and his teams finished in the first division 27 times.

He had the competitive instincts of a piranha. He was loved in the cities in which he played and managed, and hated in the other league cities. When he came to New York, the same writers who had thought him a menace to the game as a Baltimore player and manager hailed him as the most vibrant personality in the game.

He was a mass of contradictions, this small town boy who knew some of the world's great cities as an adult. He could be compassionate to a stranger and unforgiving to a friend. He seemed obsessed with baseball and yet he was not; he had many interests off the field. It was difficult to believe that the same man who incited riots on the field could be gentle and loving at home. And the final contradiction: The man who had so many enemies in ballparks around the league also had so many friends in those cities that he would hold cocktail parties in his hotel suite to greet them when the Giants were on the road.

"He was a flamboyant personality, a lot like George M. Cohan," said Garry Schumacher, who covered McGraw and his Giants as a newspaperman in New York in the twenties. "He and Cohan were great friends, too. McGraw was Broadway-wise. He was Mr. New York, make no doubt about it."

Perhaps the key to his personality was this: There was only one way to do things as far as McGraw was concerned—his way. That led to the end of his friendship with Wilbert J. Robinson, known as "Uncle Robbie" to his many friends in baseball.

McGraw and Robinson were teammates on the Orioles, and McGraw had hired Robinson as a coach for the Giants. The two had also been partners in a Baltimore saloon.

Then, two things happened. The first was relatively minor. "Uncle Robbie had been the third-base coach in the 1912 Series," said Schumacher. "He had made a decision on one play that had cost the Giants a run, and McGraw was mad as hell."

The second incident was more serious: Robinson decided to take the job as Brooklyn manager. It would seem that McGraw would have been happy that his longtime friend was getting a chance to advance, but McGraw regarded Robinson's decision as disloyalty. For the remaining 20 years of his life, McGraw hardly spoke to Robinson.

McGraw's relationship with his players was often a stormy one. He twice traded away third baseman Buck Herzog, for instance, because they could not get along. His relationship with his eventual successor, Bill Terry, was no better. "McGraw never spoke to Terry at all except to bawl him out," said Schumacher.

Some players just could not take McGraw's harangues. One player, "Shuffling Phil" Douglas, had his baseball career ended by a series of incidents that grew out of a McGraw harangue.

Douglas was a pitcher of considerable ability with an even more considerable weakness for liquor. He first came to the majors in 1912 with the Chicago White Sox, but his drinking problem had caused him to be passed along to the Reds, Dodgers and Cubs before McGraw traded for him before the 1921 season.

Douglas won 15 games during the 1921 season and added two more wins in the World Series, though he disappeared at times on what he called "vacations." McGraw used former outfielder Jess Burkett to watch Douglas in the 1922 season, but Douglas managed to evade Burkett for a four-day period. When he came back to the Polo Grounds, hung over and trembling, McGraw bawled him out in front of his teammates and told him to go home and sleep it off.

The shaken Douglas sat down and wrote a letter to a friend of his, outfielder Leslie Mann of the St. Louis Cardinals, suggesting he could "go fishing" for the rest of the season, so the Cardinals could win the pennant—if he were paid off.

The next day, Douglas called Mann to try to get the letter destroyed, but it was too late. The postal service was more reliable in those days. The letter had been delivered, and Mann had already told his manager, Branch

Wilbert Robinson, best known for managing the Brooklyn Dodgers, also set a record with seven hits in a game. *(George Brace photo)*

John J. McGraw was both a topflight third baseman for the Baltimore Orioles and one of the greatest managers of all time with the New York Giants. *(George Brace photo)*

Rickey, about it. Rickey, in turned, called baseball commissioner Judge Kenesaw Landis.

Landis conducted an investigation, during which Douglas admitted writing the letter. Landis then ruled that Douglas could no longer play organized baseball. Nobody connected with the affair seriously thought that Douglas had meant what he had written, but coming as it did so close to the Black Sox scandal, Landis's action was the only one he could have taken.

Despite McGraw's problems with his players, a lot of players on other teams wanted to play for him for a simple reason: He won. That was the only reason to play the game, McGraw thought. He was a driven man, and he admitted it. "In playing or managing," he said early in his career with the Giants, "the game of ball is only fun for me when I'm out in front and winning. I don't care a bag of peanuts for the rest of the game."

He would do anything to win. As a player, he would trip, hold and spike opposing base runners, and it was then he started his attacks on umpires. He encouraged the spectators to join him, to the extent that after one game, Baltimore fans waited outside the clubhouse for half an hour with a length of rope, threatening to hang the umpire. The umpire, no fool, waited until they left before he came out.

As a manager, he seemed to be involved almost constantly in disputes with the umpires and the league president, often almost simultaneously. He left the American League because of his conflict with league president Ban Johnson, and his behavior was no more circumspect when he joined the Giants. Here are some of the highlights of his disputatious career:

—On May 20, 1905, McGraw was ejected from a game when he accused the umpire of being influenced by Pittsburgh owner Barney Dreyfuss. He then accused Dreyfuss of welshing on bets and tried to make a $10,000 bet with him on the game.

Dreyfuss complained to league president Harry Pulliam, who eventually suspended McGraw for 15 days and fined him $150. The league directors (owners) overruled Pulliam and rescinded both fine and suspension, but that wasn't enough for McGraw and Giant owner John T. Brush, who took the matter to court in Boston. The judge ruled in McGraw's favor.

—In the 1907 season, McGraw got into a fight with a Cincinnati guard. In another game, he threw a cup of water in the face of umpire Bill Klem.

—On June 8, 1917, McGraw punched umpire Bill Byron. McGraw was suspended for 16 days and fined $500. He told New York writer Sid Mercer that league president John K. Tener was a tool of the Philadelphia Phillies and that the umpires were the poorest he had seen. When Mercer quoted him, McGraw denied it, but Tener met with Mercer and announced he was convinced that McGraw had said it. McGraw was fined an additional $1,000.

This was the dark side of McGraw's nature, but there was another, generous side to the character of this complex man. He was a soft touch for a panhandler, and the Giant's payroll was crammed with the names of former players of McGraw's who needed money.

Newspapermen, though they had their problems with McGraw, also saw another side of him, particularly when the team was traveling.

"He could be an amazingly engaging guy," remembered Schumacher, "and he had friends all over, a million friends. When we hit town, he'd hold a cocktail party in his hotel suite. There'd be four or five newspaper guys there, and the rest would be his friends.

"He was a very engaging host. The conversation was on baseball sometimes, and other things, too. Maybe about the town we were in. Sometimes we'd have some questions about the games, things we could get in our stories, but it was mostly just conversation."

Sometimes, too, there were surprises. Schumacher remembered one game in which the Giants had been leading as it grew dark. McGraw had argued that the game should be called, but umpire Bill Klem let it continue and the Dodgers won it on a home run by Babe Herman.

"At the party that night," said Schumacher, "I started to say to him, 'Oh, Mr. McGraw, it was terrible the way we lost that game. That shouldn't have been allowed.' I kept getting a dig in my ribs from Sid Mercer (another writer) so I stopped.

"I asked Sid what he was doing, and he said, 'Don't you know McGraw and Klem are good friends?' "

McGraw friendly with an umpire.? Indeed. "He and Klem were from the same area in New York," said Schumacher, "and McGraw always thought Klem was in a class by himself as an umpire. Which he was."

In the off-season, McGraw liked to travel to foreign countries, and he found a way to combine business with pleasure in November 1911, when he took his club to Cuba for a series of games against Cuban teams. It is typical of his approach to baseball that, though the games meant nothing, he became upset at some early defeats. He scheduled a morning workout and announced that any players who did not play their best would be sent home. The Giants won the remaining games on that tour.

Cuba was McGraw's favorite (for a time, he and Charles Stoneham owned a race track and casino in Havana, until Commissioner Landis ordered them to sell it), but it was hardly the only foreign country the Giants visited.

In 1913, after winning their third straight pennant, the Giants went on a world tour with the White Sox, starting in Cincinnati and ending in London, where King George V was among the spectators. The teams played 44 games in the United States, Japan, China, the Philippines, Australia, Ceylon, Egypt, Italy, France and England.

McGraw and White Sox owner Charles Comiskey tried one more tour, in 1924, but with considerably less success. The first game, at Liverpool, attracted about 3,500, but a game at Dublin had a total paid attendance of 20, causing the game to be canceled. Three games in Paris did so poorly at the gate that the remaining games, in Brussels, Nice, Rome and Paris, were canceled.

●

Though McGraw's playing career was overshadowed by his managerial career, he was an excellent player, possibly good enough to make the Hall of Fame on that basis.

As a player, he was swift and skinny, without the paunch that the best tailoring could not hide in his later years as a manager. He was an excellent base runner, once stealing 78 bases in a season (in 1894, when the rule was less strict) and 73 in 1899, when the current scoring rule applied.

He was also an excellent hitter, with a lifetime average of .344. His mark of .391 in 1899 is the highest ever for a third baseman.

He inherited the job of managing the Orioles when Ned Hanlon left in 1899 for Brooklyn, taking the Baltimore stars (except for McGraw and Robinson) with him. He finished fourth with the Orioles that year, as his former manager, Hanlon, won the pennant in Brooklyn.

McGraw was sold to St. Louis of the National League in 1900 but refused the job of managing. He was smart enough to see that the upcoming battle with the American League was going to create openings for somebody with his ability, so he did not sign a reserve clause contract. That enabled him to jump to Baltimore—by now in the American League—in 1901.

As we have seen, his problems with AL president Johnson caused him to move to the Giants, and it was with the Giants that he made his reputation. In 1902, with McGraw managing the last 63 games, the Giants finished in last place, but the next year they moved up to second, and in 1904 they won the pennant—and McGraw was on his way.

●

McGraw's managerial style was marked by extremely close control of his players, and he became known as "The Little Napoleon." His players did almost nothing without his guidance. He called pitches, and he gave signs to his batters on every pitch.

He was a great believer in the effectiveness of the low curve, and it was largely because of the success of his pitchers that the National League became known as a low ball league—as it still is today. The most spectacular example of that strategy came in the 1922 World Series when McGraw ordered his pitchers to throw nothing but low curves to Babe Ruth. Ruth chased the pitches and got only two hits in 17 at-bats, as the Giants swept the Series, 4–0.

McGraw was an excellent tactician, always a step ahead of the opposition. He was not reluctant to go against the baseball "book" if it meant a chance to win. The classic example of that came in a game against Pittsburgh, when Babe Adams was pitching and George Kelly was batting for the Giants. The count went to 3-and-0, and McGraw gave Kelly the hit sign. Kelly got a base-clearing double.

Later, McGraw was asked why he let Kelly swing on 3-and-0, when it seemed that Adams might walk him and force in a run. McGraw's reasoning went like this: Despite the three balls he had thrown, Adams was an excellent control pitcher. If McGraw conceded the strike on 3-and-0, Adams would probably be able to put the next two pitches where Kelly couldn't do much with them. Expecting that Kelly would be letting the 3-and-0 pitch go, however, Adams grooved that one.

The Giants' manager was also an excellent amateur psychologist. He played on the superstitions of his ball players, and he was managing in an extremely superstitious era.

During a game in 1904, catcher Frank Bowerman told McGraw he had seen a team of white horses driving past the Polo Grounds. "That's a good sign," he said. "Watch me kill the ball this afternoon."

Bowerman got two hits that day, and he spread the word about the white horses around the clubhouse. The next day, the horses made another appearance, and the day after that, and the day after that. By the end of the week, the whole team was hitting well.

The players never seemed to realize the obvious: McGraw had hired the driver and team of horses to ride by the park after Bowerman had first noticed them.

McGraw's teams won pennants in bunches. The 1911–13 team won three in a row, and the 1921–24 team became the first in baseball history (and still the only National League team) to win four in a row.

But the game was slipping away from McGraw. The lively ball, introduced in the 1920s, made baseball an entirely different game from the one McGraw played and managed so well. He resented the change, particularly the symbol and architect of the change, Babe Ruth. He always downgraded Ruth's talent, insisting that Honus Wagner was a far better player.

The 1922 Series was the last McGraw's Giants won, and the 1924 pennant was the last National League championship, though the Giants finished second four times and third twice in the remaining seven full years of McGraw's career.

His judgment was still good, however, as he proved when he got a phone call from a friend in Louisiana, Harry Williams, touting him on a young prospect named Mel Ott. McGraw gave Ott a tryout and signed him at the end of it.

Ott was only 17, but McGraw kept him with the Giants. "He's too young to play big league ball," he told newspapermen, "but I won't send him to the minors because I'm afraid it would ruin him. His hitting style is unorthodox, and there isn't a minor league manager who wouldn't tinker with it. But it is natural for him, and he'll get results as soon as he learns about big league pitching."

McGraw also changed Ott from a catcher to an outfielder, mainly because he believed his catchers should be bigger than Ott. McGraw put Ott on the bench beside him and gave the youngster a thorough baseball education. Ott got only 60 at-bats that first year, but by 1928, when he was 19, he was a regular. The next year, at 20, he hit 42 home runs, and he went on to set a National League record with 511 homers that lasted until another Giant— Willie Mays—broke it. So, the final irony of McGraw's career: The man who hated the long ball introduced the league's premier slugger.

More and more, though, McGraw was losing control. It showed in the last big explosion of his career, in 1931, on a hot July afternoon in St. Louis. Spotting league president John Heydler in the stands, he started a tirade because of a $150 fine he had received after being ejected from a game by an umpire.

Heydler tried to pacify McGraw, with no success. McGraw extended his tirade to the fans who were standing and listening. Finally, he returned to the field, turned the club over to coach Dave Bancroft, and went back to the hotel to regain his composure.

McGraw's health was failing him, and it was obvious that he would have to step down. But the timing of his decision and the announcement of his successor both came as a surprise.

On July 3, 1932, the Giants scheduled a press conference for three o'clock at their offices downtown. Three hours before that, Garry Schumacher, working at that time for the *New York Journal-American,* walked into the clubhouse. Because he had not phoned his office that morning, he was unaware that a press conference had been called.

"I saw a notice on the blackboard that Bill Terry was replacing John McGraw as manager of the Giants," recalled Schumacher. "Jesus Christ! I couldn't get to the phone fast enough! By the time the press conference was being held, the paper was on the street with my story in it, so I guess you could say I had a scoop, all right."

The naming of Terry as McGraw's replacement was a big surprise, though he turned out to be a good manager, because Terry and McGraw had never gotten along. Fred Lindstrom had expected that he would be McGraw's successor. At the end of the season, Lindstrom asked to be traded because "after the way I've been lied to, I don't want to stay with the club." He was then traded to Pittsburgh.

The next year, with Terry managing and McGraw watching from a spot in the center-field clubhouse, the Giants won the pennant. McGraw managed only one game that season, as the National League manager in the first All-Star game.

On February 25, 1934, McGraw died, and an era died with him. No manager, before or since, has matched his impact on the game.

John J. McGraw was a true giant.

8. The Pen Is Mightier Than the Glove

These are the saddest of possible words—
  "Tinker to Evers to Chance"
Trio of Bear Cubs and fleeter than birds—
  "Tinker to Evers to Chance"
Ruthlessly pricking our gonfalon bubble,
Making a Giant hit into a double,
Words that are weighty with nothing but trouble—
  "Tinker to Evers to Chance."
                              Franklin P. Adams

One July day in 1910, *New York Mail* columnist Franklin P. Adams needed eight lines to fill out his column. He was in a hurry to get out to the Polo Grounds for the ball game. It was his habit, as a transplanted Chicagoan, to root against the Giants, and as he thought about the game, the eight lines above popped into his head. He quickly typed them up, sent out his column, and left for the game.

Neither then nor later did Adams think much about them, but they became among the most celebrated lines of verse ever written about baseball. Because of those words, Joe Tinker, Johnny Evers and Frank Chance became the best-known double play combination in baseball history, though they certainly were not the best. They even went into the Hall of Fame together, in 1946.

Oddly, none of the three started at the position that made him famous. Chance was originally a catcher, Evers a shortstop, and Tinker a third baseman. Chicago manager Frank Selee switched all three.

Chance was the first to join the Cubs, in 1898. In his first game, he caught Clark Griffith and did so poorly that he threatened to quit. A Chicago sportswriter, Harold ("Speed") Johnson, talked him out of it.

Chance was never more than a second-string catcher with the Cubs, and he had more than his share of the broken and bruised fingers that are a catcher's lot. He was a solid right-handed hitter, however, with averages of .286 (twice), .305, and .278 in his first four years.

The Chicago Cubs' double-play combination of, from the left, Joe Tinker, Johnny Evers, and Frank Chance, was immortalized in verse. *(George Brace photo)*

When Selee became manager in 1902, he looked for a way to get Chance's bat into the lineup and switched him to first base, but Chance still caught 29 games that season.

Chance didn't want to make the change. He liked catching, despite the many injuries. Again, he threatened to quit, but Selee talked him out of it.

Defensively, Chance did not shine as a first baseman at the start, either. In his first full season, 1903, as a first baseman, he committed 36 errors and had a .927 fielding average. In subsequent years, he improved and became a better than average fielder.

As soon as he was made a starter, he justified Selee's faith in his offensive ability, hitting .327 in 1903 in the first of four straight years over .300, in an era when pitching dominated.

Chance was also surprisingly fast for a man of his size, six feet tall and 190 pounds. He stole 67 bases in 1903 and 57 in 1906, and his career total of 405 is a Cub record.

His leadership qualities became evident as soon as he got into the starting lineup, and he was named manager in mid-1905 when Selee fell ill with pneumonia. In Chance's first full season as manager, 1906, his team won 116 games, which still stands as the major league record, though the season has been expanded from 154 to 162 games. For both his playing and managerial abilities, he was nicknamed, "the Peerless Leader," by Chicago writer Charles Dryden.

Chance could be a hard man, as an incident in 1905 showed. A pitcher named Jack Harper, then with Cincinnati, hit Chance with a pitched ball in a game that season. Chance felt it was intentional, and he vowed to run Harper out of baseball.

As it happened, Cincinnati owed Chicago a player in return for infielder Honus Lobert, who had been traded to the Reds. Chance insisted that Harper be the player.

When Harper reported to the Cubs, Chance told him that his salary—$4,500 with Cincinnati—had been cut to $1,500, and he could take it or leave it. Players had no choice in those days, with the bidding war with the National League having ended two seasons before.

Harper took it and sat on the bench for two months, pitching only one inning in that time. Then, he quit in disgust and went home, which cost him a chance at a World Series share in 1906.

It was a petty, vindictive move by Chance, but perhaps understandable. Chance was often hit by pitched balls in his career, five times in one game in 1904. Toward the end of his career, he suffered from severe headaches because of that, and those headaches were probably one of the reasons for his early death, in 1924.

Tinker was the next of the famous trio to come to the Cubs, arriving in 1902. He started the season at third base, but Selee switched him to shortstop (where he had played part of the time in the minor leagues) in mid-season.

Like Chance, Tinker did not take kindly to the switch at first, grumbling that Selee expected too much of him. He seemed to have a point, too; he made 73 errors that season, with a fielding average of .907. But Selee was right once again in his evaluation. Tinker had good range and a strong arm, and those attributes eventually made him into a good fielding shortstop.

Tinker was only an average hitter, though his .263 lifetime average was certainly adequate at a position where fielding is much more important than hitting. Strangely, though, he treated the great Christy Mathewson like a batting practice pitcher, averaging .317 during his career and .421 in 1908. His key triple off Mathewson in a September 23 game decided the pennant that year.

Evers also joined the Cubs in the 1902 season, after veteran second baseman Bobby Lowe had broken his leg. Evers was a most unlikely major leaguer. He never carried more than 125 pounds on his five foot nine frame, and when he reported to the Cubs he was even lighter, perhaps about 115 pounds.

He was given the smallest uniform available, but even that was baggy on him. He played both games of a doubleheader at shortstop the day he arrived, but his teammates were so skeptical of his chances of making it that they wouldn't let him on the bus back to the hotel. He had to climb to the top and ride there.

Nevertheless, Evers made it. After three games at shortstop, he was switched to second by Selee. He was very competitive and known as "the Crab," partly for the way he moved in the infield and even more for his disposition. Evers was constantly battling with whoever was nearest—umpires, opponents, or teammates.

In one game in 1909, Evers challenged umpire Bill Klem to meet him at the National League offices the next day to settle a dispute, and he bet Klem five dollars that he would not show up. The next day, Evers was there and Klem was not.

In every Cub game in which Klem umpired after that, Evers drew a large "5" in the dirt in front of the batters' box, and he would hold up five fingers whenever he caught Klem's eye. Klem finally paid off, to rid himself of the nuisance.

Chance and Tinker would have liked to have rid themselves of Evers, too. Chance once commented that he wished Evers played the outfield so he wouldn't have to listen to Johnny's everlasting chatter.

Tinker didn't speak to Evers for years because of an incident involving a taxi before an exhibition game at Bedford, Indiana, on September, 13, 1905. Evers had hailed a cab at the team's hotel and ridden away, leaving Tinker and a couple of other players on the sidewalk. During the game that day, Tinker started arguing about that with Evers, and soon they were fighting.

The next day, Tinker told Evers that, since it was obvious they couldn't get along, it would be better if they just didn't talk. Tinker held up his end of the bargain. The talkative Evers would forget sometimes during a game and start yelling across second base at Tinker, but the shortstop refused to be provoked.

In later years, Evers mellowed, and he and Tinker greeted each other warmly when they were inducted into the Hall of Fame together. Chance, of course, had been dead for 22 years by then. Evers died the year after his Hall of Fame induction; Tinker two years later.

The famed double-play combination was by no means the whole team for the Cubs. The remaining member of the infield, third baseman Harry Steinfeldt, was a good fielder and steady hitter; he hit .327 and led the league with 83 RBIs in 1906.

Steinfeldt was probably as good a player as the other three, but he didn't have anybody writing verse about him. As a result, he is not in the Hall of Fame and he is known chiefly today as part of a trivia question: "Who was the third baseman in the Tinker-Evers-Chance infield?"

The key to the Cubs' dynasty of 1906–10, though, was the pitching staff. In 1906, the staff led the league with an earned run average of 1.76. Mordecai ("Three Finger") Brown was the staff ace with a 26–6 record and an ERA of 1.04, and Ed Reulbach added 20 wins. Six pitchers had more than 10 wins.

Brown got his nickname because of an accident in his youth, when he got his hand caught in a corn cropper. He lost half his index finger and injured two other fingers.

He turned that accident into an advantage. The stunted index finger enabled him to put an unnatural hop on the ball. He did not have an outstanding fastball, but his breaking pitches baffled hitters for years. Starting in 1906, he had six straight 20-win seasons, and his 208 lifetime victories earned him a spot in the Hall of Fame.

The Cubs had an incredible run in that period, averaging 106 wins a season for five years, winning pennants in four of those years. No National League club has ever done as well over that period of time. The one season the Cubs lost the pennant in that stretch, 1909, they won 104 games!

They were not that successful in the World Series, however. The "Hitless Wonders" Chicago White Sox upset them in 1906 in the first and still last World Series between the Chicago teams, and in just six games.

The Cubs won the World Series against the Detroit Tigers in both 1907 and 1908, but then they were soundly beaten in five games in 1910 by the Philadelphia Athletics, all of whose four wins were by a three-run margin or better.

●

How good were Tinker, Evers, and Chance? Certainly not as good as the Adams verse made them seem. At least one manager of the time, the disputatious John McGraw, thought the combination was very overrated.

McGraw once called a press conference to knock down the reputation of the trio. "You newspapermen have done very well by Tinker, Evers and Chance," he said. "In fact, you have built up a fake."

McGraw thought the Pittsburgh Pirate combination of Honus Wagner, Dots Miller and Bill Abstein was at least as good, and probably better, than the Cubs' combination, and he thought equally highly of the Philadelphia Athletics' combination of Jack Barry, Eddie Collins and Stuffy McInnis. His own combination of Dave Bancroft, Frankie Frisch and George Kelly was also a good one. But none of these combinations were celebrated in verse.

Ironically, the trait that was made famous in Adams's verse—turning a double play—was not the trio's strong point. In fact, they made very few.

Official statistics on double plays were not kept at that time, but former New York sportswriter Charlie Segar went through old box scores and concluded that in four years, there were only 56 double plays that went either Tinker to Evers to Chance, or Evers to Tinker to Chance.

By modern standards, that is a pitifully small total; any decent double-play combination would pass that mark easily in a year. But there are some factors to consider in evaluating that figure. One is that scorekeeping was erratic, and some double plays may not have been recorded. Another is that double plays were much rarer in those days, because a runner on first would either try to steal second or be moved along on a sacrifice or hit-and-run; teams did not try for the "big inning," as they do now. And smaller gloves made it more difficult to stop ground balls.

Taking all that into consideration, however, it still seems that McGraw was right; Tinker to Evers to Chance was an overrated combination. They should have taken Franklin P. Adams into the Hall of Fame with them.

9. A Bonehead Play That Wasn't

Chicago Cub second baseman Johnny Evers was a student of the game, often studying the rule book before he went to sleep at night. That devotion to his job paid off big in 1908 in the "Merkle bonehead" play, perhaps the most famous blunder in baseball history.

The Merkle play can be fully understood only against the background of the time, and of a specific game 19 days before. On September 4, 1908, the Cubs and Pirates met in a critical game in Pittsburgh. By that time, the National League race had narrowed down to those two teams and the Giants.

Going into the bottom of the tenth inning, it was a scoreless tie, with "Three Finger" Brown pitching for the Cubs and Vic Willis for the Pirates. Then the Pirates loaded the bases with two outs and Chief Wilson singled to center. Fred Clarke came home with the winning run. Seeing Clarke come home, the runner on first, Warren Gill, didn't bother to touch second.

Evers called for the ball and tagged second, contending it was a simple force-out that should have ended the inning without a run being scored. Unfortunately for Evers, the sole umpire that day, Hank O'Day, hadn't been looking. The Cubs protested, but since O'Day hadn't seen the play, their case was dismissed.

The rule was as clear then as it is now: A force play ends the inning, and the run does not count. Unfortunately, it had not been enforced like that. In that situation, the runner on first almost never touched second.

O'Day had been an umpire in the National League since 1888, but he had never questioned that play. Evers's protest made him think about it, and he decided that the rule should be enforced. He promised himself that he would call it the next time it came up.

The next time came in a game that ultimately decided the National League pennant. On September 23, the Cubs met the Giants in the Polo Grounds, with the Giants in first place by six percentage points.

The Cubs scored first in the fifth on an inside-the-park home run by Joe Tinker. The Giants evened it in the sixth when Mike Donlin singled in Buck Herzog. It stayed that way until the ninth.

With one out in the bottom of the ninth, Moose McCormick grounded into a force-out, with Artie Devlin out at second. Then Fred Merkle, a 19-year-old starting his first game only because Fred Tenney was sick, lined a ball to right center. Cub right fielder Jack Hayden knocked the ball down, keeping it from going for extra bases. Merkle stopped at first, with McCormick going to third.

Then Al Bridwell singled to center, bringing McCormick home. Seeing McCormick come home, Merkle cut short his run to second and headed for the clubhouse, to avoid the crush of fans.

But the game was not over, a fact realized by only two people, Evers and O'Day. Evers screamed at Cub center fielder Artie Hofman to throw him the ball, but Hofman's throw went past Evers and shortstop Tinker into the crowd, which had already poured onto the field.

Nobody ever knew for certain what happened after that. The Giants claimed that coach Joe McGinnity had picked up the ball and threw it into the stands. Evers claimed that he had retrieved it. At any rate, he got a ball—either the original or an extra one from the Cubs' bench—and he stepped on second base. O'Day told the base umpire, Emslie, what had happened, and Emslie called Merkle out.

With so many fans on the field, it would have been impossible to play any more of the game, and it was getting dark, anyway; so O'Day called the

Fred Merkle became known for his "bonehead play" that cost the New York Giants the 1908 pennant, though he did nothing that every player wasn't doing at the time. *(George Brace photo)*

game a tie and wrote a letter to league president Harry C. Pulliam explaining what had happened.

O'Day's decision was questioned by Bill Klem, the great umpire, who maintained that the rule as written was intended to apply only to grounders that resulted in force-outs, not to clean hits. But, of course, the rule did not say that, and O'Day had implemented the rule as written.

Both the Cubs and Giants protested to Pulliam. The Giants claimed they had won the game. The Cubs said they should have had a forfeit, first because of McGinnity's interference and then because the Giants refused to play the game off the next day, as the league rules required.

Pulliam upheld the umpires and ruled the game a tie. Both clubs then protested to the league board of directors, and the board upheld Pulliam and ordered the game replayed on October 8.

The Giants and Cubs were tied, with records of 98–55, when they met in that historic game at the Polo Grounds. Interest in the game was so high that an estimated 35,000 people watched from inside and thousands of others from the heights known as Coogan's Bluff that surrounded the field. The gates were closed an hour before the game because of the huge crowd.

The game itself was much less exciting than the buildup; the Cubs won it, 4–2. Jack Pfiester started for the Cubs but was relieved by Brown after giving up a run in the first. The Giants' ace, Christy Mathewson, was not his usual sharp self. He yielded four runs in the third, with Tinker's triple the key hit, and the game was all but over.

Until the day he died, McGraw always believed he was swindled out of the pennant, and he had a point. In retrospect, it seems it would have been fairer if O'Day had announced that he was going to enforce that rule, since that had not been done. By acting independently, he created a problem unnecessarily.

The ruling had some tragic aftereffects. It was the last straw for Pulliam, an idealist whose temperament was unsuited to the demands of his job. The constant pressure, much of it from McGraw, completely unstrung Pulliam, who became convinced that the owners were all conspiring against him.

At a banquet for major league club owners in Chicago the following February, Pulliam astounded everyone with his speech. "My days as a baseball man are numbered," he said. "The National League doesn't want me as president any more. It longs to go back to the days of dealing from the bottom of the deck, hiding the cards under the table, and to the days when the trademark was the gum shoe . . . 1 will have to quit at the end of this year . . ."

Pulliam took a leave of absence the next day. The owners, who generally sympathized with him, wanted to help him work out his problems, John Heydler, who had been Pulliam's private secretary, took over the job, but Pulliam returned to his office after the 1909 season started.

Then, on July 28, 1909, Pulliam had dinner as usual at the New York Athletic Club, where he lived. He left the table and went to his room, lay down on a sofa, and shot himself through the head. He was still alive when a club attendant found him several hours later, but he died the next morning.

Merkle's fate was not so tragic, but the controversy surrounding the play followed him for the rest of his career. He had a 16-year career and a successful one, but all that was remembered of his play was his "boner."

In part, that was because the writers of the time were very critical of Merkle. In the *Sporting Life,* for instance, the story said, "Through the inexcusable stupidity of Merkle, a substitute, the Giants had a sure victory turned into a doubtful one, a game was played in dispute, a complicated and disagreeable controversy was started, and perhaps the championship imperiled or lost."

In the same issue was another note: "Ren Mulford, *Sporting Life*'s Cincinnati correspondent, occasionally delivers a lecture called 'Running Life's Bases.' Fred Merkle might profit by hearing it."

All of this was unfair to Merkle, who had merely done what everybody else had been doing for years. He was only unlucky, not stupid.

Seven years after the controversy, Heywood Broun interviewed Merkle and asked him if he got any fun out of baseball. Merkle said he didn't.

"The worst thing is I can't do things other players do without attracting attention," he told Broun. "Little slips that would be excused in other players are burned into me by the crowds.... If any play I'm concerned with goes wrong, I'm the fellow who gets the blame, no matter where the thing went off line."

Many years later, baseball historian Lee Allen met Merkle in a bar in Daytona Beach. Merkle was then in the business of manufacturing fishing floats. "There was no point in asking the obvious question," wrote Allen, "and out of courtesy it was not asked, but Merkle, near tears and acting as if under compulsion, brought the subject up himself."

" 'You want to know about the play, I guess,' he said. 'It was a terrible thing to have happen.' "

And then he walked off, haunted by memories of people saying, each as if he were the first to think of it, "Don't forget to touch second, Fred."

10. Honus and Christy: Best of All

There were many fine players in the period between the turn of the century and the advent of the lively ball, but two stand above the rest: Honus Wagner and Christy Mathewson.

Mathewson, whose 373 wins equal Grover Cleveland Alexander's for the National League record, is generally considered the finest pitcher in the league's history. Wagner? Some of his peers thought nobody had ever played the game as well as Honus.

Wagner was born John Peter Wagner in 1874 in Carnegie, Pennsylvania. As a youngster, he was often called Johannes by his family, which was German; Honus is the German diminutive.

Legend has it that he started his baseball career on the coattails of his brother, Al ("Butts") Wagner. Approached by a semipro team in Dennison, Ohio, Al said he would play only if his younger brother came along, and so Honus's career started, for $5 a week and board. Al's major league career started and ended in the same year, 1898; Honus's lasted 21 years.

Although Wagner is always considered the shortstop on any all-time team that is named—indeed, shortstop is the one position that is decided without serious argument—he played all over the diamond, at third and first base and in the outfield. He even pitched several games in the minors and one in the majors. It wasn't until 1908, when he was 34 years old, that Wagner played only at shortstop.

Wherever he played, Wagner was a standout. Tommy Leach, his teammate at both Louisville and Pittsburgh, maintained that Wagner was the best in the league at all four infield positions and in the outfield, too. As an eight-time batting champion, he was demonstrably the best hitter in the league, and he was the best base runner, too. "The best everything," said Leach.

Leach figured in an amusing story with Wagner, although it took him some time to see the humor in it. In 1898, he was playing third base for Auburn in the New York State (minor) League. About a month before the end of the season, the owner got a chance to sell him, and he gave Leach the choice of clubs: Louisville or Washington.

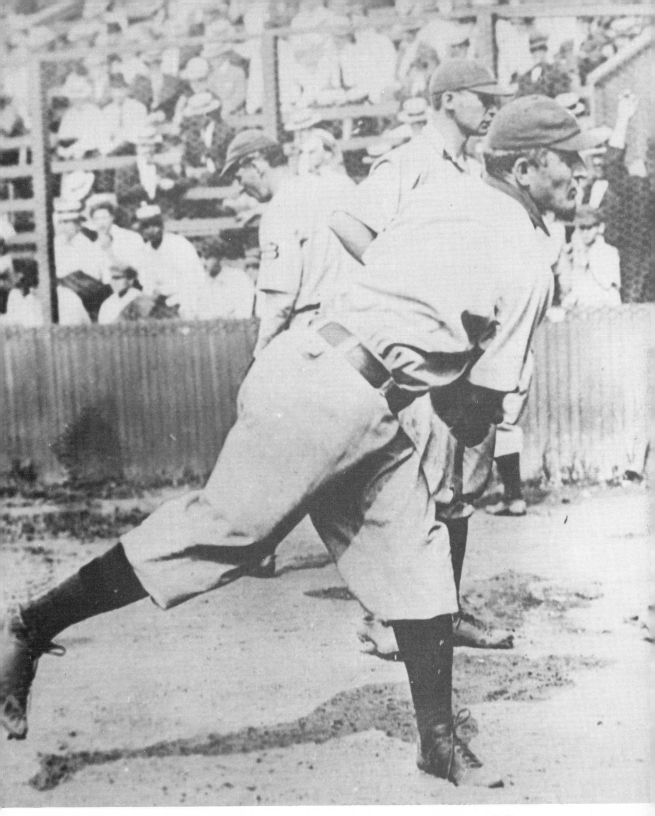

Honus Wagner, throwing in pregame warmup, is considered the best shortstop of all time. *(George Brace photo)*

As Leach told it in *The Glory of Their Times,* his manager told him to choose Louisville because Washington had a player named Wagner who was very good at third base, Leach's position. That was Al, in his first and last major league season.

The first day Leach joined Louisville, he was sitting on the bench when a batter for the opposing team lined a ball down the third-base line. "Well, this big Louisville third baseman jumped over after it like he was on steel springs, slapped it down with his bare hand, scrambled after it at least ten feet, and fired a bullet over to first base. The runner was out by two or three steps."

That was Honus Wagner. Fortunately for Leach, Wagner kept moving around, so Tommy got a chance to get in the lineup himself, but on that first day with Louisville, he would have been happy to go to Washington and try his luck against the other Wagner.

As a player, Wagner was quite unorthodox and not at all graceful. He had an odd build, with most of the 200 pounds on his five foot eleven frame concentrated in his chest and shoulders, and his arms hanging almost to his knees; Lefty Gomez once quipped that Wagner was the only person he knew who could tie his shoelaces without bending over.

"He didn't seem to field balls the way we did," said Leach. "He just ate the ball up with his big hands, like a scoop shovel, and when he threw it to first base you'd see pebbles and dirt and everything else flying over there along with the ball."

Wagner was extremely bowlegged; if his legs could have been straightened out, he would have been well over six feet tall. He seemed to be rolling rather than running when he made a dash for second base, but he was much faster than he appeared. He led the National League in stolen bases five times, and his career total of 722 is a Pittsburgh club record and fifth in major league history. His base-stealing success led writers to call him "the Flying Dutchman," ignoring the fact that Wagner's family had come from Germany, not the Netherlands. One European country was much like another to the parochial Americans of the time.

Wagner's play inspired extravagant comments. New York Giants' manager John McGraw called Honus the best of all time—as a hitter, fielder, and base runner.

"In addition to his natural ability," McGraw once said, "he had what might be termed a sixth sense in baseball. He had an uncanny faculty of being able to think where the batter would hit a certain type of ball."

McGraw's evaluation was biased, because Wagner's competition as the best of his era came from two American Leaguers, Babe Ruth and Ty Cobb. But his opinion was seconded by Ed Barrow, who had been close to both Wagner and Ruth.

Barrow had first signed Wagner to a contract with the Paterson, New Jersey minor league club and then sold him after a year to Louisville. He had two direct contacts with Ruth. He changed Ruth from a pitcher into an outfielder when he was managing the Boston Red Sox, and he was general manager of the New York Yankees when Ruth was dominating the American League, 1921–24, and changing all baseball.

"If I had a choice of all players who have played baseball," said Barrow in the twenties, "I would choose Honus Wagner."

Wagner's huge hands helped him in the field, because the baseball gloves of that era were little bigger than the hands they went on. (They weren't as specialized as now, either; Leach revealed that Wagner wore a first baseman's glove when he played third base.)

The accounts of the day described Wagner's range and arm as extraordinary. He was especially adept at going into "the hole" to get a ball the third baseman had missed and then throwing the runner out at first. He had a variety of throwing motions—overhand, sidearm, underhand—depending on the situation.

A right-handed hitter, Wagner's style was much like that of another great right-handed hitter of a later era, Rogers Hornsby. He stood in the back of the box, wiggling his bat, and he hit to all fields, depending on where the ball was pitched. He was not a finicky hitter, and he would often hit balls that were out of the strike zone. If he had a weakness, it went undiscovered by National League pitchers.

Wagner's lifetime batting average was .329, excellent for any player but especially remarkable for a shortstop. As a comparison, two other shortstops, Joe Tinker and Rabbit Maranville, made the Hall of Fame with lifetime averages of .263 and .258, respectively. Nobody ever suggested that Tinker and Maranville were better than Wagner defensively either.

Wagner's hitting was a result of his natural ability and a lot of hard work. He would take batting practice after games whenever he could find somebody to pitch to him.

At the time of his retirement, Wagner led the all-time National League list in games, at-bats, runs, hits, singles, doubles and triples. He still holds the record for triples and singles.

Only in his home run total of 101 does Wagner suffer in comparison with star players of later eras, but that was because of the dead ball being used, not his lack of power. At the time he retired, only two players in National League history, Dan Brouthers and Hugh Duffy, had more home runs. Both had 103, and most of Duffy's were inside-the-park.

Barrow contended that Wagner would have had 50 home runs a year had he been hitting the lively ball. Certainly, Wagner had plenty of power, as his career totals of 651 doubles and 252 triples attest.

Away from the field, Wagner was a shy, gentle man. He shunned publicity, though he was pleasant enough to the writers of the day, few of whom sought out personal interviews, anyway.

Fred Lieb, in *Baseball As I Have Known It,* tells two stories to illustrate Wagner's distaste for publicity. The first involved Harry Cross, baseball writer for the *New York Times,* who was told to get an interview with Wagner when the Pirates were in New York.

Cross went up to Wagner's room and requested an interview. Wagner showed him into the bathroom, which had beer and cracked ice in the tub. "Drink all the beer you want, but no story," said Honus.

In 1909, after Wagner had won his fourth straight batting championship (and seventh overall), he was invited to the National League's dinner at the Waldorf Astoria in New York. Wagner declined. "I don't make speeches," he said, "I let my bat speak for me in the summertime."

On the field, Wagner was as competitive as anybody. A legend has grown up around the first confrontation of Wagner and Cobb, in the 1909 World Series.

In the first game of the Series, Cobb was on first base and supposedly yelled to Wagner, "Get ready, krauthead. I'm coming down."

Wagner replied, "I'll be waiting," and when Cobb tried to steal, Wagner tagged him so hard that the ball split Cobb's lip. Pittsburgh won the Series, 4–3, and Wagner had a much more productive Series than Cobb, batting .333 to Cobb's .231 and knocking in six runs and stealing six bases. Cobb had only two stolen bases, though one was of home.

Wagner was not a man of extravagant personal habits. He didn't drink liquor, though he drank a lot of beer, which was no surprise, considering his heritage. He didn't get married until he was 40, and he seldom went out at night.

Thus, he did not require a large salary to cover his rather basic needs, and he seems to have thought of his salary more as a symbol than anything else. He wanted to become a $10,000 a year man, and he threatened not to play the 1908 season if he didn't get that, but when he reached that plateau, he was satisfied. He never asked for more, and he turned down a larger offer to jump to the Federal League in 1914. Then, as before, he was loyal to the National League; he had turned down American League offers during the bidding war period, 1901–02.

Wagner was playing for one of the few generous owners in the league, Barney Dreyfuss, the same man who had turned all the gate receipts over to the players after the first World Series. Ironically, however, a contract dispute ended Wagner's career.

Wagner played on through the 1917 season, although arthritis and the advancing years had robbed him of his speed and strength. At 43, he had hit .265 in 74 games. Because many of the best players were off to war in 1918, Wagner could have played another year, but he was insulted when Dreyfuss wanted to cut his salary in half, and he quit.

There was no communication between Wagner and his old club until 1933, when Fred Lieb wrote a column for the *New York Post* telling of the problems Wagner was having in the depression year. Wagner had owned a sporting goods store but had been forced to sell it when times went bad.

That led to Wagner getting a job as coach for the Pirates, a position he held until 1949. How much coaching he ever did for the Pirates is problematical, but he was the ideal public relations man for the club. He was a great favorite around the league, with adults and children both. He told a million stories, most of them great exaggerations, but all of them entertaining.

He died in 1955 in the town in which he was born, but he had lived long enough to see that his place in baseball history was secure. In 1936, he had been one of the first five players selected for the Hall of Fame, with Ruth, Cobb, Walter Johnson—and Christy Mathewson.

●

Mathewson's high standing in the National League of his day was due almost as much to his character as his great pitching ability.

Baseball was a rough game in those days and players were usually hard-drinking and hard-cursing. There were fights on the field and in the clubhouse. There was constant hazing of rookies, and veterans had ways of putting rookies in their proper place on the field. A rookie second baseman who was trying to beat out a favorite veteran, for intance, might find that the shortstop gave him the ball just a couple of beats slow on a double play attempt—which gave the runner enough time to barrel into the rookie as he made his pivot.

Pitchers threw at batters' heads regularly, and batters retaliated by dragging bunts down the first base line and trying to run down the pitcher as he moved over to cover.

In this atmosphere, Christy Mathewson seemed like Saint Francis of Assisi. He was almost too good to be true. His personal habits were impeccable; he didn't drink and seldom smoked. He was well educated, having come to professional baseball from Bucknell. He was big for his era, at six foot one and a-half and 200 pounds, and he looked like an Adonis, with blue eyes and brown hair.

Mathewson was the first baseball player to be held up as an example for young boys, and it was not uncommon for groups of boys to wait at small town train stations where the Giants would stop momentarily on their trips. Mathewson was always willing to say a few words to the boys.

Mathewson advised the boys against drinking, smoking (though he once endorsed a pipe tobacco), staying up late, and turning professional too early.

His advice endeared him to the ministers of the land, who had always been skeptical about baseball. So did his pattern of not pitching on Sunday, and his general opposition to Sunday baseball.

If there were chinks in Mathewson's personal armor, nobody ever found them—any more than opposing batters found weaknesses in his pitching. He was a paragon.

Mathewson's habits had little real effect on other players, but it did make

Christy Mathewson, here with Grover Cleveland Alexander, is the leading National League winner of all time.
His behavior on and off the diamond was often cited as a model for youngsters.
(George Brace photo)

many in the game think of changing their reputations—or images, to use a more current word. Even John McGraw was affected. He told one sportswriter that Mathewson's habit of never questioning the umpire was one he believed in!

In almost every way, Mathewson's life ran counter to that of other players. Most players, for instance, came from poverty-ridden childhoods; Mathewson's mother was wealthy, and his father was a gentleman farmer. While his peers were learning their baseball—and other lessons—in the streets, Mathewson was pitching for Keystone Academy and Bucknell, where he was also a football star.

Mathewson left Bucknell in 1899 to pitch minor league baseball, with Taunton, Massachusetts in the New England League. He was 5-2, but more important, he learned a pitch from teammate Virgil Garvin. The pitch made Mathewson famous. Called a "fadeaway," the pitch was actually a reverse curve, breaking in to a right-handed hitter and away from a left-hander when the right-handed Mathewson threw it. (When the pitch was thrown later by left-handers, it became known as the "screwball.")

The next season, with Norfolk of the Virginia League, Mathewson won 21 games and lost only 2, and his contract was purchased by the Giants. He came up to the Giants that year, 1900, but was only 0-3. The Giants then returned him to Norfolk, and he was drafted by Cincinnati. Fortunately for the history of the Giants, he was then traded back for Amos Rusie, in the trade described in an earlier chapter.

Mathewson didn't realize at first how effective his "fadeaway" could be. He was much prouder of a wide-breaking curve that had been an effective strikeout weapon during his school and minor league days. But George Davis, the Giants' manager when Christy first came up, established the proper priorities. Batting against Mathewson, he hit Christy's roundhouse curve deep to the outfield and advised him to concentrate on his other pitches.

The next season, Mathewson won 20 games for the Giants. Amazingly, at the start of the 1902 season, manager Horace Fogel decided he would make Mathewson a first baseman. Fortunately, McGraw came along in mid-season and ended that experiment immediately.

Mathewson won only 14 games that season, but in 1903, he started an amazing streak with 30 wins. He won 30 or more games for 3 straight years and 20 or more for 12 consecutive years.

Even by the standards of that pitching-dominated era, Mathewson was outstanding. He had one stretch of five years in which he allowed less than two earned runs a game for each season. He led the league five times in games won, five times in earned run average, five times in strikeouts.

His best season, oddly, was one in which the Giants did not win a pennant—the hotly-contested year of 1908. He was the loser in the game that decided the pennant, but that couldn't take the luster off his season. He won 37 games that year (which is still the modern—since 1900—National League record) and lost only 11. He led the league in eight other categories—ERA (1.43), games (56), games started (44), complete games (34), innings pitched (390⅔), hits yielded (285), strikeouts (259) and shutouts (12). He walked only 42 batters, an average of less than one a game.

Physically, Mathewson had it all. His fast ball was as good as the best when he wanted to really turn it on, his curve and "fadeaway" both broke sharply, and he had the control to throw any pitch where he wanted it.

But his main strength was his mind. He approached pitching as a science. He even wrote a book, *Pitching In a Pinch,* which was reprinted in 1977, its lessons as pertinent now as they were when he wrote it.

There is a story from Mathewson's early years with the Giants that tells most effectively how his mental attitude helped him win.

Mathewson had lost a game in the ninth when the Cubs' Jimmy Slagle hit a fast ball for a home run. The next day, McGraw asked him, "Don't you know that Slagle murders a fast ball?"

Christy hadn't known; he had just thrown the pitch his catcher had called for. But that was the last time Slagle ever saw a Mathewson fast ball in the strike zone.

The pitching mound was Mathewson's laboratory. Although his statistics are impressive, he was concerned with only one: winning the game. He seldom tried for strikeouts, because he knew that strikeout pitchers throw too many pitches; only when the situation demanded it would he throw his best fast ball.

He believed in conserving his strength and taking care of his health. He was always in good condition. The best pitcher can get beat, and Mathewson lost 188 games in his long career; but he never beat himself.

It was the 1905 World Series that really made Mathewson a star. He started the Series by pitching a four-hit shutout over the Philadelphia Athletics, winning, 3–0.

Chief Bender duplicated Mathewson's feat with a four-hit, 3–0 win for Philadelphia in the second game, but a rain delay allowed Mathewson to return for the third game. Again, he held the Athletics to four hits, winning, 9–0, this time.

Joe McGinnity shut out the Athletics, 1–0, in the fourth game, and then Mathewson came back with his third shutout, 2–0, this time yielding six hits, as the Giants won what is still considered one of the most remarkable World Series.

No pitcher has ever matched Mathewson's performance in that Series. He pitched 27 innings without yielding a run, allowed just 14 hits, struck out 18, and walked only one.

Mathewson pitched well in subsequent World Series, but without much luck. He won the opener of the 1911 Series, but then lost his next two games.

His first loss in that Series, in the third game, came in the 11th inning. Frank Baker, the Philadelphia third baseman, had sent the game into extra innings with a home run in the ninth. Baker had won the game the day before with a home run, and those two runs gave him the nickname of "Home Run Baker" for the rest of his career, a career in which, incidentally, he hit 93 regular season home runs and three in the World Series.

The next year, Mathewson's first game—second of the Series—went ten innings to a tie and was called because of darkness. He lost his next start, 2–1, on an error, and he lost the final game, 3–2, when Fred Snodgrass dropped an easy fly in the ninth inning.

In 1913—the Giants' third straight pennant, and third straight World Series loss—Mathewson won, 3–0, in ten innings, helping himself with an RBI single, but lost the deciding fifth game, 3–1.

The next year, 1914, Mathewson won 24 games, but that was his last good season. The next season, his fast ball gone, he won only eight games and was traded to Cincinnati so that he could manage the Reds.

Mathewson managed the Reds to fourth place in 1917 and had them in third place in 1918 when he joined the Army. While overseas, he got poison gas in the lungs, though it is not clear exactly how. One story said it happened when he was in the trenches; another said it was the result of an accident during a training session. The gas permanently damaged his lungs and left him with a serious cough.

When he came back home, Christy learned that Pat Moran was the Reds' manager, so he took a job as coach with the Giants. He coached the Giants for three seasons but finally had to enter a sanitorium in Saranac Lake, New York with tuberculosis.

Mathewson thought he had recovered when he left the sanitorium in 1923 to take the presidency of the Boston Braves. He was wrong. He returned to the sanitorium in 1925.

On the first day of the World Series that fall, he died.

11. The National League Fights Two Wars

When the National and American leagues reached a peaceful agreement in 1903, it seemed there would finally be an end to the battling between leagues that had almost ruined the sport. That dream was short-lived, however; the Federal League came along little more than a decade later to involve baseball in another bidding war.

The roots of the Federal League actually went back to 1912, when another players' association was formed, this one known as the Players' Fraternity and headed by New York attorney Dave Fultz, who had once been a major league outfielder.

The purpose of the organization was merely to put some pressure on owners to pay higher salaries and improve conditions in general for the players. Most major league players joined.

As an association, the group did little to change baseball. Some wealthy men outside the sport, however, saw the formation of the players' fraternity as an indication that its members were unhappy and would be willing to jump to another league if one could be organized.

The Federal League was formed in 1913 as a minor league, following the precedent of the American League. There were only six teams that first year—Chicago, Kansas City, Cleveland, Pittsburgh, St. Louis and Covington, Kentucky (across the river from Cincinnati). Cy Young managed the Cleveland team.

Before the season ended, the owners met secretly and decided to expand to eight teams and to assume a major league classification. The new line-up consisted of franchises in Indianapolis, Chicago, Baltimore, Buffalo, Brooklyn, Kansas City, Pittsburgh and St. Louis.

The league lasted two more years after that, but it was never a success. Though Federal League owners offered big money to star players, few jumped from the established leagues. The only really big name National League player to jump was shortstop Joe Tinker, who signed to manage and play for the Chicago Whales. The top players, Honus Wagner and Christy

Mathewson, stayed in the National League, and other players followed their example. The league developed only one star, outfielder Bennie Kauff, and Kauff was only an average player when he went to the New York Giants after the Federal League folded.

It was not a good time for baseball, either, with World War I starting in Europe, though the United States did not figure in the war until 1917.

●

The National League got an unexpected boost in its battle with the Federal League by an amazing pennant race in 1914. The Boston Braves put on the strongest stretch run in the history of the league to that point: even now, only the 1942 St. Louis Cardinals and 1951 New York Giants have had comparable runs.

The story is a well-known one. The Braves, in last place on July 4, came on to win the National League pennant. Actually, it was even more dramatic, because the Braves were still in last place on July 19, with a record of 35–43.

But the league was very tightly bunched that year. The Braves were only 11 games behind the league-leading Giants on July 19. By winning three games, July 19–21, they jumped to fourth.

The incredible aspect of the Braves' drive was not just that they went from last to first, but that they did it so rapidly. It actually took them only about five weeks. By August 23, they had climbed into a tie for first place.

The Braves won 34 of their last 44 games and turned the race into a rout, winning by 10½ games; in less than half a season, they had made up 22½ games on the Giants!

The team was managed by George Stallings, one of the legendary characters of baseball. Stallings hated pitchers; he once suggested that his epitaph be, "Oh, those bases on balls!" Early in the 1914 season, he told a writer, "I've got 16 pitchers and they're all rotten."

Stallings' evaluation was unnecessarily harsh; in fact, the great strength of his team was in the pitching staff, particularly the top three of Dick Rudolph (27–10 in 1914), Bill James (26–7) and George Tyler (16–14).

The Braves also had an excellent double-play combination in shortstop Rabbit Maranville and second baseman Johnny Evers, and a good catcher in Hank Gowdy.

They were not, however, the equal of the great Philadelphia A's team they met in the World Series that year. All the experts agreed on that. The A's, with their "$100,000 infield" of Stuffy McInnis, Eddie Collins, Jack Barry and Frank ("Home Run") Baker, and the great pitching of Chief Bender, Eddie Plank and Jack Coombs, were overwhelming favorites.

Stallings predicted his team would sweep the Series. No team had ever done that, but he was right: The Braves won, 7–1, 1–0, 5–4 and 3–1, to leave the baseball world in shock.

•

Meanwhile, the Federal League owners could see that their new league was not working. By 1915, the owners sued the established leagues, accusing them of violating the Sherman Anti-Trust Act. Ironically, the U.S. District Court judge assigned to the case was Kenesaw Mountain Landis, later to become baseball's first commissioner.

Judge Landis reviewed the case for the entire season of 1915 without coming to a decision. It is likely he hoped the leagues would reach an agreement without his having to make a ruling.

Harry T. Sinclair, later to become infamous for his role in the Teapot Dome scandal, threatened to move his Newark team into New York City in 1916, which forced the National League owners into a conciliatory position.

Eventually, a compromise was reached. The National League agreed to pay indemnities to most of the Federal League clubs, and Charles Weegham, owner of the Chicago club, was allowed to buy the Cubs. Except for players owned by Weegham and Phil Ball of St. Louis, who bought the American League Browns, Federal League players were all put into a pool and sold to the highest bidder.

There was an interesting sidelight to the case. No provision was made for the Baltimore club, and its owners sued baseball under the antitrust statute. In 1922, the Supreme Court, with Justice Oliver Wendell Holmes writing the majority opinion, decided that baseball was exempt from antitrust regulation "because of its peculiar nature." That opinion governed baseball for the next half-century.

•

The National League was able to cope, though at great financial cost, in the bidding war with the Federal League. The real war, World War I, proved much harder to deal with.

When the United States entered the war on April 6, 1917, nobody in baseball knew what the game's status would be. Eventually, baseball was declared a "non-essential" industry, so major league players were eligible for the draft. Boston catcher Gowdy became the first major-leaguer to volunteer in June 1917.

The fact that baseball players could be drafted was not the game's most serious problem. Since married men were exempt from the draft, there was relatively little trouble filling rosters. Only one prominent National League player was killed in battle—Eddie Grant, a third baseman with the Phillies, Reds, and Giants from 1907 through 1915—and Grant's career was finished before he went into the service.

But the 1918 season was curtailed because of the war, ending on Labor Day, September 2, and attendance dwindled during the season and the World Series that followed.

To make the situation worse, John K. Tener of the three-man National Commission, which then ruled the game, came up with a plan that was a classic example of the right idea at the wrong time.

In previous seasons, some first division teams that were out of the race had been accused of not playing their best against pennant contenders. To stop this, Tener proposed that first division teams share in the World Series receipts, a practice that has continued since.

Unfortunately, the Series receipts were very low that year; with Tener's plan in effect, the winning players received only $1,102, the losers $671.

Realizing what was going to happen, the players had asked before the Series began for a flat $1,500 and $1,000, for winner's and loser's shares, respectively. The National Commission (Tener, Garry Herrmann, and Ban Johnson) had refused.

Before the fifth game, the players remained in their clubhouses and sent Les Mann of the Cubs and Harry Hooper of the Red Sox out to negotiate a deal with the National Commission, threatening a strike if no deal was made. But Herrmann pointed out that the players' contracts required them to play World Series games and the players, obviously less militant then than now, decided to play. And everybody looked forward to a better year in 1919, not realizing that far more trouble was on the horizon.

12. The Series Is Fixed

The 1919 Cincinnati Reds are known to baseballs fans primarily as the team that was given the World Series by the Chicago "Black Sox." The Reds deserve better. It was a solid team, which won the first National League pennant for Cincinnati, pulling away from the New York Giants of John McGraw in the stretch. Though the team did not have the sustained success of the 1939–40 Reds or the "Big Red Machine" of the seventies, the 1919 Reds had a winning percentage of .686, never since equaled by a Cincinnati team.

Had it not been for what happened in the World Series that year, the National League race would have been considered one of the most interesting, though not the closest, in the league's history. It was decided in one two-week span in early August. Through a quirk in scheduling, the teams played three games in Cincinnati the first week and then three straight doubleheaders in New York two weeks later.

Feelings ran very high in both cities. McGraw demanded, and got, police protection for his players in Cincinnati, and the Reds took along their own drinking water so Giants' fans couldn't slip knockout drops into their water. That was baseball in 1919. The Reds won two of the three games in Cincinnati, four of the six (the first and third doubleheaders) in New York and never looked back, eventually winning by nine games.

Despite their strong showing, the Reds were considered a decidedly inferior team to the American League champion Chicago White Sox, though the White Sox had had a harder time winning their pennant than had the Reds. Baseball writers almost unanimously picked the White Sox to win the best-of-nine Series, perhaps in only six or seven games. The American League had won seven of the last eight Series, and the White Sox were considered one of the top teams in the league's history.

The odds didn't reflect the sportswriters' analysis, however: A rush of Cincinnati money made the Reds favorites in the Series. What was going on? Rumors began circulating that the "fix" was in for Cincinnati to win, but those with good memories remembered that similar rumors had circulated during the 1912 Series. The smart money had the Giants winning that one, but the Red Sox defied the odds and won.

Baseball and gambling had been associated from the beginning. The scandal of 1877 with the Louisville club is described in chapter 2. The lesson from that scandal had worn off in the ensuing 42 years, and there were frequent rumors of games being fixed. Indeed, the White Sox themselves had been accused (though nothing was ever proven) of bribing two Detroit pitchers to lose a doubleheader in 1917 so the White Sox could win the pennant.

The problem was that it was extremely difficult to prove that games were being thrown, without written evidence. A pitcher might be just a little off, putting a pitch where the hitter could get it in a critical situation. An infielder might be a half-step slow in covering his base, or an outfielder a split second late in starting after a fly ball. Who could say for certain that these actions were intentional?

Many of the rumors about fixed games concerned Hal Chase, sometimes known as "Prince Hal." Chase was a fine player who played for two American League teams, two National League teams, and one Federal League team in 15 years, batting .291 for his career and playing a spectacularly inconsistent first base.

Those who watched Chase insisted that nobody ever played better at first base, when he wanted to. He had great speed—he had 363 stolen bases in his career with a season high of 40—and anticipation; he was known for his ability to field bunts on the third base side of the pitcher's mound and throw a runner out at second or third.

Yet, Chase made a surprising number of errors. Fred Lieb looked up his fielding statistics for six years and discovered that Chase made between 19 and 21 errors each year, remarkably high totals.

On August 9, 1918, Chase was suspended for "indifferent playing" by the Cincinnati Reds, though he was hitting. .301 at the time. Chase himself ripped away the euphemistic curtain. He told a New York writer that he had been accused of betting on ball games.

Chase then sued the Cincinnati club for $1,650 in salary, and a hearing was scheduled for January 30, 1919, in New York, with acting league president John Heydler.

The chief evidence against Chase was an affidavit from Jimmy Ring, a Cincinnati pitcher. Ring testified that Chase had approached him during a game in 1917, shortly after Ring had been drafted from Utica, to throw the game. Ring said Chase told him, "I've got some money bet on this game and there is something in it for you if you lose."

Ring told Chase to get away, but the young pitcher went on to lose the game by one run. He said that the next day, Chase dropped $50 in his lap while he was sitting in a hotel lobby. Ring then went to Mathewson with his story.

Heydler told Lieb in an off-the-record talk that he thought Chase was guilty, but that he had no solid proof. Nobody could be found who had seen Chase give money to Ring, and Mathewson—Chase's principal accuser—was in France. Heydler announced that Chase had "acted in a careless manner" but that there was no evidence that he had bet against his club.

As soon as Chase was acquitted, he was signed by McGraw to play for the Giants, but in September, he disappeared from the club. McGraw said Chase had not been feeling well and had been given permission to go home, but the real story was apparently quite different. According to Lieb, Heydler had obtained a copy of a $500 check from a Boston gambler to Chase and had gone to Giants' owner Charles Stoneham with the evidence. Stoneham had then ordered Chase suspended, and the first baseman never again played major league baseball.

At that point, there was still no public evidence of Chase's wrongdoing, since Heydler did not show the canceled check to anybody but Stoneham. In 1920, however, a strange lawsuit involving Lee Magee made it all plain.

Magee had been a National League infielder who played with Cincinnati in 1918. The next year, he played with the Dodgers and Cubs. Though he had a two-year contract with the Cubs, Magee was given his unconditional release before the 1920 season.

Magee brought suit against the Chicago club for his 1920 salary, and the trial lasted for three days in June 1920. Magee not only failed to get the money he sought but implicated himself and Chase in the fixing of a 1918 game.

On July 25, 1918, the Reds played a doubleheader in Boston. Magee claimed that Chase had approached him about betting $500 on the Reds to win the game, but that Chase had then placed the bets with gambler Jim Costello for the Reds to lose.

Costello told a different story. He testified that Magee had first approached him with a proposition to throw the game, and that the next morning Magee and Chase both met with him and asked the gambler to put $500 down for each of them on the Reds to lose.

There are some men who cannot do anything right, and Magee was apparently one of them. The Reds won that game the next day in 13 innings, and Magee scored the winning run! Obviously, that was not the way he had planned it.

In that fateful 13th inning, a grounder off Magee's bat had hit a rough spot in the infield, bouncing up and breaking the nose of Boston shortstop Johnny Rawlings. Then, Roush hit a home run, and there was nothing that Magee could do but cross home plate, knowing his 270-foot run from first was costing him $500.

This was the kind of atmosphere that surrounded baseball as the 1919 World Series began. As it happened, this time the rumors of a fix were true.

Eight White Sox players—Chick Gandil, Eddie Cicotte, Lefty Williams, Happy Felsch, Swede Risberg, Joe Jackson, Buck Weaver and Fred McMullen—had met with gamblers to talk of throwing the Series. Their degree of involvement varied widely. Gandil, for instance, had first approached bookmaker Joseph ("Sport") Sullivan, and he had had no trouble enlisting most of the others. Weaver, though, apparently never had any thoughts of joining the conspiracy, though he sat in on the meetings, and it's likely that Jackson didn't, either.

But the one thing the eight players had in common was an utter disregard for any risk. If they ever had any doubts, all they had to do was look at the example of Chase, who had apparently gotten away with his actions for years. And, as could be expected, Chase was hanging around the fringes of this deal, too, just to find out which way to lay his money.

Cicotte was almost too obvious in his intentions in the first game. The White Sox ace, a 29-game winner with as many complete games during the regular season, was pounded at will by the Reds, who got 14 hits and won, 9-1.

Chicago catcher Ray Schalk, who was not in on the fix, was angry after the game, not only because the White Sox had lost but also because Cicotte had often disregarded Schalk's signs. Schalk wondered what was going on— or maybe he knew.

Williams was determined not to be so obvious as Cicotte in the second game, but his loss was no less mystifying to the White Sox fans who did not know, or who did not want to believe, that the fix was in. Williams gave up three runs in the fourth inning as the White Sox lost, 4-2, on three walks and a triple by Cincinnati shortstop Larry Kopf off a hanging curve. Williams' wildness was the tipoff: He had allowed only 58 walks in 297 innings during the regular season.

Dickie Kerr, another Chicago player not in on the fix, came back to win the third game for the White Sox, 3–0, but then Cicotte lost the fourth game. This time, it was only 2–0, but Cicotte made two errors in the fifth inning, in which the Reds scored both their runs. He had made only three errors on 80 chances during the regular season.

It was Williams' turn in the fourth game. This time, he pitched reasonably well, but the Reds scored four times in the sixth inning and won, 5–0. Center fielder Felsch misplayed two drives in the fateful sixth, and also committed a throwing error.

Most accounts of the 1919 World Series have concentrated on the White Sox, the initiators of the fix, but the Reds knew very early that something strange was going on.

Edd Roush, in *The Glory of Their Times,* said that he had first heard of the fix after the second game when a man he didn't know but had seen around (the description makes it almost certain that the man was a gambler) came to him and told him that Ray Schalk had accused Williams of throwing the game.

Roush's informant added that the players had not gotten the payoff (which was partially true; the Black Sox got only a part of what they had been promised) and would be trying to win the rest of the games.

Later in the Series, Roush said, the same man came to him with another report: that the gamblers had gotten to the Cincinnati players, too. There was never any evidence that this was true, but Roush went immediately to his manager, Moran, with the story.

At a team meeting that day, before the eighth and last game of the Series, Moran asked starting pitcher Hod Eller if he had been approached by a gambler to throw the game. Eller said yes, that he had been promised $5,000 if he would lose.

"What did you say?" Moran asked him.

"I said if he didn't get damn far away from me real quick," said Eller, "he wouldn't know what hit him. And the same went if I ever saw him again."

If Eller's story were true—and there is no reason to think he made it up— gamblers were working both sides of the street in that Series, because the fix was certainly still in for the White Sox to lose.

It hadn't seemed that way when Kerr won the sixth game, 5–4, and Cicotte, his pride stung by his two losses, had pitched magnificently to win the seventh game, 4–1, to bring the White Sox back to within one game of the Reds.

But before the eighth game, veteran Chicago baseball writer Hugh Fullerton was approached by a gambler who told him to bet on Cincinnati.

"It will be the biggest first inning you've ever seen," the gambler told him.

Williams had been warned before the game that the gamblers would not tolerate a repeat of Cicotte's performance of the day before. He was to lose, and it didn't matter how bad he looked in doing it.

Williams got the leadoff batter, Morrie Rath, but then gave up singles to Jake Daubert and Heinie Groh, a double to Roush, and another single to Pat Duncan before being taken out. The Reds scored four runs in the inning and won the game, 10–5. It wasn't even that close, because the Reds had a 10–1 lead before the White Sox rallied.

The Reds remained convinced, even after the evidence was in later, that they were the better team and would have won under any circumstances. Some were even convinced that the White Sox were trying to win.

Outfielder Alfred ("Greasy") Neale, who went on to greater fame as coach of the Philadelphia Eagles football team, hit .357 in the Series and was very upset when it was suggested that it was because the Chicago pitchers were on the take.

Neale thought there were some strange plays in the first game but contended that everything else was on the level. "Cicotte had more stuff than any pitcher I saw all year," he said.

"I don't know if the whole truth of what went on with the White Sox will ever be known," said Roush and he had a point. Even though there were some plays that seemed obviously designed to throw games—Williams' wildness, for instance, or the errors by Cicotte and Felsch—there was also some brilliant play by the White Sox.

Two of the Black Sox, Weaver and Jackson, had excellent Series. Weaver hit .324 and Jackson .375, and Jackson set a Series mark with 12 hits. Cicotte pitched a masterful game in his third start.

Gandil, Felsch and Risberg had poor showings, but star players often disappoint in the Series; the short time span distorts performances, good and bad. Roush, who had led the National League in hitting with a .321 mark, hit only .214 in the Series. Another Cincinnati star, Daubert, hit only .241.

Despite all the evidence that has been gathered, some questions persist. It seems likely that Weaver had no intention of ever throwing a game and played his best throughout the Series.

It also seems probable that the unsophisticated Jackson went along with the scheme when it was proposed but could not deliberately play poorly when the games started. It seems, too, that the others played well in spots, but only after making sure that the games would be lost.

"One thing that's always overlooked in the whole mess," said Roush, "is that we could have beat them no matter what the circumstances! Sure, the 1919 White Sox were good. But the 1919 Cincinnati Reds were better."

Nobody but the Cincinnati players was ever convinced of that, however. Even the Cincinnati fans were skeptical of the way the Series had gone. Indeed, some of them had been burned by betting on the Reds in the sixth and seventh games, which they lost. The victory celebration was muted, much more subdued than might have been expected in a city that had won its first World Series championship.

Despite all the speculation about the Series, nothing concrete was done for almost a year, though a Chicago grand jury was investigating the Series and related matters.

Meanwhile, the Series was the final straw for the owners. There had been talk for some time of replacing the three-man National Commission, which had ruled baseball ineffectually for years, and the owners finally did it, making Judge Kenesaw Mountain Landis the game's first commissioner and granting him sweeping powers.

Judge Landis, who had gained fame for a $29 million judgment against Standard Oil, often used those powers arbitrarily, but his stern rule helped baseball regain much-needed respect from the fans.

Landis's first major ruling, of course, came on the 1919 Series. The eight Chicago players were eventually acquitted by a Chicago jury, but Landis barred them from organized baseball.

He also barred Chase and Magee, and these actions finally convinced players that betting on and throwing games was not something that could be done without serious consequences.

13. Juice *In* the Ball, Not *On* It

The years 1920 and 1921 marked a critical turning point in the National League and baseball, as important as any in the game's history. In addition to the naming of Judge Kenesaw Landis as the game's first commissioner, changes were being introduced to make the game more popular with fans. Pitchers were handicapped, and batters were encouraged, and managers started to give up the philosophy of one run at a time in favor of the "big inning."

The first change came in 1920 when both leagues outlawed all pitches that involved tampering with the ball, including using sandpaper or emery paper, and applying spit. The penalty for violation of this rule was a ten-day suspension.

One exception was made to the rule: Any pitchers in the major leagues at the time could continue to use the spitball. There were 17 pitchers in the majors at the time who used the spitball, eight of them National Leaguers—Burleigh Grimes, Bill Doak, Phil Douglas, Dana Fillingim, Ray Fisher, Marvin Goodwin, Clarence Mitchell and Dick Rudolph.

(In a classic case of bad timing, consider the situation of poor Frank Shellenback. In 1918 and '19, Shellenback had pitched for the Chicago White Sox but had been sent down in 1920, so he did not qualify under the new rule. Since Shellenback's main pitch was the spitter, he was doomed to a career in the minor leagues, where he could continue to use the pitch. He never pitched another inning in the big leagues but won more than 300 games in the minors, 295 of them in the Pacific Coast League. He probably could have done very well in the majors—with the spitter.)

The ban against the trick pitches that involved applying something like sandpaper or emery paper to the ball was easy to enforce because the markings on the ball were obvious. The ban against the spitter remains difficult to enforce even today, and modern-day pitchers Preacher Roe and Gaylord Perry have confessed that they have used it. Roe told his story after he had retired and Perry after tougher rules had made it impossible, he said, to throw it. You can believe that if you choose; the batters don't.

Managers and hitters still complain that pitchers are throwing the spitter, and they're probably right, but it is difficult to detect. An alert catcher will throw the ball back before an umpire can get it, and the split comes off.

The beauty of the pitch is twofold: (1) It is thrown with the same motion as a fastball and thus difficult for the batter to pick up. (2) It does not put a strain on the arm; a curve does.

The pitch is most useful to a pitcher who has a good fastball but a mediocre curve, because it gives him another speed pitch. Properly thrown, the pitch breaks sharply down, much like a good overhand curve. Unlike the knuckleball, it is predictable in its movement, so it is not a difficult pitch to catch.

If the pitch was so good, why weren't more pitchers using it in 1920? Probably because it isn't always easy to control, and a pitcher with a good curve didn't need it. And there is always one problem with a spitter: When it's hit to an infielder, it may still be wet. More than one infielder has wound up throwing a curve to first because he got hold of the wet side.

The best of the spitball pitchers in 1920 was Grimes, and he was also the last to throw the pitch legally; every other spitball pitcher had retired by the time he threw his last pitch in 1934.

Grimes's technique was different from that of most spitball pitchers. He held the ball tightly, instead of loosely. He used slippery elm mixed with his saliva, as did most spitball pitchers of the day.

Grimes won 270 games in a 19-year career in the majors, good enough to earn him a spot in the Hall of Fame, and he did it as much with psychology as by the pitches he threw. He was known for his fearsome temper, and he never shaved on a day when he was scheduled to pitch, so he would appear more ominous to hitters.

As with most of his spitter-throwing colleagues, Grimes usually used the spitter mostly to keep the batter guessing. He went through the motions of throwing it on every pitch but more often than not, threw something else.

The Philadelphia Phillies once discovered that Grimes's cap moved when he actually spat on the ball, so he got a larger cap, which didn't give away his secret.

The ban on trick deliveries was the first time the hitters had been favored since the early days, when hitters could call for their pitches. The introduction of the lively ball was probably even more important.

As with all momentous changes, the introduction of the lively ball was accompanied by loud denials from those in charge that anything had actually changed. Probably because baseball is a game which revels in tradition and presents itself as relatively unchanging, those in charge don't like to admit that changes are ever made.

Talk to virtually any National League official, for instance, and he will tell you that the specifications for the baseball have always been the same. It is surely, then, simply an accident that the entire National League, pitchers included, *averaged* .303 in 1930, and that only five National League hitters exceeded .300 in 1968. They were hitting the same baseball. Sure.

It was also surely a coincidence that, about the time owners discovered that fans liked to see home runs and came out to the park in greater numbers when the games were high scoring, the baseball began suddenly flying over the fence much more frequently and going much further when it did.

In Cincinnati, for example, no ball had been hit out of the park since it had been built in 1921, until Reds' outfielder Pat Duncan did it on June 2, 1921. Duncan's home run, over the left field wall, was only his fifth in a career that had started in 1918. Strange things were happening.

The home run figures tell the story better than any narrative. In 1918, National Leaguers hit 138 home runs (in what amounted to three-quarters of a regular season, of course); in 1921, the figure had risen to 460! In less than a decade, in the hitters' great year of 1930, the figure was 892!

Still, the continued insistence that the specifications for the baseball remained the same. National League president John Heydler said that better quality wool and higher quality workmanship were responsible for a more resilient ball.

In retrospect, it seems absurd that baseball officials felt the need to disguise what was going on. The lively ball produced a game that the fans found more exciting, and wooing the fans was especially important in the aftermath of the Black Sox scandal.

Once the lively ball made its impact there was no turning back. The game was never the same again. Eventually, the lively ball changed pitching completely. It created the invaluable role of relief pitchers as we know them today, because starting pitchers could no longer coast through the lower part of the batting order. When any hitter can hit the ball out of the park, a pitcher has to work much more carefully, and that takes a lot out of his arm. A pitcher who lasts seven innings today has surely thrown at least as hard as a pitcher who went nine before the lively ball.

There was another important change coming. This one, the farm system, was given its impetus by Branch Rickey, as important and controversial a man as baseball has ever known.

14. Rickey's Revolution

Branch Wesley Rickey was a complex man, full of contradictions and, said his enemies, hypocrisies.

He was a deeply religious man who neither drank nor cursed—his strongest expletive was "Judas Priest!"—and who would neither play nor watch a game on Sunday. Yet, he willingly accepted the gate receipts for Sunday games, and his well publicized Christian conscience did not prevent him from taking advantage of those who did not understand a situation as well as he did, which was virtually everyone with whom he dealt.

He was a brilliant man and an excellent attorney, and he used his law skills to extricate himself from a contract with the St. Louis Browns when he wanted to move to the Cardinals in 1917. He approached baseball with the analytical skills of a good lawyer, and he introduced such concepts as sliding pits in spring training and chalk talks. Yet, he couldn't explain his theories to his player with any success. In ten years of managing, his teams finished in the first division only twice, never higher than third.

It was often impossible to separate his motives. Was he acting as a Christian when he broke the color barrier, for instance, or as a practical man who knew he could corner a significant part of the talent market? Probably both.

Certainly, Rickey's religious beliefs did not extend to a sharing of the wealth, either in baseball or literal terms. Old habits die hard, and Rickey's penuriousness, forced on him in the early days with the Cardinals, did not noticeably change when he had money behind him, in Brooklyn and Pittsburgh.

He used his considerable oratorical talents to convince players that they could and should play for less than they were asking. In *A Season in the Sun,* Roger Kahn tells of an episode with Rickey and Gene Hermanski, a Brooklyn outfielder. Hermanski had had a good season and was determined to get a good raise for the next season. He came out of a conference with Rickey smiling, and Kahn asked him if he'd gotten a raise. "No, but he didn't cut me!" said Hermanski.

Hermanski was lucky. Ralph Kiner led the National League in home runs with 37 in 1952, but Rickey pointed out to him that the Pirates had finished last and could have finished in the same position without Kiner. Ralph took a cut in pay.

In the long run, though, Rickey's personal traits took second place to the change he wrought in the National League and, indeed, all of baseball. Contrary to popular belief, Rickey did not invent the concept of the farm system, but he was the first executive to make the farm system successful.

Rickey saw baseball from all angles, starting as a player, and moving up to manager and finally to executive. His playing career was short and unproductive, 119 games in four major league seasons. His lifetime average was only .239.

Rickey was handicapped as a player by the fact that he would not play on Sunday. He was handicapped even more by a lack of ability. Rickey was

Branch Rickey's imaginative
mind created the farm system
and launched dynasties
in St. Louis and Brooklyn.
(George Brace photo)

catching for the New York Highlanders (now the Yankees) on June 28, 1907 when Washington stole 13 bases, a record at the time.

When Rickey fell ill with tuberculosis after that season he dropped out of major league baseball and went to the sanitarium at Saranac Lake, New York. As soon as he recovered, he went back to school and got his law degree from the University of Michigan in 1911.

Rickey had not severed his ties with the game he loved, though. While he was studying law at Michigan, he also coached the school's baseball team and recommended to the St. Louis Browns that they buy the team's star player, George Sisler.

After getting his degree, Rickey practiced law briefly in Idaho. One story had it that he became discouraged when a client told him off. At any rate, he was soon back in baseball as a scout for the Browns, who no doubt hoped he would come up with more players like Sisler.

Late in the 1913 season, Rickey was named manager of the Browns. In 1916, he moved up to the front office. Meanwhile, a group of St. Louis businessmen had purchased the Cardinals, and they hired Rickey to run the club, though it took a court battle to break his contract with the Browns.

Rickey's new job paid well—at $15,000, he was the highest-paid executive in baseball—but it seemed an almost impossible challenge. The Cardinals were woefully underfinanced, already $175,000 in debt when he joined them.

As he had demonstrated early with the discovery of Sisler, Rickey had a sharp eye for talent, but it did him little good in the beginning with the Cardinals because he didn't have the money to buy good minor league players. Many times he found he was acting only as a bird dog for John McGraw. When Rickey made an offer for a player, the club's general manager would telephone McGraw. The Giants' manager, respecting Rickey's judgment, would make a higher offer, and the player would go to the Giants.

But intelligent men can often turn adversity into triumph, and Rickey did exactly that. Seeking a way to neutralize the financial advantage of the Giants and other teams, he established a farm system.

The idea was not entirely original. In the 1890s, John T. Brush had owned both Cincinnati in the National League and Indianapolis in the Western (minor) League, and he used players from Indianapolis to stock his major league team. But Brush never bought any other minor league clubs, and no other owners followed his example.

Rickey started by buying into the Houston club of the Texas League, and then got working contol of Fort Smith (Arkansas) in the Western Association. From that modest beginning, the Cardinal farm system grew until by 1940 they owned 32 clubs and had working agreements with eight others, controlling more than 600 players.

Baseball men were split in their opinions about the worth of Rickey's revolutionary idea. Umpire Bill Klem tried to tell McGraw that it was a great idea, but McGraw, usually quick to sense trends that would help him win games, scoffed at the idea. "It's the stupidest idea in baseball," he said.

Another man who was opposed to the farm system was baseball commissioner Kenesaw Mountain Landis, who wanted minor league baseball teams to be run entirely by the bussinessmen of the towns. Landis's idea sounded fine, but it became more and more impractical as the years passed and salaries and expenses rose. Minor league baseball thrived under Rickey's system, and it probably would have withered away during that period, especially when the Depression hit, if Landis's idea had prevailed.

The judge, of course, was not a man who gave up one of his ideas simply because the facts had proven him wrong. He continued to oppose the idea of a farm system, and in 1938, he fined the Cardinals and set 73 of their minor league players free because of "secret agreements" between the Cardinals and three minor league teams.

This was like the buzzing of a flea to Rickey, of course. By that time, other clubs had long since followed the Cardinals' example and set up their own farm systems, but the Cardinals remained the most productive, no doubt because Rickey was in charge.

The farm system not only supplied the Cardinals' needs. It provided surplus players whom Rickey sold to other clubs, which kept the Cardinals in a solid financial position, a welcome change from the old days when he had even had to waive his own salary one year.

With the Cardinals (and later the Dodgers), Rickey always gave the other clubs less than they thought they were getting. He was a remarkable judge of talent, and he almost never gave away a player who became a star with another team. Rickey sometimes sold players who had been outstanding minor leaguers because he was convinced they would not get significantly better. At the same time he held onto players who lacked some skills but who were still developing. Many of these became outstanding players.

The statistics tell the story. The Cardinals had never won a National League pennant when Rickey joined them, but starting in 1926, they won nine pennants in 21 years. Though Rickey was gone by the time the last pennant in that string was won, 1946, the Cardinals were still winning with the players he had developed. Significantly, when he was no longer there to bring in the talent, the Cardinals stopped winning; not until 1964 were they champions again.

In 1942, Rickey went to the Brooklyn Dodgers. The Dodgers had enjoyed occasional success, winning pennants in 1916, 1920, and 1941, but for the most part, they had been the joke of baseball. Rickey changed that almost immediately. The players he brought to the Dodgers won pennants in 1947, 1949, 1952, 1953, 1955 and 1956, and lost two others in postseason playoffs.

Only when he went to the Pittsburgh Pirates in 1951, serving first as general manager and then as chairman of the board until 1959, did Rickey falter. Perhaps age simply caught up with him; he was 70 when he came to the Pirates. Maybe others had learned his lessons too well. The Pirates did win one pennant, in 1960, but only after enduring five last-place finishes, four of them in consecutive years, in the fifties. The club never became the dominating factor that St. Louis and Brooklyn had been under Rickey's guidance.

Rickey was voted into the Baseball Hall of Fame in 1967, an overdue honor and one that came after his death. He had died of a heart attack in 1965 while giving a speech accepting his induction into the Missouri Sports Hall of Fame.

Before that, the *Sporting News* had said, "Branch Rickey, over a period of many years, demonstrated true genius as a baseball executive."

Nearly ten years after his death, Cincinnati manager Sparky Anderson insisted that Rickey's influence was still felt, and that Rickey's influence was the reason the National League had better teams and players than the American League.

"There are a lot of people around who are Rickey's disciples who are still doing things his way," said Anderson. "Doing things Rickey's way means well-organized scouting and a good system of farm clubs. Mr. Rickey always put the highest priority on speed. He always wanted players who could throw hard, fun fast, and play defense. That's the kind of players we have in our league."

Ironically, Rickey was the biggest obstacle to his own success in his early years with the Cardinals. He had served as manager of the club from 1919 on, but though he was getting some excellent players—first baseman Jim Bottomley and outfielder Chick Hafey, for instance—he couldn't mold them into a pennant-winner.

In mid-season in 1925 the Cardinals were in last place and club president Sam Breadon couldn't take it any longer. He fired Rickey as manager, replaced him with Rogers Hornsby, and the Cardinals were on their way.

15. A Great Hitter, But . . .

Rogers Hornsby was one of those maddening individuals who believes everybody else is out of step, that his way is the only way. He was a man totally without tact, given to criticizing teammates and his players (when he was manager) while they were within listening range and calling it honesty, as tactless men will.

He quarreled with everybody, from team owners to the commissioner of baseball. Judge Kenesaw Mountain Landis didn't want anyone in baseball connected with horse racing because of its association with gambling. Hornsby liked the horses, probably because they didn't talk back, and Landis more than once tried to convince Hornsby to quit betting on races. Landis had a will of iron, and everybody else in baseball had to conform to it, but not Hornsby. He continued betting, and losing, incidentally. Naturally, he never took anybody else's advice.

Demonstrating that he couldn't get along with either sex, Hornsby was divorced twice. He was irascible, moody, petty, irritable, the last man you'd invite to a party. Which was all right with Hornsby; he didn't want to go to parties. He didn't even go to movies, because he was convinced they would hurt his eyesight, which would, in turn, hurt his hitting.

He played for five different teams because owners, though recognizing his great ability, simply could not stand to have him around for very long. He also managed five different major league teams, for the same reason.

But how the man could hit! He stood in the back corner of the batter's box, daring pitchers to sneak one past on the outside corner. Very few ever did. He hit everything—fast ball, curve, change; inside, outside; high, low. He went with the pitch, hitting to all fields so there was no way a defense could shift against him, as teams do against pronounced pull hitters.

For all-round ability, no right-handed hitter has ever equaled Hornsby. His lifetime batting average of .358 is the league record, and it seems unlikely that it will ever be approached. Seven times he led the league in hitting, and his .424 mark in 1924 is a modern major league record that will almost certainly never be equaled.

Hornsby was a line drive hitter, but those line drives often went over the fence or against the wall. He had 302 career home runs, twice led the league in home runs, and set a mark of 42 for a second baseman (since broken by Dave Johnson's 43 for Atlanta in 1973).

Four times, Hornsby led the National League in doubles, and his total of 541 ranks fifth in the league's history. Five times he led in runs scored, four times in RBIs.

As the best measure of his power, he led the league nine times in slugging percentage, a figure arrived at by dividing times at bat into total bases. Fans who have observed the more recent assaults on the record books by Hank Aaron, Willie Mays and Stan Musial probably will be surprised at one more statistic: Hornsby's lifetime slugging percentage, .577, is a National League record.

Nor was Hornsby just a powerful slugger. He had excellent speed, as his triples and stolen bases marks attest. He had nine seasons in which he was in double figures in triples, with a high of 20 in 1920; twice, he led the league in triples. Six times he stole a dozen or more bases in a season, three times getting as many as 17.

Strangely, there was little in Hornsby's early career that predicted he would be such an exceptional hitter. He weighed only 140 pounds when he came to the majors and was known primarily for his fielding, especially at shortstop, where he played most of his early career. He hit only .246 in 18 games when he first joined the St. Louis Cardinals in 1915 and, though he hit over .300 in three of his first four seasons, he didn't hit with the power that marked his later, more productive years; he didn't reach double figures in home runs until his sixth full season.

Branch Rickey encouraged Hornsby to add weight to his nearly six-foot frame, and Hornsby did, working on a farm in the off-season. Eventually, he went as high as 200 pounds, none of it fat, and the results showed in his hitting.

Hornsby's greatness as a hitter started when he was permanently switched to second base in 1920. There, despite a well-publicized weakness on pop flies, Hornsby was an excellent fielding second baseman, good enough to play even if he had been no more than an average hitter.

That year, Hornsby led the league in five hitting departments, average (.370), slugging percentage (.559), RBIs (94), doubles (44) and hits (218). But he was only warming up for a five-year hitting spree, 1921–25, that is absolutely unequaled in National League history.

In that stretch, Hornsby won the batting title every year with marks of .397, .401, .384, .424 and .403. His cumulative average for five years was .402!

Rogers Hornsby was perhaps the greatest all-round hitter in National League history, and one of its most irascible characters as well. *(George Brace photo)*

Five times he led the league in slugging percentage, three times in RBIs, twice in runs scored, twice in doubles, twice in home runs, with 42 and 39. Three times he led the league in hits, and his 250 hits in 1922 has been surpassed in National League history only by the 254 Bill Terry and Lefty O'Doul each accumulated.

Hornsby treated all pitchers alike in those years, which is to say, he destroyed them all. When he hit .424 in 1924, for instance, only the Pittsburgh and Chicago pitching staffs held him below .400—at .393 and .387, respectively.

That year, he also walked 89 times. Adding those walks to both his hit and at-bat totals, Hornsby was on base 316 times in 625 at bats, which means that he was a better than 50–50 bet to reach base any time he came to the plate.

Despite Hornsby's great hitting, the Cardinals were not doing particularly well. They slipped one notch each of his first four great years, from third in 1921 to sixth in 1924, with Rickey as manager. They were doing even worse in 1925, winning only 13 and losing 25, when Sam Bredon decided he had to make a change. Hornsby was named manager.

Not surprisingly, Hornsby and Rickey had not always gotten along. Indeed, they'd even had a fight in the clubhouse one day in 1923. Perhaps Hornsby was irritated because he was in what amounted to a slump for him in that period, finishing at .384 that season.

After that fight there was another puzzling incident. Hornsby didn't return to play when a skin infection, which sidelined him for two weeks, was cured.

"I have shown a forgiveness almost divine toward this player," announced Rickey in typical language. "I have overlooked the unspeakable names he called me . . ."

Despite all this, the two held a grudging admiration for each other. When Breadon told Rickey of the change, Rickey immediately told Hornsby, who was involved in his second favorite pastime, lobby sitting. Hornsby did not want the job and took it only because Breadon later assured him that Rickey was out as manager, and if Hornsby did not take the job, somebody else would.

The managerial change turned the Cardinals around; they won 64 and lost 51 the rest of the way, finishing fourth. That turnaround was not surprising because a team will often do better for a time under a new manager and then slip back into their familiar losing pattern. But the Cardinals continued to be successful under Hornsby in 1926, winning the first National League pennant for the city of St. Louis, beating out Cincinnati by two games and demolishing the long-standing myth that a team from St. Louis had to be far better than any other team to win a pennant because of the debilitating summer heat.

Hornsby had feared that being manager would detract from his hitting, and he seemed to be right as he slipped from .403 to .317. But he got considerable hitting help from his fellow infielders, first baseman Jim Bottomley (who led the league with 120 RBIs) and third baseman Les Bell, who hit .325 and had an even 100 RBIs. The Cards slipped past Cincinnati in early September to win the pennant; Pittsburgh was only 4½ games back in the tight race.

That was only the warm-up for one of the most exciting World Series ever, against a New York Yankees team that was a year short of its awesome peak but still good enough to win the American League pennant by three games over Cleveland.

The Series' lead swung back and forth, the Yankees taking the first game, the Cardinals the next two, and the Yankees the fourth and fifth. The Cardinals won the sixth game to set up a dramatic confrontation in the seventh between Grover Cleveland Alexander and Tony Lazzeri.

Alexander, who is co-holder with Christy Mathewson of the National League record for winning games with 373, is one of the most intriguing characters in baseball history.

His pitching feats are well understood. He won 30 games three seasons in a row in his prime, and his earned run average of 1.22 in 1915 was a National League record until Bob Gibson broke it in 1968.

Less understood were his personal problems. He was a heavy drinker, perhaps even an alcoholic, which didn't exactly set him apart from lots of other players in those days. The drinking, however, was a result of other concerns.

While serving in the Army in 1918, Alexander lost his hearing in one ear because of the constant shelling, and he first developed symptoms of epilepsy. Those problems, doctors later believed, caused his drinking, but much of this information came out many years after Alexander's career was finished.

Epilepsy is an illness that frightens people even now, and that was even more true in Alexander's day. In the climate of the times, alcoholism was more socially acceptable than epilepsy.

Alexander was a bitter man and turned even more introspective because of his problems. Because he did not talk about his problems, and because most sportswriters in the twenties were more interested in hyperbolic exaggeration than in accurate reporting, the facts surrounding Alexander remain murky. It seems likely, though, that Alexander tried to hide the fact of his epilepsy, and that at least some of his erratic behavior, attributed to excessive drinking, was due to his illness.

Despite his problems, Alexander remained an effective pitcher in the twenties, though not the great pitcher he had been earlier. Three times in the decade, the last time in 1927, he won at least 21 games.

During the 1926 season, the Chicago team for which he had pitched seven full seasons decided that Alexander was through, and the Cubs traded him to the Cardinals. The trade probably meant the difference for the Cardinals, because Alexander won nine games for them. He continued his fine pitching in the Series, winning the second and sixth games.

In the seventh game, the Cardinals were leading, 3–2, in the seventh inning. The bases were loaded, two men were out, and Tony Lazzeri was at bat. Hornsby decided to make a pitching change, bringing in Alexander to replace Jesse Haines.

Legend has it that Alexander had celebrated heavily the night before and was sleeping in the bullpen, nursing a hangover whose proportions have grown with each retelling of the story. Perhaps, but although Alexander had the reputation of pitching well with a hangover, it is hard to believe that Hornsby would risk the entire Series on Alexander if the pitcher were really in such terrible shape.

Alexander slipped a strike past Lazzeri, and then the Yankee rookie hit a shot down the left field line, into the stands—but just foul. A few inches to the other side of the foul line and Lazzeri would have been the hero, but two pitches later he had struck out, and it was the 39-year-old Alexander who was the hero.

That confrontation was such a dramatic one that most people have since forgotten that Alexander had to face the Yankees for two more innings. He retired them in order in the eighth, this athletically-old man with the supposed gigantic hangover, and got the first two in the ninth, before walking Babe Ruth, who had hit four home runs in the Series. With Bob Meusel at bat, Ruth inexplicably tried to steal second and was thrown out by St. Louis catcher Bob O'Farrell to end the Series.

Though Alexander was the hero of the Series, it was Hornsby who was the more heroic figure overall in St. Louis for both his playing and managing. He seemed set for the rest of his baseball career, at least for the playing side of it, with the Cardinals. Instead, he was traded on December 20, 1926, to the New York Giants for second baseman Frankie Frisch and pitcher Jimmy Ring.

The trade stunned everyone. Predictably, it had been caused by Hornsby's personality. During the season, owner Breadon had come into the clubhouse one day to tell Hornsby he had scheduled an exhibition game. Hornsby told Breadon what he could do with the game, and to get out of the clubhouse.

Grover Cleveland Alexander battled epilepsy and drink to win 373 regular season games and save the seventh game of the dramatic 1926 World Series. *(George Brace photo)*

Breadon decided then that Hornsby would not spend another year in a Cardinal uniform. Breadon was a courageous man, and he struck to that resolve, though he knew what the fans' reaction would be. Even on the victory train coming back to St. Louis after the Series, Breadon was negotiating with Bill Killefer to manage the club in 1928. When Killefer declined, Bob O'Farrell wound up with the job.

The trade eventually worked out well for the Cards. Frisch was a fine player, a smooth-fielding second baseman and an excellent switch-hitter, who hit .316 during his career. Although he lacked Hornsby's power, he had more speed. Frisch three times led the league in stolen bases, with a high of 49. He was also an excellent leader, one of those players who seems to be able to inspire his teammates to play their best. Eventually, he became a manager of the Cardinals, and they won the 1934 pennant for him.

Meanwhile, Hornsby went on his way, continuing to alienate people nearly as frequently as he got base hits. After only one year at New York, he was traded to Boston for outfielder Jimmy Welsh and catcher Shanty Hogan; the lopsidedness of that trade indicates how desperate Giants' owner Charles Stoneham was to rid himself of the Hornsby hairshirt.

Hornsby was gone after one year with Boston, too, though this time, it was for economic reasons. He went to Chicago for five players and $200,000, a trade that Hornsby himself advised Boston owner Emil Fuchs to make. The Cubs were the last team for whom Hornsby played full time, though he did play in emergency situations when he managed the St. Louis Browns from July 1933 to July 1937.

His frequent personality problems did not seem to affect Hornsby's play. He batted .361 for the Giants, .387 for the Braves, and .380 for the Cubs in 1929, his last great season. He was a part-time player after that, although he did play 100 games in 1931, hitting .331.

Hornsby's managerial career continued in fits and starts, but his St. Louis pennant was his first and last. He managed the Braves, Cubs and Cincinnati in the National League, the Browns in the American; in 13 seasons, he had a .460 percentage.

Four times he was fired during the season. Once, in 1932, he had the Cubs in second place with a 53–44 record when he was replaced by Charlie Grimm. The Cubs went on to win the pennant and showed their disregard for Hornsby by not voting him any share of the World Series money.

The players' insult to him probably never bothered Hornsby. After all, what did they know? They couldn't even be taught to do things the right way—the Hornsby way.

16. The Year of the Hitter

The year 1930 was one of crisis for the nation, locked in the Depression. Baseball owners, fearing that the economic slump would cut drastically into attendance, searched for a solution.

An answer seemed close at hand. Fans had reacted favorably to the more offensive-oriented game that had resulted from the use of the lively ball, so owners decided to give the ball even more juice for the 1930 season.

The results made the year a picnic for hitters, a nightmare for pitchers. And the owners? They were so embarrassed that the ball was dejuiced after the season and the experiment filed under F, for "forget it."

All year long, the hitters lined the ball off fences or lofted it over, as the pitchers longed for a quiet spot where they could hide. Records were set that have not been matched since, and at least two of them probably never will be.

The National League led the way in this hitting barrage. Six clubs—the

The Waner brothers, Lloyd (Little Poison), left, and Paul (Big Poison), terrorized National League pitchers in the 1920s and '30s, getting more than 5,600 hits between them. *(George Brace photo)*

Giants, Phillies, Cardinals, Cubs, Dodgers, and Pirates—compiled team batting averages of .300 or better. The Giants led with a .319 average, and the entire league averaged .303.

With the hitters doing so well, the pitching averages suffered in direct relationship. Only one National League pitcher, the overpowering Dazzy Vance of Brooklyn, had an earned run average under three runs a game, at 2.61.

Even more telling, no pitching staff in the league gave up fewer than an average four runs a game. Largely because of Vance, Brooklyn's staff led with a 4.03 ERA. Pittsburgh and Cincinnati yielded more than five earned runs a game, Philadelphia nearly seven.

It was the Phillies, indeed, who best demonstrated what was happening that wild year. At bat, the Phillies did some great things, averaging .315. Even the reserves were big hitters: Barney Friburg hit .342, Harry McCurdy .331, and Monk Sherlock .324, without being able to break into the starting lineup.

Chuck Klein, one of the best players never to make the Hall of Fame, hit .386 for the Phillies on 250 hits, 59 of them doubles and 40 home runs. He scored 158 runs and knocked in 170. It was an incredible year, all the more so because, of those figures, only his doubles and runs-scored led the league.

Klein was an outstanding hitter in years when the ball was less lively; his 43 homers in 1929 were a National League record. Yet, he set personal highs in five departments that year—average, slugging percentage, doubles, runs and RBIs.

Francis Joseph ("Lefty") O'Doul also had an excellent year for the Phillies, hitting .383, although 1929 had actually been a better one. In 1929, O'Doul had hit .398 with a record 254 hits.

It was typical of O'Doul that he did the unexpected, because he had done that throughout his career. He had started as a pitcher and switched to the outfield when his arm went bad. He was already 31 by the time he got his second try at the majors, as an outfielder, but he went on to hit .300 or better in six of his final seven major league seasons. Had he come up originally as a hitter, he might have been one of the all-time greats, but his .349 lifetime average was compiled during only 970 games, hardly more than the equivalent of six full seasons.

O'Doul later went on to become a very well-known minor league manager in San Francisco, a city that has often valued eccentricity more than accomplishment, and his popularity led to annual crusades by fans and writers to get him into the Hall of Fame.

Bill Terry hit .401 and set a National League record for hits in the 1930 season. *(George Brace photo)*

The Cubs' Hack Wilson set records with 56 home runs and 190 RBIs in 1930. *(George Brace photo)*

Klein and O'Doul had three teammates among the Philadelphia regulars who also hit .300 or better, and the Phillies averaged more than six runs a game, totaling 944 for the season. But their pitching staff was yielding even more—the staff's ERA was a whopping 6.71—and the Phillies finished last, 40 games off the pace.

Of all the hitters in the league, however, two stood out in that weird year, Bill Terry of the Giants and Hack Wilson of the Cubs, as different in their personalities as they were in their physiques and hitting styles.

Terry was all business as a player, probably because of hard times in his early years. His parents were separated, and Bill's formal education ended at 13. By 15, he was doing heavy work in the Atlanta railroad yards.

As early as 16, he was pitching minor league ball, but he left professional baseball four years later to work for Standard Oil Memphis. He also pitched for the company's semipro team, and he was signed four years later by John McGraw, on a tip from Tom Watkins, the owner of the Memphis team of the Southern Association.

The astute McGraw saw that Terry's future would probably be as a hitter, not a pitcher. Terry did continue his pitching with Toledo of the American Association, but McGraw had ordered the Toledo management to also play Terry at first base. Terry hit .336 and .377 in succeeding seasons at Toledo, and McGraw brought him up to the Giants to stay at the end of the 1923 season.

Terry stayed on the bench for most of the 1924 season because George Kelly was playing first for the Giants. By 1924, McGraw shifted Kelly to second to make room for Terry, but that wasn't soon enough for Terry, whose long feud with McGraw probably started at that point.

For years, Terry and McGraw didn't speak, but when McGraw decided in 1932 to step down as manager, he named Terry as his successor. Again, McGraw's judgment was excellent. Terry went on to win pennants for the Giants in 1933, 1936, and 1937, before quitting after the 1941 season.

Terry was a good manager, but it was his playing that got him to the Hall of Fame. He was a steady fielder and a brilliant left-handed hitter, remarkable for his consistency. He hit over .300 for ten straight seasons, starting in 1927, and had a lifetime average of .341. In modern National League history, only Rogers Hornsby had a higher career mark, and Terry's average is the best for left-handed hitters.

As was true for many hitters, 1930 was Terry's best season; he hit .401 with 254 hits. He and O'Doul hold the major league record for hits, and Terry is the last National Leaguer to hit .400.

It is unlikely anybody will ever hit .400 again or get 254 hits, for the same reasons. Home runs are more important to hitters than average now (Terry occasionally hit home runs, as many as 28 in 1932, but he concentrated on meeting the ball and struck out only 449 times in a 14-year career). The many night games and coast-to-coast travel make it harder on today's hitters. And, of course, it is almost impossible for a hitter to get 254 hits without hitting .401. Consider this: A .350 average is an excellent one these days, almost always good enough to win a batting title. But for a hitter who hits .350 to collect 254 hits, he would have to have 726 official at-bats. Not likely.

Wilson was much closer to the modern-style hitter, a free-swinger who led the league in strikeouts five times, though his high mark of 94 would be a half season or less for the likes of Dave Kingman.

What Wilson accomplished in 1930 was as remarkable as what Terry did; Hack set National League records of 56 home runs and 190 RBIs (the latter a major league record as well) that have never been equaled. It wouldn't be surprising if Wilson's home run record is equaled or surpassed, but the RBI total seems safe.

Terry was lean and rangy, Wilson short and stubby at five foot six and 190 pounds. He resembled a beer barrel, in part because he was so fond of the product it contained, and he was often ridiculed because of that.

Wilson was a better outfielder than is generally realized today, but his reputation rested on his power hitting. The National League was slower to appreciate the effectiveness of the big inning than the American (which, of course, had Babe Ruth) and Wilson was able to lead the league in home runs for three straight years, 1926–28, with the relatively low totals of 21, 30 and 31.

By 1929, he had raised his home run total to 39—ironically, that wasn't enough to lead the league that year, because Klein was establishing a league record with 43—to set the stage for his amazing season of 1930. His line that year read: 208 hits, 35 doubles, 6 triples, 56 home runs, 146 runs scored, 190 RBIs, and a .356 average.

Wilson didn't total that many home runs in the remaining four years of his career, shortened by his casual disregard of training rules, and Terry's highest post-1930 batting average was .354. It can be argued that the juiced-up ball of 1930 was the biggest factor in their extraordinary years, but Terry and Wilson both have a significant point in their favor. Other players were also hitting the lively ball of 1930, and nobody else did what they did. In the year in which all batters stood tall, they were the hardest outs.

17. Loonies on the Diamond

In the 1940s, the Brooklyn Dodgers and St. Louis Cardinals conducted one of the National League's great rivalries. In the two decades before that, the Dodgers and Cardinals had also been rivals, but this contest was for the reputation as the zaniest team in league history.

On balance, Brooklyn's "Daffiness Boys" probably had the edge, but the "Gashouse Gang" of St. Louis was close behind, and the Cardinals did something the Dodgers could not, winning pennants despite their antics. In one memorable year, 1934, the destinies of the two clubs were intertwined.

Any discussion of the "Daffiness Boys" has to start with Wilbert (Uncle Robbie) Robinson, who managed the Dodgers for 18 years, 1914-31, a span second only to Walter Alston in Dodger history. Alston lasted 22 years, but Robinson's longevity is more impressive because he didn't have Alston's success. Alston's teams won seven pennants and finished second seven times. Robinson's teams won only two pennants, and those came early in his career, 1916 and 1920; he had only one second-place finish, in 1924. It takes an extraordinary man to last 18 seasons with one club with no more success than that.

There was probably never a more popular figure in Brooklyn baseball history than Robinson. He was a popular choice as manager when he was selected, he was the popular choice to succeed Charles Ebbets as club president in 1925 (in what ultimately turned out to be a disastrous move), and he was popular with the fans right up to the time he was forced out as Dodgers' manager.

Almost everybody liked "Uncle Robbie," except for his one-time friend and business partner, John McGraw, who never could forgive Robinson for leaving his position as Giants coach to become Dodgers' manager.

"He was a very companionable, chatty guy," remembered Garry Schumacher, who covered the Dodgers in the early 1920s. "He used to live in the Hotel St. George, and he'd invite people to come by after the game. He was a great host."

Robinson was just as companionable in the off-season. He and some other baseball men owned a hunting lodge in Georgia, and he would spend the winter there. "He invited me down for a week one winter," recalled Schumacher. "There was a lot of moonshine drinking. The hunting was great—deer, quail—and there was lots of fishing. There was a big house with plenty of servants, and plenty of liquor, too."

Generally speaking, Robinson got along very well with the writers covering the club, but he made a couple of public relations blunders that were significant at the time, though they seem comical in retrospect.

The least damaging, but most embarrassing, gaffe came late in the 1927 season. Chatting after a September game with Boze Bulger of the *New York Evening World,* Robinson was asked how he thought the Pittsburgh Pirates would do against the New York Yankees in the upcoming World Series.

"The Yanks will murder 'em," said Robbie. "They've got the best club that ever was in baseball."

Bulger couldn't believe what he'd heard, and he asked Robinson if he thought the Yankees were better than the old Orioles, the legendary team for which Robinson himself had played. "That was thirty years ago," said Robinson. "These Yankees are better'n we were."

It wasn't until he heard from various people connected with the National League, and from old teammates and their families, that Robinson realized how damaging his words seemed when they appeared in Bulger's story the next day.

Robinson was in a quandary. He didn't want to repudiate Bulger, who had been a friend for years. He finally settled for a halfway retraction: He announced that, as good as the Yankees were, he was certain the Pirates would beat them in the World Series.

That incident, heated as it was at the time, blew over quickly. Robinson wasn't so lucky after a run-in he had with the *New York Sun* in 1926. The episode started with a sports page cartoon showing rookie pitcher Jess Petty, who was having an excellent year, with marginal portraits of Dazzy Vance and Burleigh Grimes, the veteran Dodger pitchers who were struggling.

The caption pointed out that Vance was getting more than $16,000 and Grimes $15,000 and asked how much Petty was getting. (Petty's salary was $5,000). The caption implied that Petty was worth more than he was getting, though it is baseball tradition that players get paid for what they have done in the past, not what they are doing at the moment.

Robinson complained to the managing editor of the paper, Keats Speed, and finished his diatribe by saying, "Maybe you'd like to know the bat boy's salary!"

The next day, the *Sun* had a boxed story with a headline that read: "The

Bat Boy's Salary." The last line of the item said, "The *Sun* does not care what Mr. Robinson's salary is."

From then until Robinson was fired after the 1931 season, the *Sun* never mentioned him by name, content to use "the Dodger manager" whenever a reference was necessary. Those impersonal references were never complimentary.

As a manager, Robinson was a sound tactician, and his lack of overall success (his career record was 1397 wins and 1395 losses) was probably attributable more to a lack of great talent than to any personal shortcomings. In the manner of the times, he was profane, but he was not combative. "I never saw him in any kind of ruckus with an umpire," said Schumacher.

He was particularly good with pitchers. As a coach with the Giants, he was credited with the development of pitchers Rube Marquard and Jeff Tesreau, and the strength of his best Brooklyn teams was generally in the pitching staff.

Those who knew him well respected him. "He taught me everything I know about baseball," said Schumacher.

Yet, the image that persists of Robinson is that of a comical figure. In part it is because he was a fat man who ballooned to 250 pounds on a five foot eight frame (he had played at 170). Indeed, Robinson was involved in some comical maneuvers, even before the "Daffiness Boys" came on the scene.

There was the episode, for instance, when he indignantly told his players he was going to establish a "Bonehead Club," fining those who made mental errors. The next day he turned in the wrong lineup to the umpire and became the first member of the club.

Then they was the time in 1915 when Ruth Law, the pioneer aviatrix, was flying promotional exhibitions at Daytona Beach, where the Dodgers were training. The year before, Washington catcher Gabby Street had caught a ball dropped from the Washington Monument. Now, players wondered whether it would be possible to catch a ball dropped from an airplane. Robinson announced that he could.

The next day, when Miss Law went up, the assistant trainer of the club, John Kelly, went along, supposedly to drop a baseball for Robinson to catch. Instead, he dropped a grapefruit—probably at the instigation of Casey Stengel, then a Dodger.

When Robinson caught the "ball," the grapefruit burst and the juice spread over his face and chest as he fell backward. For a few seconds, Robinson was certain the juice was his blood, and he screamed for help while the players roared with laughter.

●

Robinson, then, was a perfect manager for the "Daffiness Boys," a term coined by Westbrook Pegler, then a sportswriter, to describe the Brooklyn team which spanned roughly the 1925 to 35 decade.

The Dodgers had two pitchers who were later elected to the Hall of Fame, Vance and Grimes, and some other good players. But they were known primarily for their rather casual attitude toward the game, and their desire to get some laughs out of life. They brought laughter to others, too, though not always intentionally.

Within the club, there was a group of pranksters known as the "Big Four," a misleading name because there were far more than four members. Typical was an incident involving Jess Petty, after that pitcher had been fined for breaking curfew.

Petty was told by members of the "Big Four" that he had committed a terrible crime—getting caught. He was told to prepare his defense, in writing.

Petty took all this seriously, and he went to baseball writer John Drebinger, who typed a statement for him. Vance, speaking for the "Big Four," told Petty it was obvious he had not prepared it himself, because he didn't have a typewriter. Petty went back to Drebinger for another statement, and copied it in his own handwriting.

The next day, Petty was directed to read his statement. He labored over it, stumbling over long words. Vance told him he would be declared innocent if he could answer one question. "Here," said Vance, "you have used the word 'ignominious.' What does it mean?"

"It means I was cold sober," said Petty.

The "Big Four" provided a lot of chuckles in the dugouts, the Dodgers' and others, but the symbol of the team to the Dodger fans was Floyd Caves ("Babe") Herman, the redoubtable outfielder.

"Babe had a lot of things going for him," said Schumacher. "He could run; he could hit the home runs; he hit .393 one season. But he was always making these mental errors."

Early in his career, it was said that Herman was hit on the head by a fly ball. In an interview with the late John Lardner, Herman called that a canard, and said he would bet anybody that he had never been hit on the head by a fly ball. "What about the shoulder?" asked Lardner. "Shoulder doesn't count," said Herman. Then, wrote Lardner, Herman pulled a cigar out of his pocket and stuck it in his mouth. The cigar was already lit.

Herman's great moment was the time he tripled into a triple play. Schumacher saw it; so let him describe it.

"It was a game against Boston at Ebbets Field, and the score was tied, 5–5, in the bottom of the eighth inning. Hank DeBerry was on third base, Dazzy Vance on second, and Chick Fewster on first.

"Herman hit a line drive against the fence and over the exit gate, a legitimate triple. It was a typical Herman hit, a screaming line drive. DeBerry held up for a moment to make sure it was in and then trotted home with what turned out to be the game-winning run.

"Vance stumbled as he came toward third and tripped over the bag. About halfway home, he just fell flat on his face. Fewster saw what happened; so he pulled up for a moment.

"Meanwhile, Herman wasn't paying any attention to anybody else. All he knew was that he had a triple. The center fielder, Jimmy Welch, had made an excellent recovery and thrown in, to the third baseman, Eddie Taylor. Vance, instead of going home, had gone back to third, so all three runners came sliding into third at the same time!

"Taylor tagged out Vance and Herman. By this time, Fewster had started back to second, and he just threw up his hands in disgust, and Taylor was able to run him down, too."

It was certainly an unusual way to score a game-winning run, but Robinson took it all in stride. "Leave them alone," he said. "It's the first time they've been together all season!"

The image of erratic play by the Dodgers outlasted Robinson, who was forced out after the 1931 season, and it probably contributed to one of the best-known, and most important, phrases ever made by a manager.

Before the 1934 season, Giants' manager Bill Terry was talking to writers about other teams in the league. Roscoe McGowen asked him about the Dodgers. "Brooklyn? Is Brooklyn still in the league?" said Terry, in a most untypical wisecrack.

Terry's remark was understandable. The Dodgers had fallen on bad times. They weren't even as funny as they had been. The year before, they had finished sixth, and the one "improvement" made by the front office in the off-season was firing manager Max Carey, just before spring training was to start. Casey Stengel was hired in his place. "I guess I'm the first manager to be fired for not winning a pennant in the winter," said Carey.

Probably because it emphasized the club's sad state, Terry's remark infuriated the team's fans. When the Giants played in Ebbets Field that year, the fans booed Terry whenever he appeared on the field, and they carried banners with the hated question on it.

None of that would have been important if the Giants, going for their second straight pennant, had not fallen into a slump in September. A six-game lead had been dissipated, and the Giants were tied with the St. Louis Cardinals with only two games remaining.

Naturally, the last two Giants games were against the Dodgers. The games were played in the Polo Grounds, but so many Dodger fans came from nearby Brooklyn that there was no psychological advantage for Terry's team.

Sportswriter-scholar John Kieran, almost as if he knew exactly what was going to happen, wrote these lines for the *New York Times:*

> Why, Mister Terry, oh!, why did you ever
> Chortle the query that made Brooklyn hot?
> Just for the crack that you thought was so clever,
> Now you stand teetering right on the spot!
> Vain was your hope they forgave or forgot;
> Now that you're weary and bowed with fatigue,
> Here is the drama and this is the plot:
> Brooklyn, dear fellows, is still in the league.

Right on cue, the Dodgers took both games, 5–1 and 8–5. Was it because the Brooklyn players were angry with Terry? Probably not. More likely, it was only another example of what can happen when an inferior team, playing under no pressure, meets a superior one which feels the pressure.

At any rate, the reason was less important than the fact. While the Giants were losing, the Cardinals were winning two games from Cincinnati, and the "Gashouse Gang" had its pennant.

●

The "Gashouse Gang" is one of the most famous nicknames in baseball history, but its exact origins aren't clear. Chicago sportswriter Warren Brown used the term in print in 1935, but claimed that he had used it in conversation three years before. He said the unorthodox fielding and grubby appearance of Pepper Martin reminded him of a refugee from a gasworks.

But Brown was apparently not the first to use the term in print. That distinction went to Frank Graham of New York, who used it after an interview with team shortstop Leo Durocher.

At that time, the Cardinals often played in dirty uniforms on the road because they did not have time to send them out to be cleaned. Durocher told Graham and other New York writers, "They wouldn't let us play in the American League. They'd say we were a lot of gashouse ballplayers."

Whatever its origin, the nickname made the team. The Cardinals were a good team, not a great one. Indeed, they were not even the best in the history of the franchise; that honor would have to go to the team that won four pennants in the 1942–46 stretch. But the Gashouse Gang is certainly one of the best remembered teams in league history.

On the field, that team was an aggressive one, willing to do anything to win a game. It had great and colorful players, most notably Dizzy Dean, Pepper Martin and Joe Medwick. Few teams, if any, put on as consistently entertaining spectacles as did the Cardinals, but relatively few came to watch. This was during the Depression, of course, and St. Louis attendance dipped from 623,960 in 1931 to 290,370 and 268,404 in the next two years. The pennant-winning team in 1934 was watched by only 334,863. In comparison, the pennant-winning 1928 Cardinals drew 778,147. Many more people read about the Gashouse Gang than ever saw them play.

Off the field, the players refused to take either themselves or anybody else seriously. Playing baseball was not a way to get rich; they were doing it primarily because it was fun. That attitude stretched to their off-field activities, and they didn't worry about jeopardizing their careers because they had so little to lose. Martin, for instance, had a midget racer that he raced for years even during the baseball season.

In many ways, Martin was typical of the group. He was a good player (.298 average for 13 seasons) who could rise to the occasion: With his 12 hits, .500 batting average, and five stolen bases he was the unquestioned star of the 1931 World Series, won by the Cards.

He was a flamboyant player, inspiring two nicknames "Pepper" and "Wild Hoss of the Osage," the latter for the area in Oklahoma where he was born. His given name was John Leonard Martin, but nobody ever used that.

He started as an outfielder with the Cards, but it was as a third baseman that he gained his fame. He played the position in the manner of the Allied troops storming Normandy in World War II, on his stomach as often as his feet. Martin had little finesse, so he stopped balls by diving at them or blocking them with his chest. He looked clumsy, but he was effective.

On the bases, Martin played the same way, belly diving into bases instead of using the more conventional feet-first slide. He led the National League three times in stolen bases, but he is best remembered for the '31 Series when he told the great Philadelphia A's catcher, Mickey Cochrane, that if he

Pepper Martin, the "Wild Hoss of the Osage," was the spirit of the Gashouse Gang. *(George Brace photo)*

got on base, he would steal second. To Cochrane's consternation, Martin did exactly that five times.

His playing personality was a direct reflection of Martin's off-field personality. He was completely natural; what you saw was what you got with Pepper. He disdained the conventions and niceties. He wore no underwear under his street clothes, and no athletic supporter under his uniform; amazingly, considering his style of play, he was never hit in the unprotected area.

Martin was a colorful player. That color was often black when he appeared at spring training because for years he would pocket the expense money the Cardinals sent him to get to camp and hop a free ride on a freight train.

With Dean, he was often the instigator of elaborate pranks. In spring training one year, he decided to try barbering, and he persuaded Dean to let him give Dizzy a shave. Dean escaped intact, which is more than can be said for manager Frisch's heart when he heard about it.

One of the team's most famous stunts came on a rainy afternoon in Philadelphia, and again, it was Martin and Dean who conceived the idea. With Bill Delancey and Rip Collins, they dressed in coveralls and carried buckets of paint and brushes into the dining room of the Bellevue-Stratford Hotel, where a large group was assembled for lunch.

As the players walked into the room, Dean told the guests, "You won't bother us." Quickly, Martin and Dean were recognized, and the players were invited to have dessert with the group.

Martin and Dean would sometimes stage phony fights in hotel lobbies, and Martin had a number of other tricks that he liked, such as giving players hotfoots, sprinkling sneezing powder around the locker room, and throwing ice out hotel windows.

He was a naive, trusting man. One year, he earned $10,000 in the off-season by making stage appearances. Branch Rickey asked him what he'd done with the money and Martin patted his pockets. "I've got it all right here," he said.

"Judas Priest!" said Rickey, who had a more reverential attitude toward money.

Shortstop Durocher came to the team in mid-season in 1933 and proved to be the player the Cardinals needed to win in '34. A weak hitter, with a lifetime average of .247, Durocher nevertheless was a valuable player because he was an excellent fielding shortstop and a natural leader.

Durocher was seldom involved in the pranks, but he created a legend

Frankie Frisch became old before his time managing the Gashouse Gang and playing an excellent second base. *(George Brace photo)*

around himself with his colorful vocabulary and belligerent personality. His style was always to go for the jugular and never take a back step. Though he and the manager had their run-ins, it was a style that was appreciated by Frisch, an aggressive though much more talented player himself.

Once, Frisch accused Durocher of not hustling when the shortstop's poor throw let in a run. In the clubhouse after the game, Frisch said the poor throw would cost Durocher $50.

"Make it a hundred!" said Durocher.

"I'll make it two hundred!" replied Frisch.

"Make it three hundred!"

"I'll make it a grand!"

"Make it two grand!" yelled Durocher.

By this time, the rest of the players had gathered around and were laughing. Frisch started laughing, too, and the fine was forgotten.

Two players who later were named to the Hall of Fame played crucial roles on the 1934 championship team. One was outfielder Joe "Ducky" Medwick.

Medwick was another Cardinal player who wouldn't give an inch on the field. He was a solidly-built player who was sometimes called "Muscles," the nickname he preferred, but who was usually referred to as "Ducky" because of his waddlelike walk.

He had some great years during his 17-year career, the greatest being 1937, when he led the league in eight hitting categories: average (.374), slugging percentage (.641), at-bats (633), hits (237), doubles (56), home runs (31), runs (111), and RBIs (154). Naturally enough, he was the league's Most Valuable Player that year.

But Medwick's most lasting fame came from a play—and the resulting ruckus—in the 1934 World Series.

In the sixth inning of the final game of the Series, with the Cardinals coasting behind Dean and a 7–0 lead, Medwick lined a ball off the center-field wall. As he came into third, Detroit third baseman Marv Owen pretended he had the ball, and Medwick slid hard.

Owen raised his foot, brought it down on Medwick's leg, and then fell on him. Soon, the two were fighting, until umpire Bill Klem separated them.

When Medwick went out to the field in the bottom of the inning, the Detroit fans threw bananas, tomatoes, oranges, bottles, metal, newspapers—anything they could get their hands on.

Finally, commissioner Kenesaw Mountain Landis decided that Medwick would have to leave the game, so the game would not be forfeited. It was a curious decision from the commissioner, famed for his tough stands. Because he didn't throw Owen out, too, Landis's action made it seem that Medwick was the one to blame.

Medwick was upset because he had 11 hits, one away from the Series record, and he would have had another chance to bat, and to tie the record. The Cardinals went on to win the game, 11–0, and spared Landis the embarrassment that would have resulted if the Tigers had somehow come back and won the game.

There was an aftermath to the episode: That night, two plainclothesmen were assigned to guard Medwick until he left town, and he couldn't even go out for the Cardinals' victory dinner. He ate in his room, safe from the enraged Detroit fans, who took their baseball seriously.

But nobody, not Medwick, not Durocher, and not even Martin, better symbolized the Gashouse Gang than the irrepressible Dizzy Dean.

Dean is one of baseball's all-time great characters, and he was unusual in one important respect: He was not a drinker. The antics of many other flamboyant players resulted from hard drinking, but Dean's sprang from a frolicsome personality and giant ego.

Just getting the facts from Dean was a tough job. One legendary afternoon, he claimed three different birthplaces in separate interviews with three different sportswriters. Dean said later that he wanted each of them to have a story all his own. His given name was Jay Hanna, but he sometimes referred to himself as Jerome Herman, after a boyhood friend. His nickname never changed, though, because "Dizzy" was such a natural.

Dean had such an ego that he was sent down to Houston by the Cardinals in 1931 in hopes that it would take some of the braggart out of him. It didn't, of course. And, as Dizzy pointed out later, it's only bragging when you say you're going to do something and then can't do it.

One of his most outrageous claims was made after he had pitched a three-hitter in the first game of a doubleheader and brother Paul had pitched a no-hitter in the second game. "If I'd known Paul was going to do that," he said, "I'd have pitched a no-hitter, too."

Perhaps. Dizzy had a way of making good on his boasts. A youngster in a hospital once asked him to strike out Bill Terry in a game that afternoon, and Dizzy promised he would. He got two strikes on Terry with the bases loaded and then walked to the plate and told Terry, "I'm sorry, Bill, but I promised I'd strike you out." He threw a fast ball past Terry on the next pitch.

In the '34 World Series, Dean stopped his own warm-up before the final game to watch Detroit starter Eldon Auker. "Sorry, Mickey," he told Detroit manager Cochrane, "but he won't do." Dean was right, as he blanked the Tigers and Auker to win the Series.

Before the start of the 1934 season, Dean promised that "me and Paul" would win 45 games. That was perhaps the one time in his life when he was conservative: The Dean brothers combined to win 49 that year.

Dizzy once bet that he could strike out Pittsburgh outfielder Vince DiMaggio every time up. He got DiMaggio the first three times and then, with two strikes on him the fourth time up, Vince hit a pop foul behind the plate. "Drop it!" yelled Dean at catcher Bruce Ogrodowski, who was so surprised that he did. Dizzy then struck out DiMaggio on the next pitch.

Dean could get away with his antics and braggadocio because he was a great pitcher with a live fastball and excellent curve. In his first five seasons in the league he won 120 games. He was only 26 when a line drive by Earl Averill in the All-Star Game broke his toe and forced him to change his pitching motion. Dean soon hurt his arm and was never the same pitcher again.

His greatest year was 1934, when he won 30 games and lost only seven and led the National League in complete games (24), strikeouts (195), and shutouts (7). His 30th win and seventh shutout came on the last day of the season and clinched the pennant.

In the Series, Dizzy won the first game and the last. He taunted the Tigers as they came to the plate in that last game, and with two men on and two out in the last of the ninth, threw his fast ball past Detroit slugger Hank Greenberg to win the game and Series. That was Dizzy Dean, and that was the Gashouse Gang.

Dizzy Dean pitched and talked his way into the Hall of Fame with the Gashouse Gang. *(George Brace photo)* In later years, Dizzy became famous as a broadcaster with such phrases as "He slud into third." *(Alfred Fleushman photo)*

18. The Screwball Master

Carl Hubbell was a skinny six foot, 170 pound left-hander who won more games, 253, than any left-handed pitcher in Giants' history. Like the right-hander who set Giants records, Christy Mathewson, Hubbell threw a reverse curve; Mathewson's was called a fadeaway, Hubbell's a screwball. Like Mathewson, Hubbell was known for his control, not his strikeouts, but the feat for which he's best known is striking out six American League sluggers in the second All-Star game, in 1934.

Hubbell came to the screwball out of necessity. "My first big pro job was with Oklahoma City, then in the Western League," he remembers. "Right-handed hitters were killing me. There was a Lefty Thomas on the Oklahoma club who was winning 20 games. He threw a sidearm sinker away from right-handers. He taught me how to turn my wrist so I could break off a screwball against a right-handed hitter's power."

The screwball breaks in the opposite direction of a regular curve; left-hander Hubbell's moved away from right-handed hitters. A ball moving away from a hitter is obviously harder to hit than one coming in, so the pitch gave Hubbell an added weapon. Few other pitchers have used it successfully because it's a difficult pitch to control, and it is hard on a pitching arm because it requires an unusual motion that can twist and tear muscles. During his career Hubbell never had serious arm trouble, but years later, when he was the farm system director for the Giants, his arm was so twisted from his years of throwing the screwball that the palm of his hand faced almost directly forward.

Hubbell won 17 games for Oklahoma City in 1925, throwing the screwball, and was sold to Detroit. But Ty Cobb, then manager of the Tigers, told him to lay off the screwball. Without the screwball, Hubbell was a mediocre pitcher, and he was soon back in the minors.

Not until 1928, when he was with Beaumont, did Hubbell start to throw the screwball again. He was impressive enough to be bought by the Giants after that, and he came up that season to stay.

The screwball, though, was not the only reason Hubbell won. His remarkable control—he walked fewer than two men per game in his 16-year major league career—was another factor, and behind that control lay an excellent mind. Hubbell was a calculating pitcher. Listen to what he said about control:

"Control is thinking the pitch to a target you have in mind. No two hitters are alike. Some pitchers aim at the strike zone. Some others aim at the catcher's glove. I always looked over the man at bat and adjusted to his stance."

Some pitchers, worried about walking a man, will groove a pitch on 3-and-2. Hubbell never did. He always went for the corner, which took courage and confidence.

"And I don't mean 'aiming' a pitch," he says. "When you're merely aiming, you're throwing it up with nothing on it. You should rear back and

Carl Hubbell, the Giants' "Meal ticket," set the American League hitters on their ears in the 1934 All-Star game.
(George Brace photo)

throw hard, taking into account the hitter's strength and weakness and how the umpire calls strikes, which can vary."

When the situation was right, Hubbell even went against the "book," and his control enabled him to do something few pitchers ever could. With a runner on second, he would deliberately throw his first two pitches just a little off the plate.

"I'd never do that to the .250 hitters," he says, "because they're unpredictable. But the .300 hitters would figure I had to come in with a straight one. They'd take a toehold, and then I'd put one just slightly inside, on their fists." The result, more often than not, was a pop-up.

Hubbell was a winner from the time he came up with the Giants—he had only one losing season, 11–12, near the end of his career—and he pitched a no-hit game in 1929, only his second season. But it was not until 1933 that he became an overpowering pitcher, so reliable that he became known as "the Meal Ticket" for his ability to win the big games and stop losing streaks.

With that season Hubbell started a string of five straight years in which he won at least 21 games, averaging 23 wins for the five seasons. In 1936, Hubbell won 26 games, his seasonal high, but it could be argued that 1933 was an even better year. That year Hubbell set personal records with a 1.66 earned run average and ten shutouts.

That was also the year Hubbell pitched the finest game of his career, not excluding the no-hitter he had pitched four years earlier. In the first game of the June 2nd doubleheader against St. Louis, the team the Giants were battling for the pennant, Hubbell pitched an 18-inning shutout, allowing only six hits, striking out 12 and not walking a man. (The Giants also won the second game of that remarkable doubleheader by 1–0, with Roy Parmalee outpitching Dizzy Dean, and that gave the Giants the impetus they needed to go on to win the pennant.)

Hubbell climaxed that great year by pitching two complete game wins over Washington in the World Series, 4–2 in the first game and 2–1 in the fourth, as the Giants took the Senators in five games.

Though the Giants did not win the pennant in 1934, Hubbell had another outstanding year, winning 21 games with an ERA of 2.30, and also saving 8 games in relief. But all that paled to insignificance alongside his performance in the All-Star Game.

Few envied Hubbell his nomination as starting pitcher for the National League that year, because the American League has probably never had a stronger hitting lineup than the one that started that game. Every one of the American League starters in that game was subsequently voted into the Hall of Fame: Babe Ruth, Lou Gehrig, Jimmie Foxx, Al Simmons, Bill Dickey, Joe Cronin, Heinie Manush, Charley Gehringer and Lefty Gomez. Ruth, Foxx and Gehrig rank 1-4-6 in lifetime home runs among American League players even today.

But Hubbell had two significant advantages. One was that, of the American League starters, only Cronin had batted against him in championship competition, in the World Series of the previous year. The others knew that Hubbell threw a screwball, but they couldn't know how sharply the pitch broke or that Hubbell could make it sink, too. "He could make the ball disappear," said Garry Schumacher.

The other advantage was that the game was played in the Polo Grounds, Hubbell's home park, with its short foul lines—less than 300 feet—and distant center-field fence.

"What people forget about the situation is that the Polo Grounds made a big difference," says Hubbell. "It was so unusual, hitters would change their style. They'd try to pull the ball for homers, and you could throw them sinking pitches away."

None of that seemed to make any difference when the game started. Gehringer opened with a single and went to second on an error in the outfield. Hubbell walked Manush, and up came Ruth, with Gehrig and Foxx following. Ruth was in the twilight of his great career, but he had hit 13 home runs that season; Gehrig went on to hit 49 that year, and Foxx 44. "The odds were 500-1, no, 1000-1, that the AL would score," wrote Paul Gallico.

"I really wasn't under that much pressure," said Hubbell later, recalling the moment. "I was facing those great hitters, so from a psychological viewpoint, I had the advantage—nothing to lose. Ruth and Gehrig had hit home runs off better pitchers than me."

Not off Hubbell this time, though. Hubbell slipped a called third strike past Ruth, then got Gehrig and Foxx swinging. The fans—most of them Giants' fans, of course—went wild as Hubbell walked off the mound.

Simmons led off the next inning. The Chicago outfielder hit .344 that year, and he was a hitter who usually made contact, striking out only 58 times that year. But the screwball got Simmons, too, swinging. Cronin was next, and the Washington shortstop, who struck out only 28 times in the entire '34 season, went down swinging, Hubbell's fifth straight strikeout.

The next hitter was New York Yankee catcher Bill Dickey. By this time, Hubbell was caught up in the excitement and trying to do something he seldom tried. "I wasn't a strikeout pitcher," he says. "I never really tried to strike anybody out. I'd rather get a man out with one pitch, if I could, rather than three or four pitches." But this time, he was trying to strike out Dickey.

"I got two strikes on Dickey and figured I had him," recalls Hubbell, "but he teed off on a bad pitch and belted out a hit (single) that ended the string. I know I would have gotten the next guy out because it was Gomez, and he wouldn't bother you."

Indeed, Hubbell did strike out Gomez after Dickey's hit, giving the Giant left-hander six strikeouts in the first two innings. Hubbell pitched the one more inning allowed under All-Star rules, striking out nobody but holding the American Leaguers scoreless. Later, though, the AL hitters loosened up and went on to win the game, 9–7.

"Those of us who watched him operate," wrote Gallico, "will treasure his brief period on the mound as some of the greatest innings ever pitched."

Hubbell himself wasn't that impressed. "I actually didn't think too much of it at the time," he said. "We lost the game. Maybe if we had won, it would have meant more to me. But the next day so much was made about it in the papers, I started thinking about it. I guess it helped my career. Without it, I might have been forgotten by now. But at least people think about me once a year."

Hubbell retired as a pitcher after the 1943 season, when he was 40, and was immediately named director of the Giants farm system by grateful owner Horace Stoneham. Not all of Stoneham's sentimental appointments turned out well, but this one did. Under Hubbell's supervision, in New York and later San Francisco, the Giants farm system was extraordinarily productive.

He remained in that position into his 70s, but emphysema forced him to move to the dry climate of Arizona in 1978, where he continues his long and productive service for the Giants as a scout.

Scouting for the Giants, Hubbell has looked for pitchers with speed, because it takes too long to develop a pitcher who depends on breaking pitches. "You've got to find the guy who can throw reasonably hard," he says. "And the harder they throw, the better you like them."

And, the natural question: Does the great screwball pitcher teach the pitch to young Giants?

No, he says. "I don't teach it to young pitchers unless they have no other equipment. It is a desperation pitch. I'd prefer to see them throw hard and curve it naturally."

For Hubbell and the generation of fans who saw him pitch, it's fortunate that he didn't take his own advice.

19. Under the Lights

Larry MacPhail was a man surrounded by legends, many of them his own creation, a wild-eyed, hard-drinking, hot-tempered man who took life on a dead run. In eight years as a National League executive, three with Cincinnati and five with Brooklyn, he changed the face of baseball forever. He deserves to be in the Hall of Fame, though he is not.

At one time or another, MacPhail was involved in as many projects as half a dozen normal men. He played minor league ball, worked in a family bank, practiced law, and became head of a department store.

A captain in World War I, he and a group of officers stole a car after the armistice and drove into the Netherlands, planning to kidnap the exiled Kaiser Wilhelm and take him to the peace talks in Paris. They failed, but MacPhail grabbed an ashtray embossed with the imperial coat of arms.

After the war, MacPhail tried the automobile business in Columbus, Ohio, but quickly tired of that; so he got back into baseball by operating the city's franchise in the American Association, as a Cardinal farm club. Successful there, he was soon in the National League, first at Cincinnati and then Brooklyn, where he gained a reputation as a genuine "character."

MacPhail was a man of mercurial moods, famous for his quick temper. When he was president of the Dodgers and Leo Durocher was manager, he "fired" Durocher so many times that both men lost count. The day after the incident that had triggered MacPhail's explosion would soon be forgotten, and all would be fine—until the next "firing."

Typical was the run-in between the two men in the wake of the Dodgers' pennant-clinching win in Boston on September 24, 1941.

The Dodgers had taken a special train from Boston to New York, where 50,000 fans were waiting to greet them at Grand Central Station. MacPhail thought he would board the train at the 125th Street station, five minutes away, and be with the team when the train arrived at Grand Central.

Unfortunately, MacPhail didn't share his plans with anybody. Durocher told the train conductor not to stop at 125th Street, because he didn't want any players getting off there before the fans could greet them. So the train sped through the station, past MacPhail. When the enraged MacPhail caught up with Durocher, he "fired" Leo again, with the same eventual result as always.

Managers weren't the only ones who angered MacPhail. He left his first National League job after a heated argument with Cincinnati club owner Powel Crosley. He was so angry with *New York Daily Mirror* sports editor Dan Parker at one time that he wouldn't allow the *Mirror*'s baseball writer to travel with the team.

MacPhail seldom held grudges long—he later became good friends with Parker, for instance—but his temper often overshadowed his considerable ability. In fact, he was a shrewd man, an astute judge of talent, and an innovative promoter. On the field and at the box office, he built up the previously weak franchises in Cincinnati and Brooklyn.

In 1934, he took over a Cincinnati team that hadn't finished in the first division since 1926 and that would finish last for the fourth time in succession during that year. He rebuilt the club in his three years there, and after he had gone, the club went on to win back-to-back pennants in 1939-40. Even before that dramatic improvement, he refurbished the ball park and built up attendance, which more than doubled from his first year to his second.

Larry MacPhail, the tempestuous and pioneering Brooklyn owner in the late thirties and early forties, looks as if he's about to fire manager Leo Durocher again. *(George Brace photo)*

The challenge seemed even greater in Brooklyn. The Dodgers had been in disarray ever since the death of Charles Ebbets in 1925. Manager Wilbert Robinson was president of the club, but a continuous feud with Steve McKeever, who owned half the organization, prevented him from strengthening the team. After the 1925 season, for example, Robinson tried to buy Paul Waner from the San Francisco Seals of the Pacific Coast League, but by the time he got permission from McKeever and Joe Gilleadeau, Ebbets's son-in-law, the Seals had closed a deal for the same price with Pittsburgh. Waner, of course, went on to become a Hall of Fame player with the Pirates.

By 1938, the Dodgers had had only three first division finishes in 13 years, and the club was deeply in debt. Clearly, something had to be done.

The first move was taken by George V. McLaughlin, president of the Brooklyn Trust Company, the bank to which the Dodgers owed money. McLaughlin warned the Dodger owners that the club's credit would be severely limited unless they got somebody to run the club efficiently.

National League president Ford Frick, hearing that, advised the Dodgers to hire MacPhail, and the board of directors reluctantly agreed to MacPhail's terms, which included full authority and salary raises based upon home attendance. As it turned out, the contract was a bargain, but it was not immediately perceived as such by the Brooklyn directors, who were men of limited vision.

Limited vision was not one of MacPhail's problems. Instead of retrenching, he convinced McLaughlin that the Dodgers needed to spend more money immediately, first to refurbish the long-neglected stands at Ebbets Field and then to buy (for $75,000) first baseman Dolph Camilli from Philadelphia. The banker agreed, and the Dodgers were on their way.

MacPhail made other good deals, building the team up to its pennant in 1941. One of the best was the 1941 preseason trade that got him second baseman Billy Herman from the Chicago Cubs for outfielder Charley Gilbert and $65,000. Herman was a smart player (he taught his new teammates how to steal signs from the catcher, for instance) and he gave the Dodgers an excellent infield, with Camilli at first, Pee Wee Reese at shortstop, and Cookie Lavagetto at third.

Characteristically, making the trade wasn't enough for MacPhail: He had to embellish it with a story about how it was made.

According to MacPhail, he had worked out the trade with Chicago general manager James Gallagher and manager Jimmy Wilson in the Cubs' hotel suite in New York's Hotel Commodore.

A bottle of brandy stood on the table, and the level in the bottle went down quickly, mostly from the efforts of MacPhail. Gallagher and Wilson, believing MacPhail's judgment would be impaired by his drinking, quickly agreed to the trade.

But, said MacPhail later, he had been conning the two Chicago representatives. Instead of drinking all that brandy, he made several trips to the bathroom and poured most of it down the drain.

Gallagher denied that story strongly when he heard it, and logic is on his side. Nobody who knew MacPhail could imagine him pouring good brandy down a sink, for any reason.

If all MacPhail had done was to make good trades and build pennant-winners, he wouldn't rate much space; many club executives have similar achievements. But MacPhail was an innovator—he was perhaps the first to take motion pictures of players so that they could study and correct faults, for instance—and two of his moves made baseball history.

His 1935 Cincinnati Reds became the first major league team to play night baseball. Games had been played under the lights in the minor leagues, but never in the majors.

Typical of other big league owners' reactions to the idea of night games was that of Washington owner Clark Griffith, who said, "There is no chance of night baseball ever becoming popular in the bigger cities because high-class baseball cannot be played under artificial lights."

That didn't bother MacPhail, who got permission to play seven night games, one against each club. For the first one, May 24 against the Phillies, he got President Franklin D. Roosevelt to push a button that activated 632 lights at Crosley Field. League president Frick tossed out the first ball. The attendance was 20,422, far greater than it would have been for a day game.

When he went to Brooklyn, MacPhail staged the first night game ever played in New York City. This game was an even more spectacular event than the one in Cincinnati, but for a reason even MacPhail couldn't have anticipated.

MacPhail did everything he could to hype the game, and he could do a lot. Among the pregame festivities were sprint and broad jump exhibitions by Olympic champion Jesse Owens, and an emotional appearance by Babe Ruth, whom MacPhail had just signed as a Dodger coach. The game itself, on that evening of June 15, 1938, didn't even start until 9:45 P.M., and the Cincinnati pitcher who opposed the Dodgers that night was Johnny Vander Meer.

Four days earlier, Vander Meer, in his first full season with the Reds, had pitched a no-hitter against the Boston Bees (later Braves). It is safe to say

Cincinnati left-hander Johnny Vander Meer became the only pitcher to throw back-to-back no-hitters in 1938. *(George Brace photo)*

that nobody, including Vander Meer, gave more than a fleeting thought to the chance that he might pitch another one against the Dodgers, because nobody in major league history had ever pitched two consecutive no-hitters.

But Vander Meer did it that night. It was not an artistic game, by any standards. Vander Meer, plagued by wildness throughout an up-and-down career, walked eight. The Reds scored four times in the third and won the game, 6-0, so the issue was seldom in doubt. With that kind of lead, a pitcher often gets careless, but Vander Meer stayed on top of the Dodgers all the way. He got a scare with two outs in the ninth when the weak-hitting Durocher lined a ball down the right field line, but the ball went foul at the last moment and Durocher then ended the game by flying out to center-fielder Harry Craft.

It was a rare moment in major league history and, though Vander Meer had an indifferent career (119 wins and 121 losses in 13 years) he was always able to look back and call to memory the time he did something nobody else had ever done.

MacPhail couldn't count on spectacular happenings like no-hit games all the time, of course. An improving team would certainly help attendance, and so would more night games, but he needed something to really push his product. That something was radio.

Radio broadcasts of baseball games are taken for granted now, and it is hard to believe how leery club owners were of radio in those days. More than leery. Afraid.

There had been sporadic broadcasts of games; indeed, some Cincinnati games had been broadcast when MacPhail was with the Reds. But no team had broadcast home games on a daily schedule, and there had been no baseball broadcasts in New York City except for World Series and All-Star games.

The attitude toward radio in those days was much what it is toward television now: Broadcasts of games would keep people home listening instead of going to the games.

MacPhail knew better. Though he had no proof, he sensed that regular home broadcasts would stimulate attendance, because fan interest would be increased. As we have learned since, radio is very different from television. Television can cause people to stay home, because a telecast can show people as much—and, sometimes, more—than they would see at the park. Radio encourages the imagination, but it is not a substitute for actual live viewing.

There'd been a five-year ban on game broadcasts in New York among the three clubs—Dodgers, Yankees, and Giants—but MacPhail warned the other two clubs that he was going to broadcast games in 1939, when the ban expired. He proved that he had meant what he said when he hired Red Barber, who had broadcast games at Cincinnati when MacPhail was there, as his announcer in 1939.

Barber, in his book, *Rhubarb In the Catbird Seat,* said that MacPhail told him that Giants secretary Eddie Brannick had warned him that if he broke the antibroadcasting ban, "We'll get a fifty-thousand-watt radio station and we'll get the best baseball broadcaster in the world and, MacPhail, we'll blast you into the river."

That didn't sit well with MacPhail, of course, but he didn't waste time worrying about Brannick's threat. He went out and himself got a 50,000-watt station (WOR) and Barber, who probably was as good as anybody who has broadcast the game. He told Barber, "And I don't want to be blasted into the river."

He wasn't. Indeed, he forced the Yankees and Giants to broadcast their games, but the early Brooklyn games were so much more popular that, as Barber recalled, ". . . for a couple of years there after we all got going, the Giants and the Yankees couldn't come up with sponsors and they went off the air . . ."

As always, MacPhail was a step ahead. When the Giants and Yankees decided they had to broadcast their games in 1939, MacPhail decided to start the Dodger broadcasts in spring training. It was a master stroke, because the fans were hungry for baseball broadcasts, and MacPhail got a jump on everybody.

He was also in the right place at the right time with the right announcer. Brooklyn was a borough with an enormous inferiority complex. Manhattan was the glamor borough, the one with the tall buildings and the Broadway shows. Brooklyn was the one comedians mentioned to get an easy laugh.

To make it worse, the Giants had enjoyed great success since the turn of the century, while the Dodgers had generally stumbled. It grew worse as the century progressed. The symbol of the Giants was the pennant; seven of them had been flown at the Polo Grounds since 1920, the last time the Dodgers had won. The Dodgers were symbolized by players who wound up at the same base. Brooklyn fans were ready to support anything in which they were first.

Barber quickly felt a kinship with Brooklyn residents when he was totally ignored in a story *Time* magazine did on the radio broadcasts of baseball games in the April 17, 1939 issue. The Giants and Yankees had agreed to share a broadcaster, since their schedules provided that they would never be home at the same time, and had hired Arch McDonald. The *Time* story dealt primarily with McDonald and didn't mention either Barber or Mac-Phail, who had broken the radio ban.

Barber was furious, and he was that much more determined to do a good job. On Opening Day, he asked the station to give him an additional ten minutes time before the start of the game, and he went down to the field to interview opposing managers Durocher and Bill Terry of the Giants. Pre-game interviews are commonplace now, but they were a novelty then, and Barber's interviews became a conversation piece.

Barber's style was very easy to listen to, sprinkled as it was with remarks that became his trademark, such as "sitting in the catbird seat," which he borrowed from a winner in a poker game, and "rhubarb," which he got from Garry Schumacher, who got it from Tom Meany, who got it from a bartender.

Barber was also a student of the game, and he was able to explain the action clearly and concisely. That talent, alas, is not as common as we all wish it were. He was able to describe the action honestly because MacPhail never tried to tell him what to say, either at Cincinnati or Brooklyn. Barber learned the hard way that not all owners are that tolerant when he was fired by the New York Yankees after the 1966 season, primarily because he had dared to comment on a particularly small crowd at one game.

His impact on Brooklyn was extraordinary. Walking through the borough, the sounds of the Dodger broadcasts could be heard from car radios, kitchen radios, radios in the gardens. He created fans, and his Southern phrases became a part of the common language—"tearin' up the pea patch," "walkin' in tall cotton," etc. He was even the catalyst for a short story by James Thurber, called *The Catbird Seat,* and a book by H. Allen Smith, *Rhubarb.*

And, oh, about attendance. In the six years before MacPhail arrived, the Dodgers had averaged around 500,00 a year. His first year, they drew 666,000. The next year, with the team moving up to third and the games being broadcast, attendance rose to 955,000. By 1941, the pennant year, it had soared to 1,214,000.

Every baseball owner realizes now that night games and daily broadcasts are indispensable to a team's success. But Larry McPhail was the pioneer, the man who went ahead though others told him he was crazy. He had the last laugh, but all of baseball has profited from his determination and foresight.

20. Bums and Birdies

In the forties, the St. Louis Cardinals and Brooklyn Dodgers virtually turned the National League into an exclusive, two-team monopoly. Fittingly, they even shared a general manager. Branch Rickey, who had established the farm system that eventually provided the St. Louis team with nine pennants, went to Brooklyn in 1942, and the National League balance of power swung the Dodgers' way.

In the period from 1941 through 1949, the Cardinals and Dodgers won seven pennants. Only Chicago, in the war year of 1945, and Boston, in 1948, interrupted the flow of Brooklyn-St. Louis pennants, and the Cardinals were second in 1945 and 1948.

In successive years, in 1941 and '42, the Dodgers and Cardinals went almost to the final day of the season in ferocious two-team battles before the pennant was decided. In 1946, they were tied at season's end, necessitating the first National League playoff in modern times.

The Cardinals won the playoff, and they had greater success during the decade, winning four pennants and three World Series and finishing second five times. But the Dodgers, who won three pennants and finished second three times in those years, started the decade stronger than the Cardinals and ended it the same way. And it was the Dodgers who went on to dominate the fifties.

The Dodger team of 1941 was perhaps the best that Brooklyn had ever fielded, though the ones that followed in the next decade would be even better.

Owner Larry MacPhail had made some smart trades in the off-season to improve the club that had finished second to Cincinnati the year before, getting pitcher Kirby Higbe (who became a 22-game winner in 1941), catcher Mickey Owen, and second baseman Billy Herman.

Equally important were two players the Dodgers had brought up at the end of the 1940 season, shortstop Pee Wee Reese and center fielder Harold ("Pete") Reiser. Both played pivotal roles in the Dodgers' success in 1941.

Reese was the steadier of the two, and he had a long, productive career with the Dodgers, 16 years that extended into the Dodgers' first year in Los Angeles.

Reese had played for Louisville in his native Kentucky, which accounted for his original nickname of "the Little Colonel," and was sold by the Boston Red Sox because player-manager Joe Cronin was firmly entrenched at shortstop.

Always an excellent fielder, Reese was a weak hitter when he first came up, but he worked in characteristic fashion until he became a steady, though not spectacular, hitter by his third full season, generally in the .270–.280 range. He also became an effective base stealer, leading the league once, in 1952, with 30.

Reese's value, though, transcended statistics, because he was a smart player who made the most of what he had. In the field, he was always in position to make the play. At bat, he became adept at working pitchers for walks, at hitting the ground ball to the right side to advance a runner or the fly ball to score one, at getting the base hit at the right time; Reese was usually to be found in the middle of Dodger rallies. His stolen bases, too, came at strategic moments. He never fattened his statistics by stealing in lopsided games; he waited for those moments when he could steal to get into position to score the winning run.

Reiser, though, was much the more spectacular of the two, the kind of player everybody thought at first was stopping only momentarily in Brooklyn on his way to the Hall of Fame. The man who was nicknamed "Pistol Pete" had everything: speed, power, hitting ability, great arm.

He was good enough to lead the league in five offensive categories, including a batting average of .343, in his first full season. He was good enough to set a major league record by stealing home seven times in 1946. During his brief prime, Reiser may also have been the best center-fielder in the league, an absolutely fearless man who believed that anything hit in the air belonged to him and who was willing to challenge outfield walls to get those balls. When Reiser first came up to the Dodgers, he caused the kind of excitement among baseball men that Willie Mays did a decade later when he came up to the Giants.

But Reiser had only one year that compares with Mays's many great ones, the season of '41 when he led the league in hitting, slugging percentage (.558), runs (117), doubles (39), and triples (17).

The next year, his recklessness caught up with him. He crashed into an outfield wall in St. Louis chasing a fly ball and was hospitalized with a severe concussion. He came back to play, which was a mistake. His average dropped about 60 points as he tried to fight his way through double vision.

Reiser lasted in the majors through the 1952 season, but he left his exciting style of play behind in that St. Louis hospital. There were flashes of the old Reiser—most notably, the seven steals of home in 1946—but for the most part, he was just another ballplayer trying to hang on to his job.

The accident in St. Louis was only one of many times Reiser had run into walls trying to catch fly balls, and it may be that the collisions had a cumulative effect. Outfield walls are now padded to prevent such injuries. If the wall in St. Louis had been padded in 1942, we might talk of Reiser as one of the all-time greats. Instead, his is the sad story of what might have been.

All of this was in the future in 1941, though, and Reiser and his teammates played brilliantly in one of the most exciting pennant races of all time. It was that way from two weeks into the season: On April 27, the Cardinals took the lead for the first time; the next day, the Dodgers took the lead, also for their first time; and on April 29, the two teams were tied.

It stayed that way. The Cardinals led the league on 11 separate occasions, the Dodgers on seven; nine times, the teams were tied. The lead changed hands 27 times during the season and, although the Dodgers won 100 games for the first time in their history, they didn't clinch the pennant until their 99th win.

A pennant race as tight as that tests the tempers of even the calmest men, and the Dodgers didn't have the calmest men. MacPhail got so heated at one point that he fired the bartender in the Dodgers' press bar, Hymie Green, because Green had misinterpreted a Red Barber comment during a game broadcast.

Relief pitcher Hugh Casey, upset at a balk call by umpire George Magerkurth in one game, threw three straight pitches aimed at Magerkurth's head; none hit their target.

Asked for a comment on that the next day by Associated Press writer Ted Meier, Dodger manager Leo Durocher replied by knocking Meier down— twice, some reports said. Afterwards, they shook hands, and Meier had his story, though not the one he had sought.

On September 11, the Dodgers moved into St. Louis for a three-game series that probably decided the race. Holding only a game and a half lead, they won the opener in 11 innings, 6-4, as Dixie Walker singled in the deciding runs.

Freddy Fitzsimmons, one of the greatest competitors the game has seen, was the winning pitcher, surviving a weird ninth inning episode that tells much about the man.

Fitzsimmons had charged to the plate to protest a call on a pitch to Johnny Mize. His protest to plate umpire Al Barlick amused Mize, who was smiling when Fitzsimmons glanced his way. "He lit into me," remembered

Mize many years later, "and told me what he was going to do. 'Three fastballs and you're out of there!'"

Fitzsimmons was known as a knuckleball pitcher, and Mize never thought he'd see three straight fastballs. But the Brooklyn pitcher was true to his word and Mize, thinking each time that the next pitch would surely be the knuckler, watched three fastball strikes go past him.

The Cardinals won the next game, 4–3, and then on September 13, before the only full house of the series, the teams played a game that is one of the classics of baseball history.

The opposing pitchers for the game were Whit Wyatt of the Dodgers and Mort Cooper of the Cardinals. Wyatt was a well-traveled pitcher who'd come up with Detroit in the American League in 1929 but whose only real success came with the Dodgers, who had picked him up in 1939. With the Dodgers he finally acquired a slider to go with his excellent fastball, and he picked up 70 of his lifetime 106 major league wins in a four-year period, 1940–43, for the Dodgers. His best year by far, though, was 1941, when he won 22 games with a 2.34 ERA and seven shutouts.

Cooper was just coming into his own, pitching well down the stretch in 1941 and setting the stage for the best year of his career in 1942.

The Cardinals had their only serious threat of the game in the second inning, putting runners on second and third with nobody out. But Wyatt struck out Gus Mancuso and Cooper and got Jimmy Brown on an infield out. That was the last time the Cardinals got a runner to third, and only once more, with two outs in the ninth, did they get a runner to second.

Meanwhile, Cooper was pitching even more brilliantly for the Cardinals, not yielding a hit for the first seven innings. Then, in the eighth, Walker doubled off the right-field screen.

Before Herman had come to the club, none of the Dodgers had tried to steal signs, but wily Billy had taught them the knack. Most of the time, though, he was still the only sign-stealer, passing them along to the hitter when he got to second. This time, Walker saw a chance to repay Herman. Catching the sign for a curve, he passed it along to Herman.

"I saw Billy's owl eyes bug out," said Walker later, "and I was sure the Cardinals would catch on and switch."

They didn't. Cooper threw the curve, just below the belt and on the outside corner of the plate. Herman, a right-handed hitter who liked to go to the opposite field, doubled into the right-center alley for the only run of the game.

The game, incidentally, took two hours and 37 minutes to play, an inordinately long time for a game in which there was so little offense. There were no complaints of boredom from the fans, however.

The race was by no means ended when that series was over, but the Dodgers had established a narrow supremacy that they maintained until Wyatt clinched the pennant by blanking Boston, 6-0, for his 22nd win on the next-to-last day of the season.

The World Series that followed was a disappointing one for the Dodgers. Conceivably, they could have swept the mighty Yankees in four games; instead, they lost in five. Here's how the strange set of circumstances went:

GAME 1: In the seventh inning, with the tying and winning runs on base and nobody out, Jimmy Wasdell foul-popped into a double play. Red Rolfe, the Yankee third baseman, caught Wasdell's pop, and when Pee Wee Reese tried to advance from second to third, New York shortstop Phil Rizzuto alertly moved to third to take the throw from Rolfe and tag Reese out. The Yankees won the game, 3-2.

GAME 2: Wyatt pitched a 3-2 win for the Dodgers, with Dolf Camilli's sixth-inning single knocking in the winning run.

GAME 3: Freddy Fitzsimmons pitched scoreless ball for seven innings but had to leave the game when he was hit in the leg by a line drive off the bat of opposing pitcher Marius Russo. Reliever Casey allowed two runs, and the Dodgers lost, 2-1.

GAME 4: This is the game baseball fans remember, a game the Dodgers lost after they had had it "won." The Dodgers were ahead, 4-3, with two outs and nobody on in the ninth when Casey struck out Tommy Henrich, which should have ended the game.

The pitch, which Casey later admitted was a spitball, eluded catcher Owen, and Henrich reached first before Owen could retrieve the ball and throw him out. Casey got two strikes on Joe DiMaggio and then tried to blow a third one past DiMaggio, who singled to left. Casey got two strikes on Charlie Keller and tried the same tactic; Keller doubled off the right-field wall to score both runners and put the Yankees ahead. A walk to Bill Dickey and a Joe Gordon double added two more runs, and the Yankees won, 7-4.

GAME 5: The dazed Dodgers got only four hits as the Yankees won, 3-1, to close out the Series.

The Series was typical of the Dodgers, a star-crossed group that knew professional tragedy (Reiser), personal tragedy (Casey's suicide in 1951, two years after his career ended) and a lot of simple bad luck. The worst luck of all was running into one of the greatest of all National League teams the next year, the 1942 Cardinals.

21. Stan the Man

At the end of the 1941 season, the Cardinals brought up a young outfielder named Stan Musial whose life story at that point seemed purest fantasy It got better. Musial hit .426 in 12 games at the end of that season and went on to become one of the finest players in National League history and, quite possibly, the most popular player of all time. As a man and as a player, only superlatives apply to Stan Musial.

Musial was born in 1920, the fifth of six children of Polish-speaking immigrants, in the coal-mining town of Donora, Pennsylvania. He was christened Stanislaus, which became Stanley when he started school.

His parents, following the American dream, wanted Stan to go to college, but he only wanted to play baseball, and against his family's wishes he signed to play professional baseball, as a pitcher. He was 6–6 in his first, abbreviated season, then 9–2 and 18–5 in subsequent seasons.

His 18–5 record came at Daytona Beach in the Florida State League, where Dickie Kerr, who had pitched so well in the infamous 1919 World Series, was the manager. He was more than a manager to Musial; he was also a friend. Musial and his wife, the former Lillian Labash, were living with the Kerrs when the first of the four Musial children was born.

Musial never forgot Kerr's generosity and help. Years later, he bought a house in Houston for the Kerrs, and it was only when Kerr talked about it that the purchase became general knowledge.

Kerr was also the first to recognize that Musial's future might be as a hitter, not a pitcher. Musial played 57 games in the outfield that year, and one play in one game that year had a profound effect on his career, when Musial fell on his left shoulder chasing a fly ball.

When the next season started, Musial's left arm was dead, his pitching career ended. His playing career was not, however, because he had turned his single-minded determination to hitting. As a pitcher, he had been bothered by wildness and was not highly regarded as a major league prospect; he was still in Class D, the lowest rung on the minor league ladder, when he was hurt. As a hitter, though, he quickly proved that he could play on the highest level.

He started the 1941 season with Springfield of the Western Association and hit a scorching .379 with 26 home runs in just 87 games. That earned him a promotion to Rochester of the Triple A International League, where he hit .326 in 54 games. At the end of the season, the Cardinals brought him up, and the sore-armed Class D pitcher of 1940 was the talk of the National League just one year later. That was a script nobody in Hollywood would dare touch.

Despite his late season success in 1941, Musial appeared lost in spring training the following year. His arm was troubling him on throws from the outfield (it would always be the weakest part of his all-round game) and he seemed to have lost his hitting ability.

Fortunately, Cardinal manager Billy Southworth never lost patience with Musial. For a time, Southworth used Musial only against right-handed pitchers, until Stan regained his balance. Very quickly, Musial was in the lineup against all kinds of pitching, and he hit a very respectable .315 that season.

There are players who have good rookie seasons and never again play as well, because the rest of the league learns their weaknesses. Musial was the opposite; his rookie season was only a warm-up for much better years to come. He had no real weaknesses for others to learn about, but he benefited from learning what the pitchers in the league could, and could not, do.

His next season, Musial led the league in hits (220), doubles (48), triples (20), average (.357) and slugging percentage (.562). But even that was only warming up for his best year, 1948, when he had the finest all-round year of any National League hitter since World War II. Check these numbers: 230 hits; 46 doubles; 18 triples; 39 home runs; 135 runs; 131 RBIs; .376 average, .702 slugging percentage; 103 extra base hits. All but the home run figure led the league; although he hit 475 career home runs, Musial never led the National League in home runs during a season.

During his 22 years, Musial set major league records for most seasons of playing 100 or more games (21), extra base hits (1,377), total bases (6,134) and home runs in a doubleheader (5).

His National League records included games played (3,026), at-bats (10,972), runs (1,949), hits (3,630), doubles (725), RBIs (1,951) and most years with 100 or more RBIs (10).

The old saying is that records are made to be broken, and most of Musial's have been, with Hank Aaron doing almost all the damage; Musial's only remaining major league record is the home run mark for double headers, his only league record the one for doubles. But his career and season statistics remain remarkable, all the more so because he was also a fine defensive outfielder and an excellent base runner, abilities that are not so easily defined by statistics.

Starting with his rookie season, Musial hit .300 or better for 16 straight seasons. In one 11-year stretch, he hit .330 or better in every season but 1947, when he hit .312 despite playing with an appendix that had to be removed immediately after the end of the season and should have been removed earlier. In 1962, heading into his 42nd birthday, he hit .330, just a point below his lifetime average!

He did all that with one of the most unusual hitting stances in history. He stood back in the batter's box, his body twisted into a seemingly awkward position. He was once described as looking like a kid peering around a corner.

When the ball approached home plate, he uncoiled and lashed at it, hitting the ball where it was pitched and driving it with power to all fields. His stance and swing required such precise timing it was freely predicted early in his career that he would have frequent slumps. He did not.

Pitchers wasted little time working on his weakness, because he had none. They could only throw their best pitches and hope they would be good enough. Musial hit fast balls, curves, sliders, change-ups, knucklers with what seemed equal ease.

Stan once told writer Roger Kahn that he had memorized the speed at which every pitcher threw his different pitches, so he knew as the ball approached home plate whether it would be a fast ball, curve, or slider. That seems improbable, but Musial's hitting was improbable. Even if that were true, Musial still had to hit the pitches.

It is tempting to think that if a hitter knows exactly what's coming, he will be able to hit the ball where he wants, but baseball is not that precise a game. Anyone who has watched batting practice sees how the hitters, knowing exactly what is coming and not facing the tough pitches they will see in the game, often pop the ball up or ground it weakly to the infield. Even in the early days of the game when hitters could call for the pitch they wanted, where they wanted it, they still went out much more often than they hit safely.

At least as important in Musial's success was his willingness to work on his hitting. He spent hours in the batting cage, and he inspired others by doing so. Curt Flood, in his book *The Way It Is* says that Musial made him a good hitter by example. When Flood saw how much time Musial spent on his hitting, he could do no less.

Musial's hitting was no more remarkable, though, than his personality.

Stan Musial set a fistful of league hitting marks while winning friends wherever he went. *(George Brace photo)*

Some writers like to say that Musial remained unchanged throughout his long career. That's an oversimplification. Musial started out as a teenager who had been playing with and talking to the sons and daughters of coal miners and immigrants. By the end of his playing career, he was talking to mayors, ambassadors, governors and presidents. Millionaires were asking for his autograph. A man would have to be a clod to remain unchanged through all that.

But Musial did remain as accessible as ever to fans and writers. Success did not make him aloof or turn him into a snob. It did not make him temperamental. He did not become rude or abrupt under the pressure of a tight pennant race.

It is no exaggeration to say that Musial was loved, and not only in St. Louis. In that most partisan of baseball towns, Brooklyn, he regularly rattled the fences and drove balls out of Ebbets Field, but the Dodger fans never booed. They held him in awe and named him "Stan the Man."

When he retired, the city of St. Louis ordered a sculpture of him built, which now stands outside the stadium. It is not a very good likeness of Musial, but it pleases him that it is there; how many statues of ballplayers have you seen?

It was an irony in Musial's career that he played on pennant-winners in his first four full seasons and then never played on another. The best team of all was probably the one he played on as a rookie, the 1942 Cardinals.

That was a team that surprised a lot of people, not least the Brooklyn Dodgers in their own league and the New York Yankees in the American.

The Cardinals were not an overpowering team. They didn't destroy teams with home runs; indeed the entire team only matched Babe Ruth's best season, with 60 home runs. But they had strong pitching; a team ERA of 2.55, led by Mort Cooper's sparkling 1.77 (and 22 wins) and Johnny Beazley's almost as remarkable 21 wins and 2.14 ERA.

Defense won many games for them; Marty Marion anchored the infield at shortstop, and Musial, Terry Moore and Enos Slaughter formed a swift outfield. Baserunning won a lot of games, too. The Cardinals didn't steal a lot of bases, but they took the extra base, often, forcing the opposition to make hurried, bad throws. Most of all, the Cardinals made the most of their opportunities. When a hit or strikeout or great fielding play was needed, the Cardinals got them.

For more than half the 1942 season, however, it appeared that the Cardinals would finish no better than second again, trailing the Dodgers as they had the year before. The Dodgers, playing even better than they had in winning the '41 pennant, led by as many as 10 ½ games in August that season.

Only Brooklyn owner Larry MacPhail seriously thought the Dodgers could lose at that point. He confronted his team and accused them of complacency, warning them that the Cardinals could still catch them. The Dodgers yawned and laughed at the excitable redhead. Dixie Walker offered to bet MacPhail that the Dodgers would win.

But the Cardinals kept chipping away at the Dodger lead. It was down to 7 ½ when the Dodgers came into St. Louis for a four-game series later that month. The Cardinals won three of the four, one a 14-inning 2–1 win by Cooper, to cut the lead to 5 ½.

By Friday, September 11, the Dodger lead was only two games, and the Cardinals came to Brooklyn for a two-game series. The Dodgers needed only to split the series to remain two games in front, but Dodger manager Leo Durocher wasn't playing cautiously. He went head-to-head with his ace, Whit Wyatt, against Cooper in the first game of the series. That strategy had worked well for Durocher the year before, but not this year; for the second straight time, Cooper outpitched Wyatt, winning 3–0 for one of his ten shutouts of the season. The Dodger lead was down to a game.

The second game matched left-handers Max Lanier for the Cardinals and Max Macon for the Dodgers, and the Cardinals won this one, too, 2–1, on Whitey Kurowski's home run. The Cardinals had tied the Dodgers for the lead.

The next day, the Cardinals went on top for the first time when they split a doubleheader with the Phillies while the Dodgers were losing two to Cincinnati. The Dodgers, who had led the league for five months, never led again.

The Cardinals' drive to the pennant was one of the three most remarkable in league history, ranking with the 1914 Braves and the 1951 Giants.

The latter two were more dramatic, because the Braves had to come from last place and the '51 Giants were even further back than the '42 Cardinals (and finally won in the last inning of the third playoff game) but the Cardinals' stretch run was quite possibly the best ever. They won 34 of their last 40 games, a pace even better than the 38 of 47 by the 1951 Giants. And even though the Braves won 34 of their last 44, that excellent finish would not have been good enough for the Cardinals. The Dodgers, after all, won 104 games that year—only one Dodger team before or since has won more—and finished only two games back.

That great stretch drive by the Cardinals wasn't enough to convince many people that they could beat the New York Yankees in the World Series, and the St. Louis club was a decided underdog when the Series opened in Sportsman's Park. The Yankees had won eight straight World Series.

The Yankees started strongly in this one, too, knocking out Cardinal ace Cooper and taking a 7–0 lead into the last half of the ninth of the Series opener. The Cardinals seemed demoralized. They had only one hit, an eighth-inning single, off Red Ruffing, and they had made four errors.

Finally, with two outs in the ninth, the Cardinals came to life, scoring four times and knocking out Ruffing. Musial was at the plate with the potential winning run when he ended the rally and the game by making his second out of the inning, grounding out to first baseman Buddy Hassett.

Most experts thought the Cardinal rally meant little, since the Yankees had won the game, but Dizzy Dean thought otherwise. On a radio show that night, Dean said, "That was just the shot in the arm our boys needed. We'll never stop now."

He was right. The Cardinals swept the remaining four games of the Series, shocking the Yankees and the rest of the baseball world.

The Yankees won revenge the next year by beating the Cardinals in five games, but that couldn't detract from the Cardinals' great showing in 1942. The Redbirds had survived one of the most dramatic races of all time and launched Stanley Frank Musial on his way to the Hall of Fame.

THE BLACK REVOLUTION

22. Robinson Breaks the Color Line

There were some great and exciting moments on the diamonds of the senior circuit in the 1940s, but the most important event happened away from the field, in the offices of the Brooklyn Dodgers, on August 28, 1945.

On that day, Brooklyn president Branch Rickey sat behind his desk and poured invective across at Jackie Robinson, a black American, to see if Robinson were willing to accept abuse in exchange for the chance to play major league baseball.

Satisfied, Rickey signed Robinson to a contract with the Montreal Royals of the Triple A International League. As Rickey expected, Robinson was good enough to play for Brooklyn after one year in the minors, and in 1947, Robinson broke the color line in baseball, becoming the first black to play in the majors.

As a stone thrown into a lake will cause ripples far beyond it, the signing of Robinson affected many other people and events, and it changed the face of baseball. It meant that the Dodgers would become the dominant team in the league for the next decade, and that the National League would gain a supremacy over the American League that it still holds today. It opened the door for perhaps a seventh of the nation's citizens, and it removed a huge blot from the face of the game.

Conditions for blacks in the United States were hardly ideal at that time, but it was true that a black could serve in the Armed Forces; he could be, as Louis ("Satchmo") Armstrong was, a top jazz musician, touring foreign countries with his band; he could be, as Ralph J. Bunche was, a mediator in

• **153**

the service of the United Nations, eligible for a Nobel Prize. What he could not do, before Jackie Robinson, was play major league baseball.

This state of affairs was a curious one, growing out of custom rather than law that could have been challenged in court. Several men wanted to change the custom—or said they did—but none dared until Rickey, who was never one to do what everybody else was doing, anyway.

Before the turn of the century there had been some blacks in professional baseball, though not in the National League—perhaps as many as 20 players, according to Art Rust, Jr., in his excellent book, *Get That Nigger Off the Field!*

The first blacks to play were brothers, Moses Fleetwood Walker and William Welday Walker, both of whom played for Toledo in the American Association, which was a major league in those days. It was Fleetwood Walker who unintentionally precipitated an incident that gave Rust his book title and caused blacks to be barred from the National League.

The Chicago White Stockings were playing an exhibition against Toledo in 1882 when Chicago player-manager Cap Anson saw Walker and yelled, "Get that nigger off the field!" He threatened to pull his team off if Walker played.

Anson lost that argument, but he won the biggest battle, keeping blacks out of the National League. When John Montgomery Ward of the Giants sought to sign black player George Stovey, for instance, Anson pressured Ward until he changed his mind.

Nobody has ever been able to explain Anson's aversion to black players, but his popularity and influence was so great at the time that nobody challenged him. By the time the National League had passed its first quarter-century, major league baseball had become all white, and it remained that way until 1947.

At times, baseball people tried to say that blacks were not good enough to play in the major leagues, but those who recognized talent knew that wasn't so. As early as 1901, for instance, John J. McGraw tried to sign a black player, Charlie Grant, a second baseman with the Columbia Giants, a Chicago Negro team.

McGraw was manager of the Baltimore Orioles at the time, and he saw Grant play when the Orioles were training at Hot Springs, Arkansas. He tried to sign Grant, even working up a story that Grant was actually of Indian (Cherokee) descent.

Unfortunately for McGraw and Grant, Chicago White Sox owner Charles

Comiskey had seen Grant play and knew that he was black, not Indian. Grant never played a major league game.

Later, when the Negro leagues were formed, all-star teams from those leagues played major league all-star teams in exhibitions, and the white major leaguers were impressed.

Here are some of the opinions Rust collected in his book:

"I have played against a Negro All-Star team that was so good, we didn't think we had an even chance against them." Dizzy Dean.

"I have seen many Negro players who should be in the major leagues. There is no room in baseball for discrimination. It is our national pastime and a game for all." Lou Gehrig.

"If managers were given permission, there'd be a mad rush to sign up Negroes." Gabby Hartnett.

Rust also wrote that Dean had told him in 1938, "Boy, it's too bad I couldn't throw a bucket of calcimine on him (Satchel Paige) and make him white, because if he were, he'd raise hell in the majors." Paige pitched well in the majors when he got his chance, of course, and he was probably at least in his mid-40s by then.

Yet, with all that, the major leagues remained determinedly white. It was acceptable for whites and blacks to compete in exhibition games, but not in the championship season. Those who tried to change the status quo were pressured into dropping their challenge.

In July 1943, for instance, Pittsburgh Pirates president William Benswanger announced that three blacks—catcher Roy Campanella, second baseman Sam Hughes, and pitcher Dave Barnhill—would be given a trial. Under pressure, he called off the tryouts. Campanella later got another chance; Hughes and Barnhill didn't.

In 1944, Bill Veeck planned to buy the Philadelphia Phillies and stock the team with black players. Instead, owner Gerry Nugent turned the team over to the league, and it was then sold to William Cox, reportedly for much less than Veeck had been willing to pay. The Phillies finished last in 1944, 43 ½ games out of first place, but presumably their fans were happy because there were no blacks on the field.

At this point, Rickey came onto the scene. As always with this complex man, his motives were mixed, and only he knew which one was dominant.

On the one hand, the Negro leagues had an untouched talent pool. In 1941, for instance, Shirley Povich of the *Washington Post,* after seeing the Senators in exhibitions against Negro teams wrote, "There's a couple of million dollars' worth of baseball talent on the loose, ready for the big leagues, yet unsigned by any major league. There are pitchers who would win twenty games a season for any big-league club that would offer them contracts, and there are outfielders that could hit .350, infielders who could win recognition as stars, and there's at least one catcher who at this writing is probably superior to Bill Dickey, Josh Gibson. Only one thing is keeping them out of the big leagues, the pigmentation of their skin. They happen to be colored."

Rickey hated to pass up any prospects, and he was convinced that the Dodgers would get a big jump on every other team if they were the first to sign a black player.

Yet the situation was more complex than that. If it had been only a matter of signing the best players, Rickey had no need to hit the black market. He had, after all, built the National League's dominant team in St. Louis entirely with white players, and there is no reason to think he could not have done the same at Brooklyn. He was smart enough to know he would be under great pressure when the announcement broke that he had signed a black player. The safe way would have been to forget about signing blacks, but Branch Rickey was never one to take the safe way. There was a moral side to Rickey's decision to seek out black players, as well as a practical one.

As early as 1910, when he was a college coach, Rickey had seen an example of bigotry. The team he was coaching had a black player, Charley Thomas, and when the team stopped at a hotel in South Bend, Indiana, the hotel clerk refused to book a room for Thomas. Rickey eventually persuaded the clerk to put a cot in his room, and Thomas slept there.

When he was with the Cardinals, Sportsman's Park had a "Jim Crow" section for black spectators. Rickey tried to persuade St. Louis owner Sam Breadon to allow blacks to sit in any part of the park, but Breadon refused. He was afraid that white fans would stay away before they would sit near blacks. Given the temper of the times and the fact that St. Louis was basically southern in its attitudes, if not geography, Breadon was probably right.

In 1943, Rickey succeeded Larry MacPhail as president of the Dodgers, and he was finally in a powerful enough position to initiate action. First he called a meeting of the club's board of directors, and got the permission he sought to make the Dodgers the first team to bring blacks into the major leagues. Then he launched an extensive scouting program, evaluating the playing ability and personal backgrounds of blacks and Latins.

He could not move openly. Because of the opposition to blacks in baseball, Rickey had to act deviously, which was not hard. He announced that he was going to establish a new Negro League, financed and run by the Dodgers, because he was convinced there was potential profit in it. Everyone knew of Rickey's fondness for the dollar, so the announcement was accepted at face value by other baseball people.

One of the teams in the proposed league was to be in Brooklyn, and it was under that cover that Rickey interviewed Robinson on that August day in 1945. Clyde Sukeforth, a scout for the Dodgers who was to become a good friend of Robinson's, first approached Jackie while Robinson was temporarily out of the Kansas City Monarchs lineup because of a sore shoulder.

Robinson was an outstanding athlete. He had been the first athlete to letter in four varsity sports at UCLA—baseball, basketball, football, track and field—and he had been a good shortstop for the Monarchs in 1945, his one year in the Negro League. But he was disgusted with the travel schedule and the discrimination he faced. Teams stayed in shoddy places on the road because so many hotels were closed to blacks. They ate poorly and on the run. Robinson believed the cover story about a new league, and he was willing to listen to Rickey's pitch.

Rickey had searched for the right candidate to break the color line. He knew that most of the fabled black players—Paige, Gibson, Buck Leonard—were past their prime. Robinson, at 26, was coming into his best years.

He also knew that Robinson was a smart, well-educated man, and a strong-willed one. He knew how difficult it would be for the first black player, and he wanted one who not only had the ability to make it but the character to withstand the taunts of the fans and opposing players. He thought Robinson could be the man, but he had to test him first.

In his Brooklyn office, Rickey told Robinson that his character would be more important than his playing ability. "There's virtually nobody on our side," he said. "We'll be in a tough position, Jackie. We can win only if we can convince the world that I'd doing this because you're a great ballplayer and a fine gentleman."

As Robinson remembered in *Breakthrough to the Big Leagues,* which he did with Alfred Duckett, he asked Rickey, "Are you looking for a Negro who is afraid to fight back?"

Rickey answered, "I'm looking for a ballplayer with guts enough not to fight back."

Rickey interviewed Robinson for three hours. During that time, he assumed many roles, and challenged Robinson to say how he would react. What would Robinson do, for instance, if he were spiked by an opposing player and then called racial names? What would he do if an umpire made bad calls because of racial prejudice, or if a restaurant owner or hotel manager refused to serve him?

By the end of the interview, Rickey was satisfied that Robinson could endure the verbal taunting, the hostile treatment, the calculated insults and slurs that he would be subjected to. He signed Robinson to a $3,000 bonus and a $600-a-month contract with the Montreal Royals. In these days of big salaries, that doesn't sound like much, but it was a lot to Robinson, who was making only $400 a month with the Monarchs. He now had enough to marry his fiancée, Rachel Isum, as Rickey had advised.

Rickey's action was kept secret for nearly two months, until October 23 when he went to Montreal to officially sign the contract and hold a press conference.

The press reaction to the announcment was mixed. On one side was Jimmy Powers, sports editor of the *New York Daily News,* who wrote, "Jackie Robinson, the Negro signed by Brooklyn, will not make the grade in the big leagues next year or the next . . . Robinson is a thousand to one shot to make the grade."

But Bill Corum of the *New York Journal-American* wrote, "Members of all races and from all sorts of places have been meeting together in the boxing ring on the may-the-best-man-win basis for so long that people with any sense at all have ceased to give it a second thought. It won't be many years until the same will be true of Negroes playing in organized baseball."

It is a little known fact now that Robinson was not the only black signed to a Montreal contract that year. Pitchers John Wright and Ray Partlow were also signed, but they were both sent to Three Rivers, and Robinson was alone.

For a time, it seemed as if Robinson wouldn't be able to make it with Montreal, either. Feeling the pressure, he did very little to further his cause in spring training, either at bat or in the field, where he had been switched from shortstop to second base.

Complicating his problems was the fact that Montreal manager Clay Hopper was a native of Mississippi, and he had begged Rickey not to send Robinson to Montreal. Hopper feared that he would not be able to return home if he agreed to manage a team with a black player.

Hopper was as much a victim of bigotry in his way as Robinson. He had been so indoctrinated in the idea that blacks were inferior to whites that he was very bitter about Robinson being assigned to play for him. When Robinson made a great play early in the season in 1946, a play that Rickey labled "superhuman," Hopper turned to Rickey and said, "Do you really think a nigger's a human being?"

But by the end of the season, Hopper's attitude toward Robinson had changed completely. He told Robinson, "Jackie, you're a real ballplayer and a gentleman. It's been wonderful having you on the team."

As a player, Robinson started to show his great ability as soon as the season started. He was now confident that he could do the job, in the field and at bat, and he opened the season with a home run in his first at bat at Jersey City, finishing the day with a 4–for–4 showing and two stolen bases.

Robinson went on to lead the International League in hitting with a .349 average, and it was obvious that he was good enough to play in the National League. The question was at what position. The Dodgers already had an accomplished second baseman in Eddie Stanky, who was only 30. Rickey solved that problem by ordering Robinson moved to first base when Jackie trained with the Royals in 1947. Just before the season started, during an exhibition between the Royals and Dodgers in Brooklyn, reporters were handed a one-line press release, which read: "The Brooklyn Dodgers today purchased the contract of Jackie Robinson from Montreal."

Robinson had faced taunts from fans and players in the International League, but it was nothing compared to what he had to endure in his first year in the National League.

There was even talk among the Dodgers, in spring training, of circulating a petition asking that Robinson not be brought up. Rickey called in the leaders of that movement and told them Robinson would play for the Dodgers and that if they didn't like it, they could quit. Nobody took up Rickey on his offer, though Dixie Walker asked to be traded and was.

The first ugly incident in the regular season came in Philadelphia, when Phillies manager Ben Chapman led a stream of racial abuse from the bench so virulent that league president Ford Frick officially warned the Phillies.

Chapman lamely answered that his taunts were no worse than calling an Italian player "wop." He eventually posed with Robinson for a picture supposedly showing that all was forgiven, but he did so only on the condition that he didn't have to shake hands.

The Cardinals tried to take that a step further. Stanley Woodward of the *New York Herald Tribune* exposed a plan by some members of the Cardinals to strike, refusing to play against the Dodgers because of Robinson. Woodward said too, that the Cardinals were trying to get other teams to take the same action.

Frick confronted that one in a hurry. He told the players involved that they would be suspended from the league if they went through with their proposed action.

"You will find that the friends you think you have in the press box will not support you, that you will be outcasts," Frick said. "I do not care if half the league strikes. Those who do it will encounter quick retribution. They will be suspended, and I don't care if it wrecks the National League for five years. This is the United States of America and one citizen has as much right to play as another.

"The National League will go down the line with Robinson whatever the consequence. You will find if you go through with your intention that you have been guilty of complete madness."

There was no strike.

But that was by no means the end of Robinson's troubles. Throughout the league he found that his head was often a target for pitchers' fastballs, and that infielders deliberately stepped on his legs when he slid into a base. He heard the word "nigger" over and over from fans and opposing players, usually teamed with a reference to the jungle. He found he often could not stay at the same hotels with his teammates or eat in the same restaurants. But he survived it all.

He got help from his teammates, who were often appalled by the treatment Robinson received from others. The most significant to Jackie was an action taken one day by Pee Wee Reese, a native of Louisville. During infield practice before a game in Boston, the Braves' players were kidding Reese about playing with a black. Reese did not answer any of the remarks, but after a few minutes, he went over to Robinson and casually put his hand on Robinson's shoulder as they talked. The action spoke more loudly than anything Reese could have said.

Through it all, Robinson kept quiet, just doing his job on the field. He had a good year, batting .297 and winning the Rookie of the Year award, and one can only guess at his inner turmoil. The role he had to play that year ran counter to his true personality, as became obvious years later. When there were enough blacks in the league for Robinson to shed his role as pioneer, he became a highly vocal player, quick to dispute umpires' decisions. He had certainly earned that right.

Robinson went on to a highly successful career, hitting .311 over ten years. His best season was his third, 1949, when he led the league with a .342 average and 37 stolen bases, and also scored 122 runs and drove in 124. He won the Most Valuable Player award that year.

But Robinson was the kind of player whose value transcended statistics.

Pee Wee Reese was a key figure in the great Brooklyn Dodger teams of the forties and fifties, playing on seven pennant winners. *(George Brace photo)*

Jackie Robinson broke the "color line" in organized baseball and went on to a Hall of Fame career with the Dodgers. *(George Brace photo)*

He was the one the Dodgers looked to for the clutch hit or fielding play, or the stolen base when it was most needed. He played his best in tight situations.

He played at a time when base stealing had relatively little importance; so his stolen base statistics seem unimpressive alongside those of the modern players like Lou Brock and Maury Wills. But Robinson was a great base runner, and a big factor in the game. He would take a big lead off base and challenge the pitchers, which broke their concentration. Even when he was supposedly trapped off base by a pitcher, he was almost impossible to catch in a rundown.

He was the spirit of the Dodgers, a fiery ballplayer who challenged the opposition, first only with his deeds, later with his mouth as well. It was surely no accident that in his ten years, the Dodgers won six pennants, lost another in a playoff, another on the last day of the season, and finished as low as third only once.

On his playing record alone, Robinson deserved his election to the Hall of Fame, but his role as pioneer was even more important. Soon, the Dodgers had other black players—catcher Roy Campanella, pitcher Don Newcombe the best of them—and other clubs in the National League followed their example.

The New York Giants signed Willie Mays and Monte Irvin, the Milwaukee Braves got Hank Aaron, the Cincinnati Reds signed Frank Robinson. Much of the history of the National League in the last 30 years revolves around players like Mays, Aaron, Willie McCovey, Bob Gibson, Wills, Brock, Campanella, Newcombe, Roberto Clemente, Joe Morgan, George Foster. . . . The list is virtually endless.

Rickey's primary practical concern had been to establish the Dodgers as the dominant team in the league, but his action also had the effect of regaining dominance for the National League itself.

The American League owners, following the example of the overpowering New York Yankee teams, were much slower than the National League owners to sign black players. Only Veeck, with Cleveland, tried to keep pace, signing outfielder Larry Doby and the legendary Paige, far past his prime but still effective. The Yankees didn't play a black until Elston Howard in 1955, eight years after Robinson had first taken the field in Brooklyn. The first black to play for the Boston Red Sox was Elijah ("Pumpsie") Green, in 1959—a dozen years after Robinson's breakthrough!

In that time, the National League got a jump on the American that it has never relinquished. By the early fifties, when the infusion of black players into the league was first beginning to be felt, the National was the stronger league, and it has remained so until this day.

Some indication of the effect of the blacks in the two leagues can be seen from statistics. Starting with Robinson in 1949, 14 blacks were named Most Valuable Player in the National League in a 20-year span; the American League had only two black MVPs during the same period and Howard was the first in '63. Eleven blacks, starting with Robinson, won Rookie-of-the-Year honors in the 20-year, 1947–66 span in the National League; the American League had only two, starting with Tony Oliva in 1964. The National League had 11 black batting champions, 1949–68; the American League had three, and Oliva was the first in 1964.

It is often said there is no sentiment in baseball; the Dodgers proved that by trading Robinson to the Giants after the 1956 season in which he had hit only .275.

But Jackie had the last laugh. He decided to retire, and he had a *Look* magazine article ghostwritten for him; so he got paid for his retirement notice. It was his way of thumbing his nose at the Dodgers, because the trade was then nullified.

Robinson's retirement was profitable—he became an executive for a restaurant chain—but often an unhappy one. Despite his intelligence, he was sometimes naive, and he was often used by politicians who wanted his name but not his ideas.

He was elected to the Hall of Fame in 1962, but many in baseball were uncomfortable with him. He was no longer content to be quiet and accept what came, as he had been forced to do in his early years with the Dodgers, and he often criticized baseball for not having more blacks in the clubs' executive offices.

His personal problems seemed overwhelming. His son, Jackie, Jr., came back from Vietnam dependent on drugs, and when he had cured himself of that addiction, was killed in an automobile accident.

Robinson himself suffered from severe diabetes, and he also had a mild heart attack in 1968. His sight was failing, and he was a tragic figure when he made an appearance at the opening game of the 1972 World Series.

He died just ten days later, at Stamford, Connecticut, his place in baseball history secure.

Roy Campanella, the glue for the Dodgers in the '50s, was crippled in a tragic automobile accident. *(George Brace photo)*

23. Dominance

There is no better example of the superiority the National League gained by being the first to play blacks than Willie Mays, the league's premier center fielder for nearly two decades.

The careers of Mays and Henry Aaron paralleled each other through most of the 1950s, and on into the sixties and even, briefly, the seventies. Inevitably, there was a long-running argument over who was the better player.

Aaron had the advantage of playing his career without interruption, while Mays lost nearly two full seasons to the military. Thus, Henry won the statistical argument, retiring with four major league records. But those of us who saw Mays play are not convinced by the statistics.

As a hitter, Aaron was no more than an eyelash better than Mays. In fielding and baserunning, categories that cannot be as easily measured by statistics, Mays had a definite edge. And in the category that could be called flair or charisma, Mays had an even greater edge. Willie could do it all, and he never in his life made an easy play look easy. He did everything in a spectacular manner.

As often happens with great players, it was not enough for writers and announcers simply to describe Mays' greatness. It became necessary to create a legend around him, that he was a sweet, lovable, naive child—the "Say Hey Kid."

Possibly he was when he first came up to the Giants, but those characteristics had disappeared by the time the team moved to San Francisco in 1958. Though still in his 20s, Mays by then was conscious of his position, aware of who could help him and who couldn't, and he seldom did anything to advance any cause other than his own.

It became painfully obvious to those who were frequently around him that Mays picked his spots. He would turn away from questions asked by small-town newspapermen, or answer with a long, drawn-out vulgarity, but if approached by a syndicated columnist, he would answer questions patiently and at length.

Willie Mays shows the batting stroke that made him feared throughout the National League. *(San Francisco Giants photo)*

His attitude toward his fans was generally one of disdain. He usually went out back doors at Candlestick to avoid signing autographs.

He demanded—and usually got—special treatment from his managers, a practice that was started by Leo Durocher, who was managing the Giants when Mays came up. Durocher's attitude was understandable; he won two pennants with Mays that would otherwise have been out of reach. That didn't make it any easier for those Giant managers who followed Leo.

Mays decided how he would practice, and when he would play. One manager, Clyde King, tried to show some independence and wrote out a game lineup without including Mays, and he and Willie very nearly came to blows in the dugout when Mays found out.

Perhaps it is too much to ask of great players that their character match their ability. When it happens—as it did with such stars in the past as Stan Musial, Honus Wagner, Christy Mathewson—we are doubly blessed, but those of us who were privileged to see Mays play will take him as he was, churlishness and all.

Oh, how he could play! The record book is eloquent enough: .302 lifetime average, 660 home runs, 2062 runs, 1903 RBIs. But it cannot begin to describe what it was like to see Mays in action. Many players have been described as poetry in motion; Mays was the only player I ever saw who justified that description.

His hitting was impressive enough—he ranks in the top five all-time in the National League in slugging average, hits, home runs, extra base hits, RBIs and runs—but it was in the field and on the bases that his true artistry showed.

His greatest catches were made in the Polo Grounds in New York, because that immense center field area—nearly 500 feet at straightaway center—gave him room to roam.

The catch everybody remembers is the one he made off Vic Wertz in the 1954 World Series, over-the-shoulder on the dead run. Mays himself thought there were several other better ones and he was probably right. The publicity glare of the World Series made that one memorable, more than others in less noteworthy games.

The remarkable thing about Mays was that he made great plays look routine, and they came in such profusion that even those who saw him daily forgot some of his best. Here, for instance, is one that almost nobody remembers, in a game in the summer of Mays's rookie year, against the Dodgers.

Billy Cox was on third with one out when Carl Furillo lofted a fly to right center. Mays caught the ball on the dead-run. Realizing instinctively that he had no chance to get Cox if he stopped and set himself, Mays whirled completely around, came up throwing, and threw a perfect strike to the plate to nail the amazed Cox.

Mays played in an era when base stealing was not regarded as important, especially for a slugger of his caliber, but he still managed to steal 136 bases in one four-year stretch, leading the league each year.

But his baserunning, as distinguished from stealing, was an even more remarkable part of his game. Maury Wills, the first of the great modern base stealers, says that he took lessons from Mays on the bases. Still, many of the things Mays did could not be taught. He had a feeling of what to do on the bases that approached the mystical. He made plays that simply could not be believed.

Do those words seem too strong? All right, then, here's one play I saw myself. In an otherwise meaningless game against the Cubs, Mays scored on a passed ball that was no more than ten feet from home plate. Herman Franks, the Giants manager at the time, said later he wouldn't have sent a runner from first to second on that play.

Mays seemed to taunt outfielders by going at half-speed on the bases, waiting until they committed themselves with a throw, and then exploding into full speed to get to the next base. There were some—not many—who were faster over 100 yards than Mays in his prime, but nobody ever got to top speed as quickly, which was the secret to his baserunning success. It never seemed to take him more than two steps to reach top speed.

In another game of no particular consequence, against St. Louis, Mays was on first when a single was hit to dead left field. Bob Skinner handled the ball perfectly.

Nobody goes from first to third on that play, of course, and it seemed just another routine play as Skinner came up with the ball and Mays made a turn around second base. This time, though, he didn't stop. He just kept going and Skinner stood in left field transfixed, holding the ball. By the time he came out of his daze and threw the ball, Mays was already at third.

There is no way of knowing how many times Mays did that to outfielders. It was, quite literally, a stolen base, but it isn't recorded that way because there is no provision for a player like Mays.

Mays seemed capable of doing anything he wanted to do. Considering every aspect of play, he ranks with Wagner as the best player in the league's history.

Like Wagner, Mays was both the best defensive player at his position and the best baserunner. He hit for power, twice surpassing 50 home runs. He hit for average, leading the league with .345 in 1954 and reaching his peak of .347 in 1958.

There are players who are considered stars because they are skillful at just one of the things—hitting, running, fielding—that Mays did so well. Ralph Kiner, for example, was a weak fielder with only a .272 lifetime batting average who made the Hall of Fame because he hit 369 home runs in his ten-year career. Mays had a ten-year streak, 1956–65, in which he hit 372 home runs! Kiner had five seasons with 40 or more home runs; Mays had six.

Mays had six seasons in which he stole at least 20 bases and hit at least 20 home runs, and two more in which he hit at least 30 home runs and stole at least 30 bases. Bobby Bonds is the only other player in National League history who has equalled that feat. Not coincidentally, Bonds played with Mays on the San Francisco Giants and learned from him. But Bonds could not hit for average with Mays nor field with him, and he was not the all-round base runner that Mays was.

Most hitters make a choice between hitting for percentage or hitting for power, but Mays was able to do whatever the situation called for. If the

Giants needed a home run to win, he would go for it, and often get it. If a single were needed to start a rally, he could do that, too.

Like everything else about Mays, his batting style was spectacular. He would swing so hard that his cap would sometimes fly off, but even with that fierce swing, he was able to maintain fantastic bat control.

His one weakness was sometimes an asset. It was well known by Don Drysdale and other hard-throwing right-handers around the league that Mays had a tendency to bail out on hard, inside pitches, especially if they came sidearm. But just when a pitcher counted on that in a tight situation, Willie would hang in there and line out a hit.

One final note about Mays as a hitter: His bat was so quick and he got around so far on some pitches that he occasionally pulled a foul ball into the stands, almost directly behind him!

Mays played in three World Series with the Giants, two in New York and one in San Francisco. Only once did the Giants win, in 1954. Twice, in 1962 and 1951, the Giants beat the Dodgers in a play-off to get into the Series. Of the two, the '51 pennant is the more memorable because the Giants won it with one of the three greatest stretch drives ever.

There are some years that can never be forgotten by baseball con-

Ralph Kiner twice hit more than 50 home runs in a season and told the world: "Home run hitters drive Cadillacs, singles hitters drive Fords." *(Pittsburgh Pirates photo)*

noisseurs, and 1951 was one of them. The season was climaxed by Bobby Thomson's home run that won the pennant, later called "the home run heard 'round the world." That is an exaggeration; 800 million Chinese neither knew nor cared. But for American baseball fans, it was a play and a game and a season with such impact that many fans, even today, can tell you exactly where they were at the moment Thomson hit his home run.

The year started off badly for the Giants. After winning their opening game, they lost the next 11. Meanwhile, the Dodgers took the lead on May 13 and steadily moved further ahead of the field, apparently on their way to their third pennant in five years and the easiest of the three.

For the first month of the season, as the Giants were stumbling, Mays was in Minneapolis. That wasn't Durocher's idea. He had seen Mays play in an exhibition game between Minneapolis and Ottawa, the Giants' two top farm teams, and he wanted Willie right away. Unfortunately, Giant owner Horace Stoneham had promised the Minneapolis fans that he wouldn't bring up a player during the Millers' season, and he intended to honor that promise.

But very quickly, it became apparent to Stoneham—and everybody else in baseball—that it was unfair to Mays to leave him in Minneapolis for the season. He was hitting an incredible .477 and catching everything that stayed in the park, and he was obviously too good for the American Association. The Giants brought him up, and Stoneham took out newspaper ads apologizing.

The Giants were about to play their 34th game when Mays arrived, and he was not an immediate sensation—at least at bat. He went hitless in his first 24 at bats, and after his last hitless game, he sat crying in front of his locker, afraid that he was not good enough. Durocher assured him that he would be in center field even if he didn't get a hit the rest of the season, and Willie went out and ended his hitless streak with a home run off Warren Spahn the next day.

Mays' appearance forced Durocher to move Bobby Thomson to third base, and Leo also switched Monte Irvin and Whitey Lockman, with Lockman going to first base and Irvin to left field. With the new lineup, the Giants started to make their move.

For quite a while, though, the Giants' move seemed to be coming far too late. Between games of a doubleheader on August 12, the Giants were 13 ½ games behind the Dodgers. But the Giants started a 16-game winning streak that day, three of them against the Dodgers, and by Sepetember 9, the Brooklyn lead was cut to 5½ games.

Mays was not the dominating hitter then that he became in later years—though his .274 average and 20 home runs were good enough to earn him Rookie of the Year—but he made play after play in the field to keep the Giants' chances alive.

More and more, too, he was becoming a factor on the base paths. Durocher, in his book, *Nice Guys Finish Last,* tells of one instance, against Spahn and the then Boston Braves.

Durocher and Mays had a set of signals by which Mays could let Durocher know when he wanted to steal. In this game, two days before the end of the season, Mays let Durocher know that he wanted to steal against Spahn, who had the best pick-off move in the business.

"I tell you," wrote Durocher, "it was just as if he had cut the tension with a knife. I'm sweating, and this rookie, all he wants to do is run?"

Mays stole second and third, and scored on Don Mueller's single, and the Giants went on to win the game. "He took the pressure right off the club," wrote Durocher. "Especially their dandy little manager."

The Giants won 16 of their last 20, 38 of their last 47 in that season, as the Dodgers played .500 ball for the last month and a half. The race was forced into a play-off, a pattern that was becoming all too familiar to the Dodgers. They had lost the 1946 pennant to St. Louis in a play-off, the first in National League history, and they had lost the 1950 pennant to Philadelphia on the last day of the season. (The Dodgers, of course, had also been caught and passed by the Cardinals' great stretch run in '42, but that was of no concern to this team; not one player remained from those days.)

Jim Hearn won the opener for the Giants, 3–1, but the Dodgers came back to win the second game of the playoffs, 10–0, behind Clem Labine. Both teams had their aces ready for the final game, Sal Maglie for the Giants, Don Newcombe for the Dodgers.

Maglie had been nicknamed "the Barber" for his habit of "shaving" hitters by throwing fastballs where their chins would have been had they stayed in the batter's box. He won 23 games that year, the league high, but this was not his day. The Dodgers got to him for eight hits and four runs, and the Giants were trailing, 4–1, as they came to bat in the last of the ninth.

Stoneham, convinced the game was lost, had already gone down to the clubhouse because he wanted to tell his players that he was proud of the effort they had made, even though it wasn't quite enough to win. Durocher gave his players a little pep talk in the dugout, but he thought the pennant was lost, too, as he later admitted.

The Giants weren't dead yet, however. Alvin Dark and Don Mueller both singled to lead off the inning. Monte Irvin, who had led the league in RBIs that season with 121, popped up, but then Lockman doubled, scoring Dark and sending Mueller to third. Mueller twisted his ankle on his slide, and Clint Hartung ran for him.

Charlie Dressen decided that was enough for Newcombe, and Ralph Branca came in to face Thomson. Branca was primarily a starter, but he had been used 15 times in relief that year, and one of his 13 wins came in relief and he had had three saves.

At that point, Thomson was the game's goat for the Giants. His baserunning error in the second—he got caught in a rundown after heading for second without realizing Lockman was already there—had taken the Giants out of a potentially big inning.

Thomson, who had his biggest home run year that season with 32, had faced Branca in the first play-off game and hit a home run. Remembering that, Durocher told Thomson to watch for a fast ball, high and tight. Thomson got the fast ball, in his power zone, but, caught in the tension of the moment, did not swing. Strike one.

Branca came back with virtually the same pitch, and this time Thomson swung and hit a sinking line drive to left field. The hit caught and held

Bobby Thomson hit the "home run heard 'round the world" to give the Giants a win in the dramatic 1951 pennant playoff with the Dodgers. *(George Brace photo)*

players frozen in time for an extended moment. At shortstop, Pee Wee Reese stood and watched, unmoving. Durocher, coaching at third, first told Hartung to tag up in case the ball were caught, and then motioned Lockman to start coming when he realized the ball was not going to be caught. He didn't realize the ball was going into the lower deck—because of the upper deck overhang, balls seldom got into the lower deck—until Thomson's hit got just over.

And then, everybody went crazy. On the radio, Giants' announcer Russ Hodges was screaming over and over, "The Giants win the pennant! The Giants win the pennant! The Giants win the pennant. . . ."

On the field, Giants second baseman Eddie Stanky jumped on Durocher's back and they leapfrogged down the third base line together. Other players mobbed Thomson as he crossed home plate, and fans came swarming onto the field. The whole mob moved toward the center-field clubhouse.

Trivia question time: Who was the on-deck hitter when Thomson hit his home run? Willie Mays, praying, he said later, that he would not have to come to bat.

The principal players in the drama, Branca and Thomson, went on to different fates. Branca's career was effectively ruined by that one pitch. Only 25 at the time, he won only 12 more major league games and was through by the time he was 30. Wherever he went, he was haunted by questions about that pitch.

Thomson went on to have two more good years for the Giants, knocking in more than 100 runs in both 1952 and '53. But his greatest contribution to the Giants in the post-1951 years came before the '54 season, when he was traded to the Braves for Johnny Antonelli, whose 21 wins helped the Giants win the pennant that year.

For a time, it seemed that the Giants would continue their miracle right through the World Series, when they won the first and third games, behind Dave Koslo and Jim Hearn.

But then the fourth game was delayed by rain for a day, which gave the Yankees' Allie Reynolds, the first game loser, an extra day of rest. He used it well, winning, 6–2, and the Yankees went on to win the next two games and the Series.

Any doubt of the importance of Mays to the Giants was dispelled dramatically in the next three years, during which the Giants' fortunes rose, fell, and then rose again in direct ratio to Mays' presence.

The Giants had Mays for the first 34 games of the 1952 season, and they were 26–8. They had won seven straight, including three over the Dodgers, and had a 2½ game over Brooklyn.

And then Mays went into the Army.

The Giants lost eight of their first ten without Mays and slowly drifted down into the standings, eventually finishing 4½ games behind the Dodgers.

The next year was far worse. Playing without Mays the whole season, the Giants finished a badly beaten fifth, a whopping 35 games behind the Dodgers, who won their second straight pennant. Durocher lost interest, as he usually did when his team was not in contention.

And then Mays came out of the Army.

There was a lot of happy talk going around the Giants' camp when Mays

With Charlie Fox, then the Giants' manager, Mays poses with baseballs spelling out 3,000 after he reached that hit plateau. *(San Francisco Giants photo)*

showed up. "It's only 240 days to World Series time," said Durocher. "In order to avoid the last-minute rush, let's start printing the tickets now."

Mays had come out of the Army stronger than when he went in, and he had the kind of season players dream about: .345 batting average, 41 home runs, 110 RBIs, Most Valuable Player award, of course. And the Giants won the pennant by five games.

That, the experts agreed, was as far as they would get. The National League hadn't won a World Series since 1946, and this didn't figure to be the year to change that pattern. The American League champions, the Cleveland Indians, were awesome. The Indians had won an American League record 111 games that year, and their pitching staff was awesome. Three members of that year's staff, Bob Lemon, Early Wynn and Bob Feller, were later elected to the Hall of Fame.

The Indians' big three consisted of Lemon and Wynn, who won 23 games apiece, and Mike Garcia, who had 19. Art Houtteman, 15 wins, and Feller, 13, backed them up. In the bull pen, Don Mossi and Ray Narleski were an ideal lefty-righty combination, appearing in 82 games between them.

The first three Cleveland starters were allowing less than three runs a game, and Mossi (1.94 ERA) and Narleski (2.22) were even stingier. As a staff, the Indians led the league with a 2.78 ERA.

The Indians had some hitters that year, too. Bobby Avila led the league with a .341 batting average, and Larry Doby led in the power categories, with 32 home runs and 126 RBIs. Al Rosen hit .300, with 24 home runs and 102 RBIs.

Cleveland was heavily favored to win the Series, and there were some who thought it might be a sweep. The writers covering the Series, contemplating the magnificent Cleveland pitching and strong hitting, also favored the Indians; more than two-thirds of those polled by the wire services thought Cleveland would win. They had forgotten that the Giants had Dusty Rhodes.

James Lamar ("Dusty") Rhodes was a colorful personality from Alabama; he sometimes had a powerful thirst. One of those oddities of baseball history, he played seven mostly indifferent seasons in the majors, but he was a tiger in 1954.

Oddly, the Giants had tried to trade him before the start of the season, but there were no takers. Rhodes had hit no higher than .250 in his two big league seasons, and he was a terrible fielder, the worst, Durocher says, he had ever seen.

So the Giants kept him, and Durocher used him almost exclusively as a pinch hitter. Probably nobody has ever had a more productive pinch-hitting year. In only 164 at bats, Rhodes produced 15 home runs and 50 RBIs and hit .341. As it turned out, he was only warming up for the World Series.

The first game of the Series, in New York, was the best. There were two highlights. The first came in the eighth inning. With the score tied, 2–2, and Doby and Rosen on base with nobody out, Vic Wertz hit a long drive to center that seemed a cinch triple. Mays caught the ball going away, and he came up throwing; his throw came back to the infield so fast that neither runner could advance, the part of the play that made Mays proudest.

Then, in the tenth inning, with runners on first and second, Durocher sent up Rhodes to pinch-hit for Irvin against Lemon. Lemon threw a slow curve on the outside corner, but Dusty got around on the pitch and lofted it down the right field line. The ball dropped just over the fence, at 258 feet the shortest in the major leagues.

Rhodes's magic came earlier in the second game. The Giants were trailing, 1–0, against Wynn when Mays walked and Hank Thomson singled with one out in the fifth. Durocher sent in Rhodes, who dropped a single in front of Doby in center field to score Mays.

Durocher was the kind of manager who stayed with a hot hand and backed his hunches, and he left Rhodes in the game. Sure enough, in the seventh, Rhodes came up again and this time hit a Wynn knuckler against the facade in right field, giving the Giants an insurance run in their 3–1 win.

In the third game, Durocher went to Rhodes even earlier. Behind, 1–0, the Giants had loaded the bases against Garcia in the third inning, when Dusty came up to hit for Irvin. This time, he slashed a single to right that scored two runs, and the Giants went on to win, 6–2.

In his first four at bats, then, Rhodes had had four hits, including two home runs, and had knocked in seven runs, all of which had been instrumental in Giants wins.

Rhodes didn't get a hit in his remaining two at bats in the third game, and he wasn't needed in the fourth game; the Giants jumped out to a 7–0 lead over the demoralized Indians and coasted to a 7–4 win. But Dusty's heroics in the first three games were enough to win him recognition as the Series MVP.

The sweep was the first for a National League team in 40 years, since the Miracle Braves of 1914. The tendency initially was to think of it as a fluke, perhaps because of Rhodes's incredible performance, but as the years passed, it became more apparent that this was simply the first indication that the National League had gained an edge over the American League that is still unquestioned a quarter-century later, the Yankees' 1977 and 1978 wins notwithstanding.

24. A Dynasty Grows in Brooklyn

There has never been a baseball town like Brooklyn. Residents of the borough had a relationship with the Dodgers, win or lose, that was unique in baseball, and perhaps in all sports. It was as if they were all part of an extended family.

The fans truly cared about the players. The term, "the Bums," was used affectionately and with resignation, as if the players were errant but loved children. When Gil Hodges was on his way to going 0-for-21 in the 1952 World Series, a church congregation prayed for him. To no avail.

Brooklyn fans were fierce partisans, but above all, they were knowledgeable. Good players from other teams were treated with the respect they deserved. Stan Musial hit so well against the Dodgers in Ebbets Field that fans groaned when he came to bat, but they appreciated Musial's unique talents almost more than his home town fans did.

Ebbets Field contributed in many ways to the baseball atmosphere in Brooklyn. Situated in the middle of a residential area of the borough, it was easily accessible. It was said, in only slight exaggeration, that nobody in Brooklyn was more than 20 minutes away from the park by public transportation. Many fans walked to the park. Few drove, because there were no parking facilities.

The park, built in 1913, was obsolete almost immediately. There were only 18,000 seats, though another 3000 fans squeezed in to stand and watch the 1916 World Series. By 1920, when the Dodgers won another pennant and Sunday baseball was legalized in New York City, it was obvious more seats had to be built.

Ebbets Field had double-decked stands from the right field foul line almost to the left field fence. Right field was up against Bedford Avenue, a major thoroughfare, so no stands could be added there, but Ebbets was able to add 6,000 seats in left field. (Eventually seating capacity was expanded to 31,900.)

The park had a small playing area—straightaway center was less than 400 feet from home plate—and it sloped downhill, so that the top of the center field fence was about on a level with home plate. In 1913, when the ball was dead, this did not seem important, but it became a big factor when the Dodgers had sluggers like Hodges, Duke Snider and Roy Campanella four decades later. Ebbets Field was a hitter's paradise.

But the advantage the park gave Dodger hitters was canceled by the pressure it put on their pitchers. The team had some excellent pitchers in the forties and fifties but few of them could put good seasons back-to-back. Sore arms and shattered psyches were the trademarks of Dodger pitchers.

Ebbets Field had many disadvantages for the fans. It was crowded and dirty, nothing like the antiseptic stadiums of today. But it had one big advantage: The fans were close to the players, to the point of being part of the action.

Charles Ebbets, who owned the Brooklyn Dodgers in the early part of the twentieth century, had a ballpark named after him.
(George Brace photo)

Hilda Chester rang her cowbell, and fans shouted insults and advice at players, managers, and umpires, confident that they could be heard, if not always heeded. A day at Ebbets Field was fun. Except for the pitchers, of course.

The loyal Brooklyn fans had little to cheer about for two decades following the 1920 pennant as the Dodgers, often little more than a half step away from insolvency, were seldom even in contention.

All that changed with the arrival of Larry MacPhail, who built the team that won the 1941 pennant. It changed even more when Branch Rickey arrived in 1942. The Dodger team that Rickey built was the best of his long and successful career, and it was probably the best National League team of all time. For a decade the Dodgers dominated the league in a way no other team had before or has since.

In a ten-year period, 1947–56, the Dodgers won six pennants, more than any other NL team in that time span. (The Giants twice, 1904–13 and 1915–24, and the Cardinals in the forties had won five pennants in a decade.)

The Dodger record could easily have been more impressive. In 1946 and 1951, they lost play-offs for the pennant. (There were only four league play-offs before divisional play was started, and the Dodgers were involved in all four, losing three of them.) In 1950, they lost the pennant on the final day of the season, to the Philadelphia Phillies. In 1954, they were second, only five games out. Only in 1948, when they finished third, 7½ games back, were they out of the race.

To realize how strong the Dodgers were, consider this: If they had won just four more regular season games over 11 seasons, they would have won nine pennants. Ten more regular season wins could have given them ten pennants; 19 more wins could have won every pennant in that 11-year stretch!

Or this: In that time, the Giants (twice), Cardinals, Braves and Phillies also won pennants; but cumulatively, the Dodgers won 120 more games than the Cardinals, 124 more than the Braves, 162 more than the Giants, 212 more than the Phillies.

Only the lack of consistent pitching kept the Dodgers from winning every pennant in that stretch. Don Newcombe and Carl Erskine were the only Brooklyn pitchers with any sustained success. Erskine won at least 11 games for six straight seasons. Newcombe three times won 20 games, and five times 17 or more in a six-year stretch. But neither pitcher was effective after their 30th birthdays, which came in 1956 for both—Erskine because of a sore arm and Newcombe because of an alcoholism he could not admit until long after his playing career had ended.

Preacher Roe had one spectacular 22–3 season, and Clem Labine had two excellent years in relief, but the Dodger pitching records of those years are sprinkled with names like Ralph Branca, Rex Barney, Joe Hatten, Erv Palica, Russ Meyer, Roger Craig, Don Bessent, Billy Loes, Clyde King and Ed Roebuck, all of whom had their moments, but not enough of them.

That was in marked contrast to the rest of the team. For most of the decade, the guts of the team remained intact, with Campanella, Hodges, Snider, Jackie Robinson, Pee Wee Reese and Carl Furillo.

It was in 1947 and '48 that the Dodger dynasty really took shape. Of the players who formed the backbone of the team for the next decade, only shortstop Reese and right fielder Furillo played for the '46 team.

In 1947, Robinson joined the team as a first baseman. The next year, second baseman Eddie Stanky was traded, and Robinson moved to second. Gil Hodges moved in at first base, Campanella became the catcher and Snider the center fielder. Billy Cox, obtained in a trade with Pittsburgh, became the third baseman.

After that, there were remarkably few changes, except in left field, where the Dodgers ran a shuttle service with Gene Hermanski, Andy Pafko, George Shuba, Cal Abrams, Sandy Amoros and even Robinson.

Campanella, Hodges, Reese, Snider and Furillo remained at their positions until the Dodgers moved to Los Angeles in 1958. Cox was with the Dodgers until 1954. Robinson was the second baseman until Jim ("Junior") Gilliam took over in 1953; after that, Jackie shifted between the outfield and third base for the remaining four years of his career.

For most of a decade, Dodgers managers Leo Durocher, Burt Shotton, Charlie Dressen and Walter Alston could start each game with six positions filled by players as good as anybody in the league.

The Dodgers were superb, offensively and defensively. Offensively, they had outstanding power; the trio of Snider, Hodges and Campanella had five seasons in which they combined for more than 100 home runs. Robinson and Reese were the best base stealers in the league. Defensively, at one time or another, Campanella, Hodges, Robinson, Reese, Cox, Snider and Furillo were all considered the best in the league at their positions.

Reese was the only holdover from the Larry MacPhail era at Brooklyn. The rest of the team was built by Rickey, through the farm system and trades, and his breaking of the color line was very important. Certainly, the Dodgers would not have been the same team without Robinson, Campanella, Newcombe, and later, Gilliam.

But it would be a mistake to lump the black Dodgers together, especially in the case of Robinson and Campanella. They were very different men.

Campanella, perhaps because he had an Italian father, never seemed to think in racial terms. He was an easygoing man, friendly with everybody. "To play this game good, a lot of you has got to be a little boy," he said.

Campanella was signed by Rickey shortly after the signing of Robinson, with much less attention, of course. He was assigned to Nashua of the New England League, where he roomed with Newcombe and was managed by Alston.

Campanella was 24 and had played nine years in the Negro leagues by the time he reported to Nashua. He was a standout from the beginning, winning the league's Most Valuable Player award after hitting .290 and driving in 96 runs.

He was promoted to Montreal the next season and had another good year, but Rickey wanted him to break the color line in the American Association and therefore assigned him to St. Paul for the 1948 season. He was much too good for that league, though, hitting .325 with 13 home runs and 39 RBIs, and Rickey brought him up, at the insistence of manager Durocher. Ironically, Durocher was gone only about a month after Campanella came up, with Shotton taking over when Leo went to the Giants.

Campanella played 83 games for the Dodgers that year, hitting .258, but it was the next year, 1949, that he became the big man behind the plate for the Dodgers, the first of nine consecutive years in which he caught at least 100 games.

Three times, Campanella was named the Most Valuable Player in the National League, in 1951, 1953, and 1955. The best year of the three was '53, when he hit .312, knocked in 142 runs and hit 41 home runs, a record for catchers until it was broken by Johnny Bench of Cincinnati, with 45 in 1970. (Bench played 36 games at other positions that year.)

Catching is by far the most rigorous position in baseball. Campanella frequently played when he was tired or suffering from various injuries, and that affected his statistics, which varied more from year to year than those of other Dodger stars'.

But Campanella was much better than his career statistics indicate, and that fact has been recognized by the baseball writers, who voted him into the Hall of Fame in 1969. As great as that Dodger team was, he and Robinson are the only players on it who have made the hall so far.

Not coincidentally, the Dodgers were at their best during the 1951–56 stretch when Campanella was at his most productive. In '51, of course, they lost to the Giants in that memorable play-off, but they bounced back with pennants in '52 and '53, by a whopping 13 games the second year.

That success convinced manager Charlie Dressen that he deserved more than the one-year contract that was the Dodgers' custom. Dressen was never a man who undervalued his own importance. Others might think that the Dodgers' great lineup had a lot to do with their success, but Charlie was convinced his managing was the difference. He demanded a three-year contract from Dodger president Walter O'Malley (who had bought out Branch Rickey in 1950) "or else."

Dressen soon found out what the "or else" was. O'Malley said goodbye and hired Alston out of the Dodger minor league system. Alston was the antithesis of Dressen, a quiet man who never spoke without purpose and let his ballplayers grab the spotlight. He had never managed in the major leagues before and many predicted he would never last, but he lasted 23 years, each year signing a new one-year contract.

That first season, though, it did seem that the one-year contract he signed might be his last. After winning so easily the year before, the Dodgers finished behind the Giants in 1954. That wasn't all Alston's fault, by any means. The Giants were a strong team playing their best ball that year and the Dodgers had what amounted to an off year for them; they scored 177 fewer runs than they had the year before, and the team's pitching ERA soared to 4.31.

The next year, though, the Dodgers were back on the track, and they won pennants in 1955 and '56, giving them four in five years. Alston went on to five more pennants, proving his managerial ability by taking quite different teams to pennants in Los Angeles.

Despite their regular season success, the Dodgers continued a long-standing Brooklyn tradition by losing in the World Series; the first seven Brooklyn pennant winners all lost in the Series, the last five losses coming against the hated crosstown Yankees.

That all changed in 1955, and fittingly so, because of the six Dodger pennants in a decade, this was the easiest. The Dodgers had won their first ten games, lost one, then won 11 of their next 12, standing 21-2. By mid-season, they were 55-22, and they coasted to a 13½ game margin over the Milwaukee Braves at the wire.

In sharp contrast to previous Series, everything worked for the Dodgers in the seventh game in 1955, even Alston's gamble in starting Johnny Podres instead of Newcombe, 20-5 that year. Alston was aware that Newcombe had been no mystery to the Yankees, either in the first game of that Series or in previous ones; Newcombe was 0-3 against the New Yorkers in World Series competition. Podres, only 9-10 during the season, had won one game earlier in the Series and he upheld Alston's decision by shutting out the Yankees in the deciding game.

Hodges knocked in two runs for the Dodgers, with a single in the fourth and a sacrifice fly in the sixth, and Amoros made one of the most memorable defensive plays in Series history to clinch the win.

In the bottom of the sixth, Billy Martin walked and Gil McDougald beat out a bunt for the Yankees. Yogi Berra, normally a pull hitter, sliced a drive down the left field line. Amoros, playing in left center, sprinted after the ball and, at the last moment, stuck out a glove to catch it, his momentum carrying him to the railing of the stands. He recovered quickly and threw the ball to Reese, who had come out for the relay, and Reese fired the ball to first to double up McDougald. That killed the Yanks' rally, and they never again threatened.

Brooklyn fans went wild that night, celebrating the first—and as it happened—last World Series win in the borough's history. Neither the Dodgers nor their Brooklyn fans have been treated well by time and events.

Robinson suffered from a series of illnesses before dying in 1972. Hodges died the same year, felled by his second heart attack, minutes after finishing a round of golf. Erskine has a mongoloid son. Furillo, released by the club when he was injured, sued baseball.

The most tragic fate, though, was that which befell Campanella. On January 28, 1958, as he was heading home to Long Island, his car hit a patch of ice as it came down a steep hill and skidded into a power pole. The car turned over, and Campanella was pinned beneath the steering wheel.

His fifth and sixth cervical vertebrae were snapped, and he was paralyzed from the chest down. His wife Ruthe, unable to cope with the situation, divorced him. (She subsequently died of a heart attack.) It says something about the strength of Campanella's character that he later dictated his autobiography and entitled it, *It's Good to Be Alive.*

Meanwhile, the Brooklyn fans have lost their club. Before the 1958 season, Walter O'Malley moved the Dodgers to Los Angeles, setting up a chain of events that has forever changed baseball. Ebbets Field, that wonderful-terrible place, has long since been destroyed, and the Brooklyn fans are left with only their memories.

Gil Hodges was a key figure in the Dodger dynasty of the fifties and later managed the Mets to their '69 championship. *(George Brace photo)*

25. Westward Ho!

For the first 53 seasons of the twentieth century, the National League lineup had been the same: New York, Brooklyn, Chicago, Cincinnati, St. Louis, Pittsburgh, Philadelphia–and Boston.

Then, a week before the start of the 1953 season, the Braves got permission to move to Milwaukee, where they had operated an American Association team. The move was startling, especially since Boston had been a charter member of the National League back in 1876, but Braves owner Lou Perini felt he had no choice.

Only five years before, the Braves had won the National League pennant as nearly 1.5 million fans cheered them on, but the enthusiasm of the fans had evaporated rapidly. By 1952, when they finished seventh, the Braves attracted only 281,000, and Perini reportedly lost $600,000. "We were playing to the grounds keepers," said manager Charlie Grimm.

An exciting chapter in league history was about to be written by the fans of Milwaukee, who nearly overwhelmed the Braves with their enthusiasm. Thousands greeted the players when they arrived, and the turnstiles clicked merrily. After the first nine home games, the Braves had been seen by more fans than had watched the entire 1952 season in Boston, and the attendance figures only hint at the frenzied enthusiasm of the fans. County Stadium was described as "an insane asylum with bases."

By season's end, more than 1.8 million fans had come through the County Stadium turnstiles, assuring Perini a $500,000 profit. The Braves had responded with an excellent year, rising from seventh to second place, though a distant 13 games behind the pennant-winning Dodgers.

The Braves had some exciting players that season. Eddie Mathews, in the second year of what became a Hall of Fame career, hit 47 home runs. Center fielder Bill Bruton won the first of three consecutive stolen base titles. First baseman Joe Adcock, who some thought to be the strongest man in baseball, hit 18 home runs. Lew Burdette won 15 games, the first of ten consecutive seasons in which he won at least ten games.

But the star of stars was pitcher Warren Spahn, who had been a key figure in the 1948 pennant and would go on to pitch in the National League through the 1965 season.

Warren Spahn became the winningest left-hander in history with 363 wins. *(George Brace photo)*

Spahn had one of his best years in 1953, winning 23 games; it was one of 13 seasons in which he won 20 or more games. His earned run average of 2.10 then was the lowest of his remarkable career.

Eventually, Spahn finished his career with 363 wins, more than any left-hander in history, and his dedication to perfection was as much a reason as any. "If he lost a game," notes Don Davidson, then the Braves' traveling secretary, "the next day he would be down early with a bullpen coach trying to find out why."

Early in his career, Spahn relied chiefly on a live fastball. As the years passed, he lost much of the zip on that pitch, but he more than compensated with guile and sharpened control.

By the midpoint in his career, Spahn no longer even considered the middle of the plate as a location for his pitches. He moved the ball up and down, and out, but always on the corners. Hitters complained that he was always "on the black," referring to the black edges around the plate.

The best indication of how smart a pitcher he became is this: In 1963, at age 42, his fastball only a memory, Spahn won 23 games and pitched seven shutouts!

At Boston, Spahn had teamed with Johnny Sain so effectively (42 combined wins in 1947, 39 in 1948), that somebody had described the Braves' pitching rotation as "Spahn and Sain and two days of rain." In Milwaukee, he and Burdette were even more effective; starting in 1956, they combined for 38 to 42 wins for six consecutive seasons.

The Braves got better and better. Henry Aaron joined the team in 1954, and by 1957–58, the Braves were good enough to win back-to-back pennants, winning the World Series the first year. It seemed the circus would never stop.

But, of course, it did. The Braves slipped after that '58 pennant, slowly at first and then more rapidly. They lost a pennant play-off to the Dodgers in 1959, finished second in '60, fourth in '61 and then had finishes of fifth, fifth, sixth, and fifth.

And the fans stopped coming.

There were a lot of reasons. The old favorites were mostly gone. The Green Bay Packers became a National Football League power, diverting attention from the Braves. Attendance slipped below a million and, in 1966, the Braves moved again, to Atlanta.

This time, hardly anybody outside the two cities cared. Far more startling moves had come eight years before, while the Braves were in their glory years in Milwaukee: The Brooklyn Dodgers had moved to Los Angeles, and the New York Giants had moved to San Francisco.

Transplanting the Dodgers and Giants had far more significance than the Braves' move to Milwaukee, startling as that first move had seemed at the time. By going to Milwaukee, the Braves had kept the National League where it had always been: east of the Mississippi River. Indeed, Milwaukee was not even totally virgin territory, having had a National League franchise one year, in 1878.

By moving to California, though, the Dodgers and Giants had made the National League true to its name. The moves, naturally, were surrounded by controversy, greeted with predictable dismay and outrage by fans, writers and politicians in the New York area and with equally predictable glee by their counterparts in the California cities.

The two principal characters in the drama were Dodger owner Walter O'Malley and Giant owner Horace Stoneham. It was an unlikely coupling, to be sure; Stoneham was an old-style baseball man, for whom the game was everything, and O'Malley, the very prototype of the modern businessman.

Stoneham's roots in baseball, and the Giants, were very deep. His father, Charles, had bought the Giants in 1919. When his father died in 1936,

Horace took over as club president. At 32, he was the youngest club president in the league.

O'Malley's involvement with baseball had come later. In the forties, he became the club's attorney, and he later bought into the club because he thought it was a good investment. Before the '51 season, he bought out Branch Rickey and took control of the Dodgers. That was, of course, the year Bobby Thomson's home run defeated the Dodgers in a play-off for the pennant. Some months later, O'Malley was riding in an elevator with Thomson. When Thomson got out, another man in the elevator gestured to him and said, "That man cost me $25." The elevator operator gestured at O'Malley. "He cost that man a quarter of a million."

By the late fifties, both O'Malley and Stoneham had decided that the future of their clubs was elsewhere, but they had come to that decision separately and by very different routes.

The Giants had been one of the most successful organizations in the National League in the twentieth century, and had won two pennants in the fifties, the second as recently as 1954.

Stoneham had played an important role in the team's success, too, because it was his willingness to make risky trades that had turned the Giants from an also-ran into champions. The '51 pennant was set up when he traded for Alvin Dark and Eddie Stanky, and the acquisition of Johnny Antonelli for Thomson was a big factor in the '54 pennant.

But Stoneham had one blind spot, which ruined him in New York and eventually in San Francisco, too: He thought the team was all that counted. He did not believe in any kind of promotion, and so when the team went down, attendance plummeted. And, after that '54 pennant, the team went down, to second division finishes in both 1956 and '57.

Meanwhile, the Polo Grounds was deteriorating, and so was the neighborhood around it. And there was another, new bogeyman: television. Once, Stoneham was watching a Mass on television, and the priest told the viewing audience that the telecast could not be considered a replacement for Catholics; they must go to the church. "Gee," Stoneham said wistfully to a friend. "I wish we could put in that kind of rule."

By 1957, attendance had dropped below 700,000. Stoneham was a New Yorker through and through; he had seen his first Giants game as early as 1912. The last thing he wanted to do was leave, but he felt he had no choice. The logical choice seemed to be Minneapolis, where the Giants had an American Association team. As with the Braves' move to Milwaukee, there would be no concern over territorial rights.

By that time, O'Malley was also ready to move. His problem was different from Stoneham's because the Dodgers were still a strong team and drawing well—more than a million in their last year in Brooklyn, 1957.

But O'Malley could see problems ahead. Ebbets Field had been outmoded almost from the time it was built. Though it was fun to watch a game there, it was small (under 32,000) and the neighborhood around it was rapidly deteriorating. Ironically, considering what soon happened, O'Malley was concerned that the Braves would have more money to work with because of their success at the gate in Milwaukee, and would thus have more money to spend on bonuses for young prospects. He was also aware that baseball in Brooklyn had traditionally been a boom or bust affair, and more often bust.

O'Malley wanted to build a new park. He even had a site picked out, at Atlantic and Flatbush Avenues. Under the Urban Renewal Act, it was possible to acquire substandard or slum areas for a better use. The land, once condemned, would have been sold to the Dodgers. O'Malley, in fact, sold Ebbets Field in anticipation of buying the land at the new site and building a new park.

"We conducted an eight-year campaign to build our own stadium in Brooklyn at the Atlantic-Flatbush site," says O'Malley. "The stadium contemplated would have been built over the Long Island Railroad terminal, which was also the one spot in the city where all subway systems intersected. This would have given us a central location serving all of the city and Long Island. The Pennsylvania Railroad owned the Long Island Railroad and its property and was most agreeable to the idea."

For a time, O'Malley thought he would get his new park in Brooklyn. "At one point," he says, "we were successful in getting legislation passed in Albany creating a Brooklyn Sports Center Authority, which would have condemned the land needed for a new stadium, with the approval of the produce market renters, who were all in favor of being relocated to a better area.

"Gov. Averell Harriman came to Borough Hall, Brooklyn, to sign the bill and that encouraged us enough to have architectural and engineering plans prepared. But the project was successfully sabotaged."

O'Malley was certainly no stranger to politics, but in this case, he was outflanked by urban planner Robert Moses, who had the ear of New York mayor Rober Wagner. Moses wanted O'Malley to build on another site, which would have been accessible only by parkway. O'Malley didn't want that, and he started to make other plans.

In 1956, O'Malley bought the Los Angeles franchise in the Pacific Coast

League from the Chicago Cubs. The next year, convinced he had no chance to fulfill his Brooklyn plans (he was even toying with the idea of a domed stadium, perhaps financed by pay-TV rights), he approached Stoneham.

"Horace had just about made up his mind to move the Giants to Minneapolis," says O'Malley. "I talked to Horace and said that if he left New York, we also would probably move because the one practical site in Brooklyn was no longer available.

"I asked Horace if he was legally committed to Minneapolis or if he would consider San Francisco. He had an open mind and I then arranged a meeting for Horace to meet the mayor of San Francisco (George Christopher) in New York. At that meeting, proposed terms for the rental of a stadium to be built in San Francisco were considered, and I then proceeded to contact mayor Norris Poulson of Los Angeles."

But though O'Malley was the motivating force behind the movement to California, it was Stoneham and the Giants who made the first announcement. On August 19, 1957, the Giants' board of directors voted, 8-1, to move to San Francisco for the 1958 season; the lone dissenter was minority stockholder M. Donald Grant, who was later to serve as chairman of the board for the New York Mets.

A reporter asked Stoneham, "How do you feel about the kids in New York from whom you are taking the Giants?"

"I feel bad about the kids," replied Stoneham, "but I haven't seen many of their fathers lately."

On October 8, the Dodgers also made it official: They were moving to Los Angeles.

The moves were both made so quickly that the new major league cities did not have major league facilities for the clubs. The Dodgers had to play in Los Angeles Coliseum, built in 1923 for football and never considered before for baseball, and the Giants played in Seals Stadium, a fine minor league park but one with only 23,000 capacity. The Giants were the first to get into a permanent facility, Candlestick Park, in 1960, but the Dodgers wound up with much the better park when they moved into Dodger Stadium two years later.

Much of what has been written about the Dodgers' deal in Los Angeles has implied that it was a giveaway; so it is important to examine the situation and put it into perspective.

O'Malley bought the land, 300 acres in Chavez Ravine, for $2 million and built Dodger Stadium with his own money. The Dodgers pay real estate taxes on the land, as much as $1 million a year, but the land is zoned to prohibit any other commercial structures. Contrary to what has been written frequently, the Dodgers did not get mineral rights to the land; those rights still belong to the city of Los Angeles.

The fact that the land O'Malley purchased is in downtown Los Angeles sometimes leads those from other areas of the country to think that O'Malley got choice property. But downtown Los Angeles is not downtown Manhattan. It may be, in fact, that there really is no such thing as downtown Los Angeles. Los Angeles is a city of suburbs, and many Dodger fans never get downtown, except to Dodger Stadium.

Chavez Ravine was, in fact, virtually deserted when it was bought by the Dodgers. "The total income from taxes on the property prior to our acquiring it totaled less than $1,000 per year," says O'Malley.

O'Malley's deal with the city of Los Angeles was blocked first by litigation, which was dismissed, and then a referendum, which he won. When that was behind him, he laid plans for a stadium that is incontestably the best baseball facility in the country.

Dodger Stadium is a triumph of design. It is used only for baseball, not as a multipurpose stadium, so there are no awkwardly designed seats. Tickets are color coded, so fans know which levels to enter; if it's necessary to go up a level, there are escalators. Parking lot areas are matched to seating areas, so that fans have relatively short distances to walk, an important consideration to southern Californians, who feel disoriented when they have to leave their cars.

Inside the park, bright colors abound. There is real grass on the field, not artificial turf. Outside the park, trees and flowers proliferate.

The fans have poured into the stadium in record-breaking numbers. In 11 of the club's first 16 years at Dodger Stadium, more than two million fans came to games; in the 17th year, 1978, the Dodgers became the first club in major league history to exceed the three million mark for the season. The record they broke was their own, set the previous season, and even O'Malley was surprised.

"Frankly," he said, "I did not envision a three million gate (when the Dodgers moved to Los Angeles) but Vince Flaherty, then a Los Angeles columnist *(The Los Angeles Examiner)* did."

Fans seldom come just to see a park, though, no matter how beautiful. A more important factor in the Dodgers' success has been the fact that they have almost always been contenders since they moved to Los Angeles; they finished first or second in 14 of their first 21 years in California.

Appropriately, the Los Angeles Dodgers became a completely different team from the Brooklyn Dodgers. Only Jim Gilliam, who had come to Brooklyn in 1953, really bridged the gap between the two, playing nine years in Los Angeles. None of the Brooklyn stars became stars in Los Angeles.

Jackie Robinson, of course, had retired two years before the Dodgers moved. Roy Campanella was paralyzed in an automobile accident and never played in California. Pee Wee Reese played one ineffectual year and retired. Don Newcombe, the Dodgers' best pitcher in Brooklyn, was 0–6 in Los Angeles before being traded.

Duke Snider played five years in Los Angeles, Gil Hodges four, and Carl Furillo three, but none of them approached the success they had in their best years in Brooklyn. The Dodgers in Los Angeles had to develop their own stars, as they surely did.

The Los Angeles team became different in style as well as players. Especially after the Dodgers moved into their new stadium, their emphasis went to pitching, instead of the power hitting of the Brooklyn years.

In a six-year period, 1961–66, the Dodgers won three pennants and finished second twice, one of those second-place finishes coming after losing a play-off to the Giants. That six-year success also coincided with Sandy Koufax's best six years, but that is really no coincidence. The Dodgers had some other fine pitchers during that time: Don Drysdale twice won 20 games or more and finished with a Dodger record of 209 wins; Ron Perranoski was the best relief pitcher in the league for most of that stretch; Claude Osteen won 32 games for the back-to-back pennant winners in 1965–66.

But it was Koufax who was the main man. Clearly, as he went, so went the Dodgers. When he was sidelined with a finger ailment after winning 14 games in little more than half a season in 1962, the Dodgers lost the pennant. When he won 25 games the next year, they won the pennant and the World Series; when he was sidelined again the next year, after winning 19 games, they slid to fifth.

When he won 26 and 27 games the next two years, they won the pennant both years. When he retired after the 1966 season, the Dodgers plummeted from first place to eighth.

Koufax's period of brilliance was relatively short, and his career totals are not particularly impressive. With 165 wins, he is one of only three pitchers in National League history to make the Hall of Fame with less than 200 wins. (Dazzy Vance, 197, and Dizzy Dean, 150, are the other two.)

Still, Koufax certainly deserves his spot in the Hall. During those six years, he was overwhelming. He was without doubt the best pitcher in baseball and, adjusting for the differences in the game, probably as dominating as any National League pitcher has ever been, not excluding Christy Mathewson and Grover Cleveland Alexander.

Consider this: In the last four years of his career, pitching for a team that got him few runs, Koufax won 97 games and lost only 27. In the 1963 season, his first great one, he won 25 games and lost only five. After facing him in the World Series, Yogi Berra said, "I can see how he won 25 games. What I don't understand is how he lost five."

In his last four years, Koufax's earned run averages were 1.88, 1.74, 2.04, and 1.73. The best way to appreciate those figures is to compare them with the records of two other great National League left-handers from the lively ball era, Carl Hubbell and Warren Spahn. Hubbell had only one year when his ERA was under two runs; Spahn's lowest ERA was 2.10.

Koufax set a National League record with 18 strikeouts against the Giants in a 1959 game, and a major league record of 382 strikeouts in the 1965 season. He averaged more than a strikeout an inning and yielded less than seven hits a game. He usually finished what he started, with 89 complete games his last four years. He was the first pitcher to pitch four no-hitters, and the last one, in 1965, was a perfect game.

He did it all basically with two pitches, an overwhelming fastball and a curve that looked just like the fastball until it broke off sharply just in front of the plate. Once in a while, he would struggle to get his rhythm in the first inning and would be momentarily vulnerable; in one memorable game I witnessed, the Giants knocked him out in the first inning and went on to score eight runs. But once past the first inning, he was as close to unbeatable as any pitcher could be.

Because he was so good, Koufax was an outstanding gate attraction. The Dodgers estimated that he was worth an extra 10,000 admissions for a home game. That cut both ways, though. When Koufax retired and the Dodgers fell far out of contention in 1967, attendance dropped a half million, from 2.167 million to 1.663 million.

Koufax was not quite 31 when he retired, seemingly on the brink of accumulating some great career statistics; he had 44 more wins than Hubbell at a comparable age, 43 more than Spahn, and in four more seasons he could have eclipsed Walter Johnson's major league career strikeout mark.

But the arthritis in his pitching arm and shoulder had grown worse and worse. He had to soak his arm for hours after pitching, and he frequently could not raise his arm to comb his hair. He feared what would happen in the future. "If you had one good arm and one bad arm," he said, "and somebody said you could buy back the use of your bad arm, I think you'd do it. In a sense, that's what I'm doing."

Even though attendance fell sharply when Koufax retired and the Dodgers finished eighth and seventh—their only consecutive second division finishes in Los Angeles—in 1967 and '68, the low mark was a still respectable 1,581,093 in 1968. That's a tribute to the Dodger organization, which realizes there is more to getting good attendance than merely opening the gates.

The Dodgers are probably the best organization in all of professional sports, considering all aspects, from putting a good team on the field to making it easy and pleasant for the fans to come. They have kept their ticket prices low—only $4.50 for box seats, $3.50 for general admission as late as 1978—and they have run countless promotions, getting fans into the stadium for bargain prices.

O'Malley can afford to discount ticket prices, of course, because he owns his stadium and doesn't have to share concession or parking money with anybody. That's one of the reasons he's a rich man; he estimated his worth at $24 million when talking to writer Roger Kahn.

The Dodgers' promotional work could serve as a model for any organization. Even in bad years, that kind of promotion puts a floor under attendance, preventing the kind of disasters that have forced clubs to move to other cities.

And in good years, the results have been phenomenal for the Dodgers. In 1977, the Dodgers had perhaps the best all-round team since arriving in Los Angeles. Their pitching was well balanced with Tommy John (20–7), Rick Rhoden (16–10), Don Sutton and Doug Rau (both 14–8), and Burt Hooton (12–7). They were the first team with four hitters with 30 or more home runs—Steve Garvey (33), Reggie Smith (32,) and Dusty Baker and Ron Cey (30 each). And they set a major league attendance mark with 2,955,087.

The next year, helped by what was a tight race with the Giants and Reds for most of the season, the Dodgers did even better at the gate; averaging more than 80 percent of the stadium's capacity for every game as they drew 3,347,845.

For most of the first California decade, the Dodgers-Giants rivalry was as bitter as it had been in New York and probably more competitive than it had been for a similar period of time.

In 1959, there was a three-way battle between the Dodgers, Giants, and Milwaukee Braves. Eventually, the Dodgers beat the Braves in a playoff, with the Giants third, only four games back.

In 1961, the Dodgers finished second, the Giants third. In 1962, the Giants beat the Dodgers in a play-off. In 1963, the Dodgers won and the Giants were third. In 1965 and '66, the Dodgers won and the Giants were second, two games and a game and a half back, respectively.

Inevitably, the closeness of the rivalry created some very tense moments. The most celebrated came in an August 1965 game in Candlestick Park.

The trouble began when Giant pitcher Juan Marichal threw brushback pitches at Maury Wills and Ron Fairly. The Dodgers wanted Koufax to retaliate against Marichal when Juan was at the plate, but that wasn't Koufax's style. So, Dodger catcher John Roseboro zipped a return throw after a Koufax pitch very close to Marichal's head. Marichal later claimed the ball actually tipped his ear; Roseboro said it went about three inches away from Marichal's nose. Roseboro's view is the more likely; it would have been very difficult for the ball to tip Marichal's ear without hitting his head.

Marichal screamed at Roseboro, "Why you do that? You better not hit me with that ball."

Roseboro came up out of his crouch and apparently tried to hit Marichal, but Marichal swung his bat, hitting Roseboro on the left side of the face. Roseboro kept coming and landed at least one punch.

Eventually, other players got into the action and broke it up, but by that time, blood was streaming from Roseboro's face. Willie Mays grabbed Roseboro and pulled him away, telling him, "Your eye is out." Dodger manager Walter Alston later said he feared the same thing. Mays went into the Dodger dugout with Roseboro, cradling his head as the Dodger trainer examined Roseboro. As it turned out, fortunately, Roseboro's eye was all right.

As a result of the fracas, National League president Warren Giles fined Marichal $1,750 and suspended him for eight playing days. The Dodgers regarded that as insufficient penalty, and Roseboro sued Marichal for $110,000, later settling out of court for $7,000. But whether Marichal's punishment was sufficient or not, it was certainly costly to the Giants because he lost two starts.

Those years were frustrating ones for the Giants in many ways, because they could win only one pennant, while finishing second four times in a row, 1965–68, in league competition. (They then finished second once more, this time in the Western Division when the league split into divisions in the '69 season.)

They were also profitable years. The Giants have never had the over-

Sandy Koufax's prime was cut short by an arthritic arm, but while he was pitching he was the league's best since the advent of the lively ball. *(George Brace photo)*

Juan Marichal, shown with his characteristic high leg kick, won 20 or more games six times for the San Francisco Giants in the sixties. *(San Francisco Giants photo)*
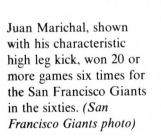

whelming gate success of the Dodgers, for understandable reasons—they operate from a considerably smaller population base and the windswept San Francisco area is much less pleasant for night baseball than balmy Los Angeles—but they were very popular in their first decade. Even when they had to play in small Seals Stadium their first two years, they went over a million, and they averaged better than 1.5 million a season for the first decade.

That changed drastically in 1968, when the A's moved from Kansas City to Oakland, just across the bay, and cut sharply into the Giants' market. Attendance dropped below a million, to 837,000, for the first time since the Giants had come to San Francisco.

There were other problems. Stoneham, the most congenial and generous of men, was also very shy. He did not get out into the community very often. He was a shadowy figure to San Franciscans, thought of as a transplanted New Yorker who wasn't happy in the west. In San Francisco, a very provincial town, that was a serious liability. Unlike O'Malley, Stoneham did not believe in promotion, and so the Giants had nothing to fall back on when the team went bad.

And it did go bad. After winning a divisional championship in 1971, before losing in the league play-off to Pittsburgh, the Giants slumped below .500 for five of the next six years.

The extraordinary farm system, under the direction of Hubbell and Carl Schwarz, kept producing good players, but Stoneham just as consistently traded them away. Young players like George Foster, Garry Maddox, Bobby Bonds, Dave Kingman, Steve Stone, Ken Henderson were all traded away. So was Gaylord Perry, who went on to win 100 games in the American League, as he had done in the National. Orlando Cepeda was traded; so was Willie McCovey.

Almost as bad as the trades he made were the trades he didn't make. He waited until Mays had no value left before selling him to the New York Mets (a borderline pitcher, Charlie Williams, was thrown in by the Mets.) Marichal had been a great pitcher, though overshadowed by Koufax, six times winning 20 or more games for the Giants. But he had nothing left by the time Stoneham was forced to sell him to the Boston Red Sox in 1974.

This was in sharp contrast to Stoneham's early years in San Francisco, when he had been an astute trader. Three-fourths of the starting rotation on the 1962 pennant winner—Jack Sanford, Billy O'Dell and Billy Pierce—had come in trades.

What happened? Perhaps Stoneham simply got old. Perhaps he relied too

Willie McCovey was the most popular San Francisco Giant and second only to Willie Mays as the best. *(San Francisco Giants photo)*

Vida Blue switched to the National League and led a Giants' challenge that fell short only in the final month of 1978. *(San Francisco Giants photo)*

much on his long-time friends, whose judgment was also clouded by age. Farm system secretary Schwarz thinks that the lack of operating money—Stoneham did not have the financial resources of many others in the game—forced him to make uneven trades in which the other clubs tossed in money as a sweetener.

Whatever the reasons, a bad situation became worse. As the Giants drifted out of contention, San Francisco fans became apathetic. They listened on the radio but did not come to the games. Attendance fell below the figures that had caused the Giants' move from New York, to 519,991 in 1974 and 522,925 the following year. When the FBI was searching for Patricia Hearst, somebody suggested she was probably hiding in the upper deck at Candlestick.

The Giants, it seemed, would repeat the story of the Braves, becoming the second team in the National League to move twice. By 1976, rumors became fact: Stoneham announced that he had sold the club to a Canadian brewery, which would move the Giants to Toronto for the '76 season.

San Francisco mayor George Moscone got a temporary injunction to prevent the move, and that turned out to be just enough time to save the Giants for San Francisco.

During the winter, financier Bob Lurie had been trying to find a partner to go 50-50 in buying the club. Just a couple of hours before the court deadline, he found one—Arizona cattleman Bud Herseth. The Giants stayed.

The next two years were rocky ones for Lurie and Herseth. The club was an also-ran and attendance increased only slightly, to 700,000 in 1977.

But just before the expiration of the March inter-league trading deadline in 1978, the Giants made a dramatic trade for A's pitching star Vida Blue, With Blue and the improvement of some young players, most notably Jack Clark, the Giants jumped back into the pennant race for the first time in seven years, and the fans responded with numbers and enthusiasm. Attendance jumped to 1,740,477.

And, once again, the Dodger-Giant rivalry heated up. The rivalry between Los Angeles and San Francisco is as bitter in its way as that between Brooklyn and Manhattan—Mort Sahl once cracked that in the event of a bombing attack, neither city would warn the other—and when both teams are in the pennant race, enthusiasm runs high. The first two weeks in August 1978, the teams played four games in San Francisco and then another four in Los Angeles. Those eight games drew more than 400,000 fans. The National League's Westward Ho! movement was once again an overwhelming success.

26. The Amazin's . . . and Others

There was a new look to the National League in 1962. For the first time in more than six decades, the league had more than eight teams. Two expansion teams were added, the New York Mets and the Houston Colt 45s (later renamed the Astros). The schedule was lengthened from 154 games to 162. Another chapter was added to the league's history and, thanks to the Mets, it was a bizarre one.

On the playing field, the Mets were an absolute disaster. Some called them the worst National League team in history. Trying to acquire competence by osmosis, the club's ownership had hired former Yankees George Weiss and Casey Stengel as general manager and manager, but the magic was gone for both men.

Looking over the culls available in the league expansion pool, Weiss went for aging veterans—who contributed little to the Mets—instead of gambling on younger players. Realizing that this team was even worse than the dogs he had been saddled with at Brooklyn and Boston early in his managing career, Stengel just went through the motions, sometimes even falling asleep in the dugout.

Stengel had had his pride hurt when he was fired by the Yankees two years before, primarily because he had reached his 70th birthday. No doubt, he wanted to prove he could still manage, but the Mets players never gave him an opportunity. They would have benumbed a much younger man.

Those who want to argue that the Mets were the worst of all time have plenty of statistical ammunition. That first year, the Mets lost a record 120 games, and that seems to be a record that will never be broken. All expansion teams have rocky first years, but no other expansion team has come within ten losses of the Mets' mark.

There were other records. The Mets immediately tied a National League record by losing their first nine games. They hold the league records for losses in two consecutive years (231) and three consecutive years (340).

The Mets were incredibly inept. They ended their first season 60½ games behind the pennant-winning San Francisco Giants. They finished tenth for the first four years, climbed to ninth the fifth year and fell back to tenth the next season.

In their first seven years, they had only two seasons in which they finished closer to the top than 40 games!

The Mets, in fact, were so pitiful that they were funny, and New Yorkers took the team to their hearts, It became fashionable to go to the newly built Shea Stadium to laugh at the Mets and see what implausible moves they would make next.

Some players were funnier than others. The most famous—or infamous—was first baseman Marv Throneberry, nicknamed "Marvelous Marv" because as a player he was anything but.

Throneberry was a mild-mannered prematurely balding young man of 29 who had come to the majors in 1955 with the Yankees. He had an older brother, Faye, who had an equally undistinguished career. Oddly, they finished with almost identical batting averages, .236 for Faye, .237 for Marv.

Marv hit with occasional power—16 home runs for the Mets in '62—but hardly enough to make up for his low batting average and erratic fielding. He had already been with three American League teams before he wound up with the Mets early in the '62 season.

As a player, Throneberry's style was much like that of Inspector Clouseau, as played so brilliantly by Peter Sellers in the Pink Panther movie series. Marv tried so hard to do the right thing and almost invariably did the opposite, which is the essence of comedy. He could be depended upon to throw to the wrong base, or perform other mental blunders. Fans looked forward eagerly to Marv's next mistake, and they cheered him when he obliged.

Throneberry took it all good-naturedly, which is how it was intended by the fans, and the whole scene eventually turned to his favor. His playing career ended the next year and, without the publicity about "Marvelous Marv," he would have been just another ballplayer, forgotten the moment he retired. Instead, he had a name that was recognizable long after his retirement, and he was doing beer commercials 15 years later alongside players and coaches known for their positive achievements.

The reverse psychology employed by the Mets' fans enabled the club to disprove one of the oldest theories in baseball; that a team has to be a winner to draw well. The Mets drew close to a million fans their first year and averaged 1.5 million through the first seven seasons. In 1964, when they finished 40 games out in tenth place, they outdrew the crosstown Yankees, who had won the pennant, by more than 400,000!

And just when the jokes appeared to be wearing thin, the Mets turned around and became the best in baseball. That happened in 1969, and it remains one of the most amazing stories in baseball history.

The National League split into divisions for the first time that year because of the expansion to 12 teams, San Diego and Montreal joining the league. The Mets were placed in the Eastern Division.

The St. Louis Cardinals, who had won back-to-back pennants in 1967 and '68, were in the same division, but the Cardinals were never in contention that year, and it was the Chicago Cubs who first seemed to be the division's strongest team.

With Leo Durocher spurring them on as only he could, the Cubs got off to a big early lead. The Cubs had a solid team that year, one with far more big name players than the Mets. Ron Santo, Ernie Banks, Billy Williams and Jim Hickman all hit more than 20 home runs that year. Glenn Beckert and Don Kessinger gave the Cubs great defense up the middle. They had an excellent 1-2-3 pitching combination in Ferguson Jenkins (21 wins), Bill Hands (20 wins) and Ken Holtzman (17 wins, one of them a no-hitter).

In contrast, the Mets had only one real star, right-hander Tom Seaver, probably the best pitcher of his generation, who won 25 games with a 2.21 earned run average and 208 strikeouts.

Manager Gil Hodges, who had ended his playing career with the Mets in 1963, did an admirable job of platooning; outfielders Tommie Agee (146 games) and Cleon Jones (137) were the only Mets who played more than 130 games.

When they took two of three from the Cubs in a series at Shea Stadium in early July, the Mets gave an indication of what would happen later in the season. One of the Met wins then was a one-hitter by Seaver, who lost his no-hitter with one out in the ninth. The next week in Chicago, the Mets again took two out of three from the Cubs.

But then the Cubs went into high gear and the Mets slumped, and the Cubs led by as many as 9½ games in early August. Then the Cubs slumped and the Mets started to move.

By early September, the Cubs were dying like a speed horse in the stretch, and it was obviously only a matter of time. On September 8, they came into New York for a doubleheader with their lead shrunk to 2½ games. The Mets swept both games and, two days later, were in first place to stay. The eventual winning margin for the Mets was eight games, a swing of 17½ games from early August. The Mets' total of 100 wins was the best in the National League, and 27 more than they'd had the previous year.

The powerful Atlanta Braves took the National League West, led by Hank Aaron, who'd matched his uniform number with 44 home runs. The Mets and the Braves met in the first National League championship series for the right to represent the league in the World Series, and the Mets proved two baseball axioms: In a short series, go with the team that has (1) the best pitching; and (2) the momentum. The New Yorkers won three straight.

Most baseball experts thought the World Series would be another matter. The Baltimore Orioles had been very impressive during the American League season, winning the East Division by a whopping 19 games as they won 109 games, high in baseball. Like the Mets, the Orioles had swept through the championship series, downing the Minnesota Twins in three straight.

The Orioles won the first game of the Series 4–1, as Mike Cuellar bested Tom Seaver at Baltimore. Then the Mets surprised everybody by winning the next four games.

The Mets won another pennant four years later (losing to the Oakland A's in the World Series). Since then a series of ill-advised economies and trades have dragged them back down to the bottom of the league. But nothing can take away the glory of that marvelous year of 1969 when they stood the baseball world on its ear.

The Mets also have the distinction of being the only expansion team to win as much as a divisional title, let alone a league pennant or World Series, in the first 17 years of the expansion era. The battle for most expansion clubs has been to achieve respectability.

The Houston Astros are a good example of that. The Astros (then the Colt 45s) started off much stronger than the Mets, a full 24 games better that first year of 1962. Yet, the Astros have never been able to poke their heads much above .500, and those seasons have been followed by periods of regression. In 1972, for instance, the Astros won a club record 84 games, but three years later, they had slipped to 64–97, a half-game worse than their first year. In 1977 they were a respectable third, exactly at .500, but by the next season they were struggling to stay out of the cellar again.

Bad luck and bad trades have dogged the Astros. Before the 1969 season they traded Rusty Staub to Montreal for Don Clendenon and Jesus Alou,

Above left, "Marvelous Marv"
Throneberry represented the futility
of the New York Mets in the early
sixties. *(George Brace photo)*

Above, Tom Seaver epitomized the
excellence of the Mets in '69,
when his pitching was the key
to their world championship.
(George Brace photo)

Left, Don Wilson seemed on his way
to an outstanding career when he died
of carbon monoxide poisoning.
(Houston Astros photo)

but Clendenon would not report. Montreal substituted pitchers Jack Billingham and Skip Guinn and money, and Clendenon eventually wound up with the Mets, to become a World Series hero.

After the 1971 season the Astros traded Joe Morgan, Billingham, Denis Menke, Cesar Geronimo and Ed Armbrister to Cincinnati for Lee May, Tommy Helms and Jimmy Steward.

The Cincinnati papers and fans criticized the Reds' management for the trade, and the Astros had their best year in '72, finishing a strong second in their division. The division and pennant winner was Cincinnati, which had been strengthened even more. The Reds went on to dominate the National League for much of the seventies, aided greatly by Morgan and Geronimo, and the Astros headed downhill again.

Tragedy also hit the Houston club on three separate occasions. Pitcher Jim Umbricht and first baseman Walter Bond both died of cancer in the club's early years, and pitcher Don Wilson died of carbon monoxide poisoning before the 1975 season.

The loss of Wilson was the hardest blow to the Astros. The hard-throwing right-hander had shown flashes of brilliance in his career, throwing two no-hitters and winning 104 games. A month short of his 30th birthday when he died, he still had time to become the standout the Astros thought he would be.

The Astros, though, have one distinction: In the Era of the Stadium, theirs is still the most unusual in baseball.

The 1960s and seventies brought virtually a complete change in stadiums for National League teams. It is startling to realize that San Francisco's Candlestick Park, opened in 1960, is the second-oldest park in the league. Only Wrigley Field (1916) is older.

The new stadiums are a mixed blessing. They are usually multipurpose arenas, built for baseball and football and not wholly satisfactory for either. They often put the fans too far from the players, which detracts from the enjoyment of the game. They are devoid of distinction and interchangeable, virtually the same from one city to the next.

Still, the new parks were necessary. They offer the fans far more comfort and parking than their predecessors and in most cases they give the owners more seats to sell.

Nowhere was a new stadium more desperately needed than in Houston. There the team played for three years in a small, minor league park besieged by the terribly humid Houston weather and swarms of fleas and mosquitoes so thick that games sometimes had to be stopped.

The Houston Astrodome, the world's first indoor baseball stadium, is billed as the "Eighth Wonder of the World." *(Houston Astros photo)*

Judge Roy Hofheinz came up with a novel idea: An indoor stadium. It seemed like a joke when it was proposed, but on April 9, 1965, the first indoor baseball game was played, an exhibition between the Astros (re-named from the Colt 45s) and the New York Yankees.

The first year in the Astrodome, nicknamed "the Eighth Wonder of the World," was a wild one. Outfielders discovered they couldn't follow the ball when it was hit high, because of the light through the roof. Darker roof panels were installed to eliminate that problem, and then the grass died.

So, an artificial turf field ("Astroturf," naturally), was installed. Nobody else in the National League has built an indoor stadium, but most clubs have followed the Astros' lead and installed artificial turf.

●

In 1969, the National League expanded again, to San Diego and Montreal. Each finished last in its division, with identical 52–110 records, but the resemblance ended there.

Montreal had been a solid minor league town as a farm club of the Brooklyn Dodgers, and the fans were determined to show they could support a major league team in style.

Though the Expos played in Jarry Park, hurriedly expanded from only 2,000 to 28,000 seats, the fans came out in great numbers, 1.2 million the first year and more than a million for each of the first six years. Their enthusiasm was remarkable.

Shortstop Bobby Wine remembered, for instance, a game that didn't even start until 10:30 P.M. because of the rain. "The game finally ended at one or two in the morning," he said, "and nobody had left."

The player who benefited most from the fans' adulation was the team's one star, Rusty Staub, who came from Houston. Staub developed into a power hitter in Montreal, with 78 home runs in three years to go with two .300 years. He'd have been a shoo-in if he had run for mayor.

"He related to the people and had a sense of being a star," noted Montreal club president John McHale. "His reddish hair, his stature, his unselfishness made him an easily identifiable figure. He was a very important factor in the success of this club."

Staub was called "Le Grand Orange" by the French Canadians, but his popularity didn't prevent the Expos from trading him to the Mets in 1972 for shortstop Tim Foli, outfielder Ken Singleton, and first baseman Mike Jorgenson. "We had the star," said McHale. "We were able to trade him for three key people who made us competitors for the next two-three years."

The Staub trade did not dampen the fans' enthusiasm. Attendance dipped below one million in 1975 and to 646,000 in 1976, but that was because the Expos had a disastrous year, 55–107 and 46 games out. The Montreal fans had grown more sophisticated and would not tolerate a showing like that.

But when the Expos bounced back and won 20 more games the next season—and moved into the stadium built for the 1976 Olympics—attendance also bounced back, to more than 1.4 million. On the field, and at the box office, the club seemed on solid footing.

Rusty Staub was a good player at Houston who became a hero when he was traded to the Montreal Expos. *(Houston Astros photo)*

The San Diego Padres were, at first, an entirely different matter. There was no instant love affair between the fans and the team in San Diego. Apathy was the word. For their first five years, the Padres' attendance ranged from 549,000 to 644,000. Some said there weren't enough people in the area to support a major league club. Others thought there were too many retired people on fixed incomes who didn't have the money to spend on entertainment. Still others thought San Diego, with its great beaches and climate, had too many counter-attractions,

What nobody apparently considered was that the fans were not eager to spend their money on the team until the owner did. C. Arnholt Smith, who had bought the Padres for $10 million, was in deep financial trouble, and the club had to sell players or trade those with high contracts just to keep afloat.

After the 1973 season, Smith made plans to sell the club to a group that planned to move it to Washington, D. C. The National League had drawn up a schedule with Washington included (in the Western Division!), but the city of San Diego would not let the team go.

Mayor Pete Wilson, aided by city attorney John Witt, went to court to prevent the team from being moved. That was the first stage in the Padres' redemption. The second stage came when Ray Kroc, who had built the McDonald's hamburger chain, bought the club.

As an owner, Kroc has often reacted as a fan. In his first year as owner, he was so displeased by what was happening in one game that he got on the public address system and apologized to the fans, berating the players in the process. At other times, he has criticized his players as being pampered and overpaid, accusations with which most fans would agree.

But Kroc pumped life into a moribund franchise, spending money for free agents Rollie Fingers and Gene Tenace in his most dramatic move, and attendance has been well over one million every year since he bought the club.

The Padres have had their moments. The most spectacular came on August 1, 1972, when Nate Colbert hit five home runs in a doubleheader against Atlanta, driving in 13 runs and collecting 22 total bases. The first mark tied a major league record, the second and third broke major league records for a doubleheader.

Ironically, Colbert had watched Stan Musial hit five home runs and collect 21 total bases in a doubleheader in St. Louis 18 years before, when Nate was only eight. "I never thought anyone would equal that record," he said.

Randy Jones became the first Padre to win a top league prize when he won the Cy Young Award in 1976. He was 22–14 with an ERA of 2.74; the year before, he had been 20–12 with a 2.24 ERA.

Jones confounded the hitters with a succession of slow and slower pitches; his "fastball" was timed at a mere 76 mph. But he had great control, tying Christy Mathewson's National League record of 68 straight innings without a walk in 1976.

Unfortunately, Jones had to have arm surgery after the 1976 season, and he has not been the same pitcher since. But even without Jones, the Padres were an improved team, as was Montreal.

More important for the league, all the expansion clubs were finally on a firm financial footing, and the league's future seemed even brighter because of that.

The well-traveled Dick Allen was one of the leading hitters in the National League in the sixties and seventies.
(Paul H. Roedig photo)

Nate Colbert set or tied
National League records with
five home runs, 13 RBIs,
and 22 total bases in a 1972
doubleheader.
(San Diego Padres photo)

Randy Jones was a Cy Young
Award winner for the expansion
San Diego Padres at a time
when the Padre fans had little
else to cheer about.
(San Diego Padres photo)

27. The Year of the Pitcher

In the point and counterpoint of National League history, the years of 1930 and 1968 are inextricably linked. The first was the Year of the Hitter, the second the Year of the Pitcher, and the statistics are so diametrically opposed that it is hard to believe the same game was being played.

In 1930, for instance, the Philadelphia Phillies finished last but had five .300 hitters; in 1968, there were only five .300 hitters in the entire league. In 1930, the best team earned run average (Brooklyn) was 4.03; in 1968, the worst team ERA (Cincinnati) was 3.56, and there were six teams under three runs.

For the National League hitters, 1968 was a year of torment. Henry Aaron (.287), Willie Mays (.289), Frank Robinson (.268) and Roberto Clemente (.291) all hit below .300, and they were the finest hitters in the game.

For connoisseurs of pitching duels, 1968 was the year; there were 185 shutouts in the 810 games played, more than one-fifth of the total. Gaylord Perry and Ray Washburn combined to throw no-hitters in successive games, which had never been done in major league history. (Ironically, Jim Maloney and Don Wilson repeated that feat the next year.)

Even mediocre pitchers were impressive in 1968, and the quality pitchers were untouchable. Juan Marichal won 26 games and pitched 30 complete games, but he was overshadowed by Bob Gibson and Don Drysdale, who set major league records.

Gibson was unquestionably the top performer of the year. He won 22 games, 13 of them shutouts, led the league with 268 strikeouts, and had an earned run average of 1.12.

Since 1912, when earned run averages were first kept, no National Leaguer had ever done that—not even the stars of the dead-ball era, Christy Mathewson and Grover Cleveland Alexander. Gibson's ERA was also a major league record for those who had pitched at least 300 innings.

Gibson's statistics that year bordered on the unbelievable. He started 34 games and completed 28, and he was never knocked out; he was lifted for a pinch hitter in the six games he failed to complete. He yielded only 198 hits in 305 innings, an average of less than six hits a game. And he capped his year by striking out a record 17 hitters in the first game of the World Series.

That Gibson should have been the top pitcher of the year was no surprise. He and Marichal were the best right-handed pitchers of their era, and he and Drysdale were the most feared, because of fastballs which sometimes went through the batter's box instead of across the plate.

Gibson was a fine all-round athlete who had been a basketball player before turning to baseball, and he was a much better hitter than the average pitcher, managing a .303 average one season, 1970. He was also a courageous man. The year before, a line drive had broken his leg, and he completed the inning!

His chief weapon was a fearsome fastball that eventually led him to a National League career record of 3,117 strikeouts. Lack of direction on that fastball handicapped him his first two years, but by 1961 he had enough control of the pitch to win 13 games, starting a run of 14 straight seasons in which he won more than ten games.

Gibson won 251 games in his career and had five seasons in which he won 20 games or more, but none matched his great 1968 showing. His 13

The hard-throwing Bob Gibson baffled National League hitters during his great 1968 season— and before and after, as well. *(George Brace photo)*

shutouts that year were more than he recorded in any other two seasons combined. His ERA was more than a run lower than his second best. His hit-per-inning ration was easily the best of his career, and his 28 complete games were a career high, too.

Drysdale and Gibson were both 32 in 1968, but whereas Gibson was in his pitching prime, Drysdale—who had come to the majors when he was only 19—was in the twilight of his career. It didn't seem that way in '68, when he won 14 games and had the lowest ERA (2.15) of his career, but he pitched in only 12 games in 1969 and was out of baseball by 1970.

That unusual year gave Drysdale one last chance for glory, and he made the most of it. The legendary sidearm fastball that sometimes seemed to be coming from third base had lost some of its zip, but Drysdale was able to compensate with guile. He threw eight shutouts and set two major league records—six straight shutouts and 58⅔ consecutive scoreless innings.

There should, however, be a parenthetical note attached to both records: "Accomplished with the aid of an umpire." An unusual call by plate umpire Harry Wendelstedt kept Drysdale's streak alive before he had broken either record.

It happened, fittingly, in a game between those great rivals, the Dodgers and Giants. On May 31, 1968, in Los Angeles, the Dodgers were leading, 3–0, but the Giants had the bases loaded in the ninth with nobody out.

With the count 2–2 on Dick Dietz, Drysdale threw an inside fastball that hit Dietz, who started to first base as the runner on third trotted home. But Wendelstedt ruled that Dietz had not made a reasonable effort to avoid the pitch, and it was therefore only ball three.

"It was a gutsy call," said Dodger catcher Jeff Torborg. Charles S. ("Chub") Feeney, then the Giants' vice-president, disagreed. "It would have been gutsy if he had made it in San Francisco," said Feeney.

Giant manager Herman Franks, testy under the best of circumstances, protested loudly and long enough to get himself ejected, without changing the call, of course.

Dietz then popped up to short left field, not deep enough to score the runner from third, and Drysdale got the next two Giant hitters to preserve his shutout, tying the major league record set by Guy White of the Chicago White Sox in 1905.

The next time out, Drysdale broke White's record with his sixth straight shutout and Walter Johnson's mark of 56 straight scoreless innings, set in 1913. This time, Drysdale needed no help from an umpire.

The fiercely determined Gaylord Perry
threw the first of two consecutive
no-hitters at Candlestick Park
in 1968. Ray Washburn of the
St. Louis Cardinals notched the
second. *(San Francisco Giants photo)*

The Candlestick Park scoreboard
announces Perry's feat.
(San Francisco Giants photo)

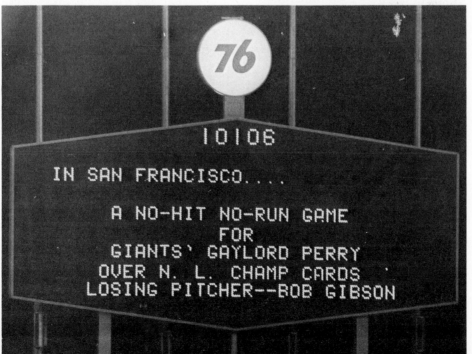

History of another sort was made by Perry and Washburn in their back-to-back no-hitters at Candlestick Park, the first of their careers for both men; 1968 was like that.

Perry had pitched brilliantly that season, throwing two two-hitters and two three-hitters and missing a perfect game by the margin of one hop against the Chicago Cubs on August 26. In the seventh inning of that game, Glenn Beckert had hit a bouncer through the middle that just eluded Giant shortstop Hal Lanier and second baseman Ron Hunt. Beckert was the only base runner for Chicago in a game in which Perry threw only 75 pitches, and only 22 of those balls.

Despite his brilliance, Perry was only 14–14 when he took the mound against the Cardinals the night of September 17. Like everyone else, the usually hard-hitting Giants were having a great deal of trouble scoring. It didn't help Perry's disposition any to learn that he had to face the overpowering Gibson. Pitching coach Larry Jansen told Perry, "If you shut out the Cardinals, you might get a draw."

Jansen's wry prediction was almost dead-on. Hunt hit a first-inning home run for the Giants, and that was the only run of the game. Perry walked two batters, but that was it for the Cards; Gaylord ended the game by striking out Curt Flood.

The no-hitter was only the second at Candlestick Park—the first was Marichal's in 1963—but the third came less than 24 hours later, when Washburn no-hit the Giants in an afternoon game.

Washburn struggled much more than Perry had the night before, walking five batters and throwing 138 pitches, but the Giants didn't come close to a base hit. He faced the heart of the Giants' batting order in the ninth—Hunt, Willie Mays, and Willie McCovey—but had a 1-2-3 inning and preserved his no-hitter.

As Washburn came into the clubhouse, he saw Perry, "I was watching you last night," he said.

"So I noticed," replied Perry.

Not surprisingly, National League attendance fell to a five-year low in 1968; most fans pay to see hitting, not pitching. The next year, the pitching mound was lowered, the ball was juiced up, and batting averages went up again. So did attendance.

Overall, league attendance was up 3.3 million (about 1.8 million of that because of the expansion clubs, Montreal and San Diego). Club officials breathed a sigh of relief. The Year of the Pitcher was only a bad memory.

28. Snag a Bag: The Rise of the Base Burglars

One spring day in 1962, Los Angeles Dodgers manager Walter Alston had a conversation with his shortstop, Maury Wills, which would make Wills a star and revolutionize baseball.

Alston was a man of few words, and he didn't waste any that day. He just told Wills that he could try to steal a base any time he wanted, instead of waiting for a sign.

Base stealing lost much of its appeal with the advent of the lively ball. A few runners such as Max Carey, whose careers had started in the dead ball era, still stole bases frequently, but managers discouraged others from doing it. The big inning was the way the game was played, and you didn't have big innings if runners got thrown out trying to steal. The idea was to hold your base until somebody hit the ball up against the fence, or over it.

Carey set a National League record with 738 stolen bases in his career, and that mark lasted for nearly five decades after his retirement in 1929. He stole as many as 63 bases in a season during the dead ball era and had three seasons of more than 50 stolen bases in the twenties. But the last time he did that, with 51 stolen bases in 1923, was the last time a National Leaguer topped 50 for almost forty years.

More often than not, the stolen base leader in the National League in that interim period stole fewer than 30 bases. Three times in that stretch, the leader didn't exceed 20. The low point was reached when Stan Hack led the league with 16 in 1938 and tied Lee Handley with 17 in 1939.

Even the best runners were cautious. Jackie Robinson, for instance, was the most feared runner of his baseball generation, but Robinson used his ability more as a psychological weapon than anything else. He would dance off base, daring the pitcher to throw his way.

In fact, Robinson did not often try to steal. On the average, he only attempted a steal once every 3 or 4 games during his career. His season high was 37 steals, and that was the only time he stole more than 30. In his ten-year career he stole only 197 bases. Obviously, he could have stolen far more if he—and his managers—had been so inclined, but with the Dodgers' home run potential, base-stealing was considered an unnecessary risk.

There were some definite rules for even the best base stealers. One was that you didn't embarrass the other team by stealing if your team was far ahead, though baseball is a game where no lead is ever totally safe.

This was the atmosphere when Wills came to the majors in 1959. He seemed an unlikely revolutionary; he seemed, in fact, an unlikely major leaguer. He was five foot eleven and 170 pounds but appeared smaller, and his only recommendation was a good glove.

Wills had bounced around the minor leagues for more than eight years, starting in 1951 as a second baseman. Before the 1959 season, the Dodgers sold him conditionally to the Detroit Tigers, but the Tigers returned him after taking a look in spring training. The Dodgers then sent Wills back to Spokane for his ninth minor league season.

But the Dodgers had serious shortstop problems in '59. The great Pee Wee Reese had retired after one anticlimactic season in Los Angeles. Don Zimmer, at one time considered a potentially outstanding shortstop, fell into a slump at the beginning of the year and the Dodgers next tried Bob Lillis, who wasn't the answer, either.

Meanwhile, Wills was having the best year of his career at Spokane, hitting over .300 and fielding brilliantly. In mid-season 1958, Spokane manager Bobby Bragan had turned the right-handed hitting Wills into a switch-hitter, and the change made Wills much more dangerous. With his speed, he was able to leg out more hits from the left side of the plate, and he also eliminated his weakness against a right hander's curve.

The Dodgers brought him up in mid-June, when he was nearly 27, old for a player getting his first good shot at the major leagues. The eternally skeptical Los Angeles sportswriters were sure the Dodgers had made a mistake, particularly when Wills failed to get a hit in his first 12 times at bat.

Alston wasn't sold on Wills, either. He benched Maury after his weak start, and Wills was in and out of the lineup for a time. Finally, Alston made Wills the regular shortstop because of his glove, and Wills responded by bringing his batting average up to .260. The Dodgers won the pennant, sweeping a playoff series with Milwaukee, and Wills went on to play well in the World Series, which the Dodgers also won.

Stolen bases? Wills had all of seven in 83 games. The next two years he led the league with 50 (highest since Carey's 51 in 1923) and 35, but that was only a warm-up.

In those years, the Dodgers were playing in the Los Angeles Coliseum, a

Maury Wills started a
base-stealing revolution
when he set a record with
104 stolen bases in 1962.
Los Angeles Dodgers photo)

stadium that had been built for the 1932 Olympics, not for baseball. The configuration of the Coliseum forced a very uneven layout, practically an overnight trip to the right-field fence but only the minimum 250 feet down the left-field line, where a huge screen was erected.

What followed might have been fun, but it was hardly baseball for the connoisseur. Batters regularly hit pop flies that went over or off that fence. The Dodgers' Wally Moon, a left-handed hitter, even worked out an inside-out swing, much like a golf swing, that enabled him to pop balls over that fence. In that stadium, the Dodgers had to go for the big inning. Wills's base stealing was only an irritant to the other teams, not an important part of the Dodger offense.

In 1962, all that changed when the team moved into Dodger Stadium. The new park, with its 330-foot foul lines and 375-foot power alleys in right and left center, made it possible to play a balanced game. Baserunning became important again.

"We didn't have a lot of power that year," remembers Wills, "except for Frank Howard (who hit 31 home runs). Moon couldn't hit balls over the left-field wall any more, and Tommy Davis was primarily a line drive hitter."

Turned loose, Wills changed the game. He stole 104 bases, won the Most Valuable Player award, and almost stole the pennant for the Dodgers, who lost to the Giants in a postseason play-off.

Other teams tried everything to stop Wills. The most radical technique was that used by Giant manager Alvin Dark. Before a play-off game at Candlestick Park, Dark had grounds keeper Matty Schwab water the area around first so thoroughly that Wills would have had to use the Australian crawl to reach second. Umpires ordered extra dirt on the basepaths to dry them out, and Dark earned the nickname of "Swamp Fox."

Wills demoralized other teams. "Speed is the greatest weapon in baseball," he says, "Good pitchers can always stop good hitters, but nobody can stop speed. It causes a change in everybody's game. A pitcher changes the tempo he's worked on for years. Infielders tighten up. Outfielders are pressured into hurrying their throws."

Wills turned his base stealing into a tactical weapon around which an offense could be generated. The weapon was good at any time.

"Walter Alston used to come to me in the ninth inning and ask me if I thought I could steal on the pitcher, because he trusted my judgment," says Wills. "If I told him I could, he'd say, 'All right, then, we won't bunt you down. We'll let you steal second and bunt you to third.

"That was a tremendous compliment to me, but he knew I wouldn't take an unnecessary chance in that situation. I might feel, for instance, that with most pitchers, I had an 80–85 percent chance of stealing. If there was a particular pitcher in the game with a good enough move to cut my chances to 75 per cent, I wouldn't go. That wasn't enough of an edge in that situation."

Alston, in fact, always respected Wills's judgment. "He never criticized me if I tried to steal and got thrown out," says Maury.

Wills also had the benefit of having Jim Gilliam hitting behind him. Gilliam always took a couple of pitches to give Wills a chance to run. Maury learned how different it could be without that kind of help when he was traded to Pittsburgh. "Many times I had a base stolen, but the hitter fouled off a pitch over his head," says Wills in disgust.

Wills's technique was a daring one. He always took the maximum lead. "Everybody says baseball is a game of inches," he says. "If I could take six inches more lead than somebody else, I had that much more of a chance to steal."

Pitchers continually drove him back to the base—"as many as 15 throws in a row," says Wills—and some thought his continual dives back into first wore him down. He denies that.

"My knees took a pounding for a while," he says, "but then I got knee pads." He couldn't have been slowed down too much; he had back-to-back years of 52 and 40 steals when he was 36 and 37. Ty Cobb had only nine and nine again at that stage of his career.

It was the little things that made a difference for Wills. "I always took my lead from the back side of the bag, not the front side," he says, "because the first baseman had that much further to swipe with his glove. I always slid for the outside of second base, for the same reason. And I was always a good slider, so I gave myself every chance to get in under the throw."

Wills was always alert. When he was on first, as soon as he saw that the pitch was in the catcher's glover he took two hard steps back to first. "That way, if the catcher decided to throw down, my momentum was going back to the base and he couldn't pick me off."

Wills regards base stealing as a mental game played with the pitchers and catchers. "The important thing is not to worry about being embarrassed. You have to wipe out all thoughts of failing out of your mind. You have to make up your mind to be decisive, whether you're right or wrong. You can't play it safe when you're trying to steal.

"And if you get picked off or thrown out, you have to go right back the next time and challenge the pitcher. It's like getting thrown off a horse; you have to get right back on."

Wills's success inevitably spawned imitators, and two who came later surpassed him: Joe Morgan, who holds the National League record for percentage of successful stolen bases, and Lou Brock, who holds the major league records for career and season stolen bases.

Morgan is the most complete player of the three. He does everything well. In 1978, he set a major league record for most consecutive errorless games, 90, and the year before he committed only five errors all season, the lowest in the National League's history.

He hits for a good average, twice going over .300 and around .280 for his major league career. He hits with surprising power for his size (five foot seven, 165 pounds), as many as 27 home runs in a season. Morgan both knocks in runs, as many as 111 in a season, and scores them, as many as 122. He seldom swings at a bad pitch, and he usually gets more than 100 walks in a season.

In 1975 and '76, Morgan won back-to-back Most Valuable Player awards, only the second National Leaguer to do that; Ernie Banks was the first. Teammate George Foster was the MVP in '77, which didn't surprise Morgan, who had said even before the season started that he didn't expect to win a third straight MVP award.

"The pitchers simply won't let you win three in a row," he said. "They try to pitch you so you won't be the one to knock in a run. They'll try for a perfect pitch or they'll walk you. They don't care. For a while, I started trying to get base hits on balls out of the strike zone, but that's not the way Joe Morgan hits."

Early in his career, with Houston, Morgan was just an average ballplayer, a good fielding second baseman but not particularly distinguished in any aspect of his offensive play. Then he tore up a knee in 1968 and missed all but ten games of the season. That gave him time to think about what he should be doing, and the one aspect of the game that he gave the most thought to was base stealing. He did not become the all-round hitter he is now until he went to Cincinnati in 1972, but he became a good base stealer as soon as he returned to the Houston lineup in '69.

"I looked around at the parks that were being built," he says, "and I saw how big they all were. I knew that base stealing was going to be much more important to teams, so I really started studying the pitchers. Nobody ever taught me anything about stealing bases, so I had to teach myself."

He had a good teacher. Before '69, Morgan had never stolen more than 29 bases in a major league season. That year, he stole 49, starting a decade-long string in which he stole at least 40 bases a season. Twice, he stole 67.

Morgan studies pitchers so he knows exactly what they will do when he is on base. When a pitcher comes into the league for the first time, Morgan watches him warming up before the game. "That's when he's going to be trying to get into his rhythm," says Joe.

His base-stealing style is the same as Wills's. He takes a long lead, daring the pitcher to drive him back. "Most guys won't take a lead like that because they're afraid they'll get picked off," says Morgan. "You can't think like that. If I get picked off, the next time I'm going to be out there with just as big a lead, going for the steal again."

Sometimes, even before the pitcher starts his motion, Morgan has started for second, as fast as a sprinter out of the blocks. "A lot of guys, like Lou Brock, are faster than I am, but I can get to second base as fast as they can because I take a big lead, get a good jump, and I'm at full speed in two steps instead of five or six."

Because he plays on a team with power hitters like Johnny Bench and Foster, Morgan doesn't try to steal as often as Wills did, but he usually makes it when he goes. "One of the things I'm proudest of," he says, "is my percentage. I believe I should steal at least four out of five times.

Nothing—and nobody—bothers Morgan in his pursuit of stolen bases.

Left-handed pitchers? "They're easy to steal against because everything they do is right out in front of you. They've always got some giveaway. Like, Steve Carlton lifts his foot slower if he's coming to first base."

Good pitchers? "It's easier to steal against good pitchers. Like Tom Seaver. When Seaver was with the Mets, he was easy for me to steal against. Good pitchers are good because they do everything the same all the time. They get into a rhythm. Well, once you spot that rhythm, the rest is easy."

Good catchers? "If a team has a catcher I consider a better than average thrower, the only difference it makes is that I won't go if I don't get just the right jump. But no catcher can stop me if I get the right jump. When I was with Houston, I had no trouble stealing against Bench, and he was the best-throwing catcher in baseball."

Joe Morgan won back-to-back Most Valuable Player awards in 1975 and 1976, and the Cincinnati Reds won back-to-back World Series. *(Copyright Cincinnati Reds, Inc., 1978)*

Pitchouts? "Pitchers usually give them away because they throw with a slightly different motion. If the catcher calls a pitchout on the first pitch and I don't go, well, then, I've really got them because if he tries to call another, the pitcher is going to say, 'Oh, no, I'm not going to be 2–0 on the hitter.'"

As you've read from the comments made by Wills and Morgan, it takes a special kind of player to be a base stealer. The physical ability is necessary, of course, but beyond that, what's needed is a mental toughness approaching arrogance, and a desire to challenge pitchers and catchers. Certainly, that's true, too, of Lou Brock, the all-time champion base stealer.

"You're doing something that is an option," he says. "For me, that's always made it an enjoyable challenge. I don't have to steal bases, you see, to play. I steal bases because I want to."

As with Wills and Morgan, there was nothing in Brock's early major league career to indicate that he would become a prodigious base stealer. Indeed, most of his early career, with the Chicago Cubs, was marked by frustration. The Cubs were frustrated because Brock was not living up to his potential; Brock was frustrated because the Cubs seemed to expect too much.

As a rookie, Brock hit .263 for the Cubs, stole 16 bases, and scored 73 runs. It was hardly a great season, but it was acceptable for a rookie, except that his rookie season was Brock's best as a Cub.

The next year, Brock hit .258. Swinging for the fences, he hit only nine home runs and struck out 122 times. His speed helped him steal 24 bases, but he was a liability in the outfield. When he hit only .251 for the first 52 games of the 1964 season, the Cubs traded him with pitchers Jack Spring and Paul Toth to the Cubs for pitchers Ernie Broglio and Bobby Shantz and outfielder Doug Clemens. Brock and Broglio were the key men; the other players were marginal, on both sides.

The trade was one of the most lopsided in baseball history. Broglio, who had won 21 games in 1960 and 18 as recently as 1963, had nothing left; he won only seven games for the Cubs in 2½ years and retired after the 1966 season.

Meanwhile, Brock became an instant star for the Cardinals. He hit .348 for St. Louis in 103 games, finishing at .315 overall, and stole 33 bases; counting the ten he had stolen for the Cubs, he had 43 for the season. The Cards won the pennant, which they couldn't have done without Brock, and Lou went on to bat .300 in the World Series, which the Cardinals also won.

In St. Louis as in Chicago, Brock remained a free swinger. He has struck out more than 100 times in six separate seasons in St. Louis, with a high of

134, very high figures for a man who has only once hit more than 16 homers in a season (21 in 1967).

But every other phase of his game improved dramatically in St. Louis. His lifetime batting average as a Cardinal has hovered around the .300 mark; he has hit with substantially more power; his fielding has improved; and of course, he became an outstanding base stealer. In 1965 he stole 63 bases, starting a string of 11 consecutive years in which he stole at least 51 bases; seven times in that stretch he stole more than 60 bases.

Those numbers are all the more impressive because Brock reduced his total stealing opportunities by hitting regularly for extra bases. In 1968, for instance, he had 46 doubles and 14 triples (both league-leading figures) and still managed to steal 62 bases.

Brock's style is very different from Wills's and Morgan's, because he doesn't believe in taking a big lead. "Willie McCovey taught me that," he says, wryly. "One time at Candlestick, I took a long lead and got chased back. McCovey tagged me on the back of my head, and I saw stars for a couple of innings after that. That can happen with other first basemen, too. They're all 220-pounders, and they all tag hard. That's what wears a base stealer out, the constant diving back to the base."

His great speed enabled him to take a short lead and go when it was unexpected. He talks almost mystically of baserunning as an art and turning sight into sound, but what he means is not at all mysterious: There is a split second when the pitcher and catcher do not know he is going, until they are alerted by a yell. By then, it's usually too late.

Brock is deep into the psychological implications of stealing. "A lot of players are afraid to steal bases, because they're afraid of getting caught. Instead of being upset because they've been caught, they should be thinking, 'The next five or six times I won't be caught.'

"But players are afraid of being embarrassed. That's why so few ever play to their potential. They feel naked when they make a mistake out there, so they'll do a lot of things to keep from making a mistake. That's why so few players even try to steal. They know they won't be criticized unless they try and fail."

If you take him at his word, Brock doesn't prepare as thoroughly as Wills and Morgan, though it's easy to believe that he works harder at his craft than he is prepared to admit.

"There are no more than about four different types of moves," he says, "so when you learn those, you know it all. There are things that give away any pitcher's move."

Because he was speaking during the 1978 season, Brock wouldn't go beyond generalities. "I'm not going to talk about the giveaways until I'm through playing; there's no sense giving away secrets.

"I don't have to study a pitcher for a long time to know what he's going to do, because I know the basic moves. That's why you'll hear a pitcher say, 'Brock never saw me pitch before, but he stole on the first pitch I threw with him on base.' I already knew his move, even though he didn't realize it."

It says something about Brock's character that he had his best year, and the best year any base stealer ever had, at age 35, when he should have been slowing up. He stole 118 bases, which is one of those figures that is so incredible it is hard to comprehend. That was 48 more than he had stolen the year before, 44 more than his previous best, 14 more than Wills had in his best year, 22 more than the legendary Cobb's best.

"I did it because it was a challenge," he says. "You can look at a challenge as hard work, or you can look at it as fun. I prefer to look at it as fun. The book says you can't steal like that at 35; so I did it, just to go against the book."

That year was one long triumphal march for Brock, who was named "Man of the Year" by the *Sporting News* and "Player of the Year" by both the *Sporting News* and *Baseball Digest.*

He reached high gear during a nine-day home stand, September 2–10, when he broke Wills's record for the Cardinal fans, including a group in the left field stands called the "Brock Base Burglars."

He reached 103 against the New York Mets on September 8. On September 10, against the Phillies, he singled in the first inning off Dick Ruthven. After a strike to Ron Hunt, Brock stole second. That tied Wills's mark and broke Carey's league career record simultaneously.

In the seventh inning, Brock singled again. Again he waited for a strike to Hunt and took off for second, sliding in safely with No. 105 and a new major league record.

On September 17, against the Pirates in Pittsburgh, he recorded his 109th steal, and reached second place on the all-time major league career list. Number 110 came the next day; Number 115 on the 23rd. His final theft came on September 29 in Chicago, enabling the Cards to tie a league record by leading the league in stolen bases 13 seasons.

The next two seasons, Brock had identical marks of 56 stolen bases, bringing his total to 865 before the 1977 season, just 27 short of Cobb's career record, which had seemed insurmountable a few years before.

Age was finally taking its toll on Brock, and he moved slowly toward

Cobb's record. He stole two bases against the Giants on August 25 to move within one of a tie, but was then blanked in a three-game series against the Dodgers.

On August 29, against the Padres in St. Louis, he walked in the first inning and stole second with Jerry Mumphrey at bat, going to third when catcher Dave Roberts threw the ball away.

In the seventh, with Randy Jones pitching, he reached first on a force-out and then stole second for Number 893. The game was stopped as he was mobbed by teammates, and Jones gave him the record base. When the Cardinals returned home, he was honored with a civic parade through downtown St. Louis.

Brock ended his campaign with an even 900 stolen bases, 35 during the '77 season, by stealing second in the eighth inning of the first game of a doubleheader against the Mets on September 30.

What next? Will Brock's records hold up as long as Cobb's did? Or will some young player who has learned the art by watching the great modern base thiefs break them? Nobody can tell, but Brock is certain he won't be forgotten: The National League has named its annual prize to the top base stealer the Lou Brock Award, the first time an active player has been so honored.

Lou Brock erased all the records
with his base-stealing spree
in the seventies
(*St. Louis Cardinal photo*)

29. A Flood Against *the Man*

Historians have long debated whether men shape events, or vice versa. Curt Flood is a good argument for the first theory. Flood was an excellent player, the best fielding center fielder in the National League at one time and a steady hitter, averaging .293 over 12 full seasons and 21 games spread over another three partial seasons. But that's not how he is remembered. Curt Flood is remembered as the man who challenged baseball's reserve clause. He didn't win and, as a matter of fact, the battle ended his career. But because he took his stand, the organizational structure of baseball and other professional sports were irrevocably changed.

In many ways, Flood was typical of the black players who have excelled in the National League since Jackie Robinson broke the color line. Born in Houston, Flood grew up in Oakland, California, where his family had moved when he was two. He lived in what he called a "typically squalid ghetto" in his book, *The Way It is,* and his athletic skills enabled him to break out of the ghetto.

Flood was a superb athlete in his youth. The Oakland-Alameda area produced such players as Frank Robinson, Joe Morgan, Vada Pinson, Tommy Harper and Willie Stargell. In his youth, Flood was considered better than any of them.

Flood played on the same American Legion team with Robinson and Pinson, and that team won championships. Baseball was the biggest part of his life, and it was not surprising that he signed to play professionally after he graduated from high school in 1956. Nor was it surprising that he signed with Cincinnati; Robinson had done that the year before.

He did not expect to go far at that point. George Powles, his American Legion coach, had talked to him before he signed and tried to prepare him for possible disappointment. Curt was small, five foot seven and 140 pounds, when he graduated from high school, and being black he would get no special favors. Flood himself thought at the time that the best he could hope for would be to play for the Oakland Oaks of the Triple-A Pacific Coast League.

The Reds started him out at High Point-Thomasville in the Class B

Carolina League. He had an excellent year, hitting .340, with 128 runs batted in and 29 homers; the first two figures led the league. He came up to the Reds for five games at the tail end of the season.

The next year, the Reds sent Flood to Savannah of the Class A South Atlantic League and had him playing third base; they thought he might be more valuable to them at that position in the future. Flood had a good year at Savannah, hitting .299 and making the league All-Star team, but two developments made him expendable as far as the Reds were concerned. The first was that Don Hoak, obtained in a trade before the 1957 season, had had an excellent year, and the Reds no longer thought they needed Flood as a third baseman.

The other development was more important. The Reds had signed Pinson the year after signing Flood, and they thought the bigger, faster Pinson had more potential than Flood. They traded Flood to the St. Louis Cardinals.

The Cardinals sent him to Omaha at the start of the 1958 season but quickly brought him up after he hit .340 in the first 15 games. He earned a starting spot with his fielding and hit .261, good enough for a rookie.

He had problems at the plate, however. Despite his lack of size, he had been a power hitter in American Legion ball, and the 29 home runs he had hit in his first minor league season had convinced him he could be a power hitter as a professional, too. He had developed a hitch in his swing, trying to hit everything out of the park. Finally, teammate George Crowe took him aside and explained what he was doing, so he could correct it.

Once he learned to concentrate on making contact, Flood became a good hitter for the Cardinals. In 1961 he started a string in which he hit better than .300 for six of eight seasons, with a high of .335 in 1967, when the Cardinals won the pennant and the World Series.

The Cardinal team of that era was a strong one, winning pennants in 1964, '67, and '68 and the World Series in the first two of those seasons. It was also an unusually close group of players. "We had a camaraderie you don't often see on teams," Flood says now. "I still miss that feeling."

Neither the camaraderie nor the success of the Cardinals was long-lived. The first break came when the favored Cards lost the 1968 World Series.

The Cards slipped back the next year, finishing fourth in their division. In the second half of the season, manager Red Schoendienst started playing two youngsters, first baseman Joe Hague and catcher Ted Simmons, batting them third and fifth.

That bothered Flood, especially since he knew that he would see fewer good pitches, batting ahead of Hague. He told Jack Herman of the *St. Louis*

Globe-Democrat that management had given up on the season. Herman wrote what Flood said, attributing it to an anonymous veteran. Cardinal general manager Bing Devine retaliated. "The only reason the regulars are complaining," he said, "is that they are afraid of losing their jobs."

It was obvious the Cardinals would make some trades after the season. Did Flood think he would be one of those traded? He can't answer that, even now.

"I think probably at the back of my mind, I realized that I might be traded," he says, "but no player ever really admits to himself that he's going to go. I had been with St. Louis for 12 years and I had had a good year, though not my best."

Curt Flood defied baseball and brought about a revolution when he challenged the reserve clause. *(St. Louis Cardinals photo)*

So, it came as a shock when he got a call on October 8, 1969, from Jim Toomey, Devine's assistant, informing him that he had been traded to Philadelphia with Tim McCarver, Joe Hoerner and Byron Browne for Richie Allen, Cookie Rojas and Jerry Johnson.

Now, Flood understands the trade. "The Cardinals wanted Allen, and I was the only player the Phillies really wanted," he says. At the time, though, his pride was stung. "I had given the Cardinals my best for 12 years. All my friends were in St. Louis. I felt I had been let down."

Up to that point, Flood's reaction was typical of most traded players, and the comments he made were not taken seriously. Even when he threatened to retire, few people paid much attention. He was, after all, making $90,000 a year (the Phillies offered him a contract that would have brought him more than $100,000) and he was still only 31, which meant he should have several more years to play. Who could turn his back on that kind of money?

Then, Flood decided to sue baseball. His grounds: Baseball's reserve clause was illegal.

Baseball's reserve clause was unique in professional sports. In other sports, players were signed to contracts that included an option year beyond the length of the contract. A player could thus play out his option year (at a cut in pay) and become a free agent. In baseball, though, the reserve clause bound a player to a team for life.

"I just decided that there comes a time in a man's life when he should have some say in where he goes to work," says Flood. "In any other business, a man wouldn't just be sent off to another city without even talking to him. I had no gripe with the Phillies. They were very generous in their offer to me. I just didn't want to go to Philadelphia. It was a selfish thing, really."

Baseball, of course, is not just another business. Unlike other enterprises, it depends on balance. If one team dominates a league, it hurts every club, because attendance declines everywhere. Owners have always feared that one club might get all the best talent if players were free to go wherever they chose.

And baseball is not even like other sports. Football and basketball, for instance, get their players from the colleges; the only significant labor expense they have is what they pay their players while they are playing. In contrast, baseball has had a minor league system for player development; few players go directly from a college team to the majors. A team has an investment in its players before they ever appear in a major league game.

The question has been: How do you balance the need for relatively equal competition and the club's need for a return on its investment in players with the players' desire to have some voice in where they play? The answer to that question is different since Flood filed his suit.

Flood's first move, once he thought of suing, was to talk to Marvin Miller, the head of the Players' Association. Then, Curt talked to the Executive Board (players) of the association, before Miller put him in touch with Arthur Goldberg, former associate justice of the Supreme Court. Goldberg agreed to argue his case.

The suit first came up in Federal court in New York, before Judge Irving Ben Cooper. Former players Hank Greenberg and Jackie Robinson testified on Flood's behalf, as did Bill Veeck, at that time out of baseball, though he returned later as owner of the Chicago White Sox.

Robinson said, "We need men of integrity like Curt Flood and Bill Russell, who are involved in the area of civil rights, and who are not willing to sit back and let Mr. Charlie dictate their needs and wants for them. . . ."

Outside of court, players and former players were divided in their views. Robin Roberts said he felt going to court was the wrong way to attack the problem. Carl Yastrzemski said the association's executive board should not have supported Flood's suit without calling for a referendum of players. Willie Mays said he wouldn't object to being traded (as, indeed, he was little more than two years later) if his salary were high enough.

Meanwhile, though, such players as Ed Kranepool, Bob Gibson, Dal Maxvill, Lou Brock and Richie Allen supported Flood. Kranepool called Yastrzemski a "yo-yo for the owners."

The trial went on into the 1970 season, and Flood left the country for Copenhagen. Finally, on August 12, 1970, Judge Cooper denied Flood's bid for an injunction and for damages in the $4.1 million antitrust suit. He upheld the reserve clause and suggested that any change should be made through player-owner negotiations.

Judge Cooper noted, in a 47-page decision, that the effect of the reserve clause was to deny a player career freedom, but he was more impressed with management's argument that it was needed to maintain balanced competition and fan interest.

"Clearly the preponderance of credible proof does not favor elimination of the reserve clause," he wrote. He suggested that "arbitration or negotiation" might modify the system.

Judge Cooper's decision was upheld by a Court of Appeals on April 7, 1971, and by the U.S. Supreme Court on June 19, 1971.

Meanwhile, Flood was back in baseball, albeit briefly. Bob Short, then owner of the Washington Senators, traded for the rights to Flood and persuaded him to return, for a salary of $110,000. Flood, assured his return would not jeopardize his case, came back, but played in only 13 games, getting seven hits in 35 at-bats, and retired for good. "I had laid out a year and it was really hard coming back," says Flood. "Plus, my mind was all screwed up."

But baseball's legal troubles were just beginning. In 1972, a player strike delayed the opening of the season by ten days. In 1973, another strike was narrowly averted, and players won two important concessions: (1) A player with ten years' major league experience, the last five with the same club, could not be traded without his consent. (2) Owners agreed to outside arbitration in salary disputes. And in 1975, pitchers Andy Messersmith of the Los Angeles Dodgers and Dave McNally of the Montreal Expos followed Flood's lead and attacked the reserve clause.

Instead of going to court, Messersmith and McNally went to the three-man arbitration board—Miller, John Gaherin, the owners' representative, and impartial arbitrator Peter M. Seitz—that had been established to handle player-club disputes.

Messersmith and McNally had both refused to sign new contracts and claimed they were free agents. The baseball argument was what it had always been: The reserve clause bound a player to a club for the length of his career.

As expected, Miller sided with the players and Gaherin with the owners. Not as expected, though, Seitz broke the tie by ruling there was nothing that "explicitly, expresses agreement that the player's contract can be renewed for any period beyond the first year." Messersmith and McNally were free agents, and the reserve clause was no more than a one-year option.

Seitz' ruling was sharply criticized by commissioner Bowie Kuhn. Many baseball executives felt it would ruin the game. It has not, of course, though it has certainly changed it radically.

Players have more freedom than ever before. An agreement between the owners and the Players' Association, reached before the 1976 season, provides that players with six years' major league experience can declare themselves free agents, if they are not under contract beyond that time.

Several players have taken advantage of the free agent provision and have gone to other clubs; Messersmith, in fact, has done it twice. Some of the contracts the free agents have received have been incredibly lucrative.

Yet, the new order had surprisingly little effect on the competition in the

National League in the first three years. Philadelphia, Los Angeles, Cincinnati and San Francisco did well with little or no help from free agents. The most active clubs, San Diego and Atlanta, did not become contenders.

Of the three players who created this situation, only Messersmith benefited financially, though he suffered professionally. After winning 39 games in two years before he became a free agent, he won only 15 in the next two years for Atlanta. He played out his option and went to the Yankees in '78, probably with the Braves' blessing. He has since been released by the Yankees.

McNally, once a fine pitcher, hurt his arm in 1975 and was only 3–6; no club wanted him when he became a free agent, and he retired.

Flood's case is the saddest. He advanced the players' cause, but only at his own expense. He used up most of his savings in his suit and threw away a chance for perhaps 3 or 4 years of six-figure contracts. The case left psychic scars that are still obvious. He is a high-strung man, reluctant to talk of his past. He finds it difficult to look even a friendly questioner in the eye.

After his abortive comeback with Washington, Flood returned to Copenhagen, leaving that city in the winter to go to Spain. He operated a bar on the island of Majorca for five years, and his only connection with baseball was through conversations with the American sailors who were frequent visitors at his establishment.

Then, in the fall of 1977, he returned to Oakland, so quietly that only family and friends knew he was back. "I had a good time in Majorca," he says, "and I recommend that kind of experience, living in a foreign land, to everybody. But the U.S.A. is the best country in the world, and Northern California is the best place to live. And I wanted to be back near my mother."

In 1978, he even got back into baseball, doing the color commentary for the Oakland A's radio broadcast. He welcomed the chance to get back into the game he still loves, though he found it odd at first. The players were almost all strangers to him; it had been seven years since his brief appearance with Washington, nine years since his last full season.

He hadn't even heard much from his old baseball friends in the interim. "But a lot of that is my own fault," he says. "I didn't do anything, either. There were times when I could have written a letter or a postcard, or sent off a Christmas card, and I didn't."

Would he do it all over again, knowing what he knows now? He says yes, but it doesn't really matter. What's done is done. Curt Flood's life will never be the same again, and neither will baseball.

Andy Messersmith carried Flood's challenge one step further, and was ruled a free agent when the reserve clause was declared void by arbiter Peter Seitz. *(Los Angeles Dodgers photo)*

Rollie Fingers was one of several players to capitalize on the free-agent market as he switched from Oakland to San Diego, where he continued as one of the game's best relievers. *(San Diego Padres photo)*

30. The Great Roberto

Roberto Clemente was many things. He was the first Latin to be elected to the Baseball Hall of Fame. He was Branch Rickey's last great discovery. He was once voted the National League's Most Valuable Player, and four times its batting champion. He was only the 11th man in major league history and seventh in the National League to get 3,000 hits.

He was a superb fielder, a fine base runner and a team leader. He could rise to the occasion; he hit .362 in the two World Series in which he participated, .414 in the second one—and the Pirates won both. He had the reputation of being a hypochondriac, but he played in almost constant pain from a bad back and bone chips in his elbow.

He felt certain that he did not get the publicity he deserved because the writers disliked him, and yet almost every baseball writer admired him extravagantly. He was a mass of contradictions, surly one moment, warm and generous the next. He was a sensitive man, always looking for a slight, real or imagined. He was so complex a man that Phil Musick, after covering Clemente and the Pittsburgh Pirates for the last four years of Clemente's career, could write a book entitled, *Who Was Roberto?* and wonder if he really knew Clemente.

From the start, Clemente's career was an unusual one. He was signed by the Brooklyn Dodgers and could have become a member of one of the finest outfields in league history, with Carl Furillo and Duke Snider. But a miscalculation on the part of the Dodgers and a "bonus baby" rule sent Clemente to the Pirates.

Clemente was signed by the Dodgers on February 19, 1954 to a minor league contract of $5,000 and a bonus of $10,000. The major league rule at the time provided that a player who was signed for more than $4,000 had to spend the year on the major league roster or be subject to draft by another club after one year in the minors. That was one of several rules that had been established to cut down on large bonuses to untried players.

The Dodgers did not have room on their roster for Clemente, so they sent him to Montreal, and Royals manager Max Macon was obviously instructed to keep Roberto under wraps. When Clemente was in a slump, he was kept

The moody Roberto Clemente was one of the best players in National League history before his tragic death. *(Pittsburgh Pirates photo)*

in the lineup. When he was hitting well, he was taken out. One day Clemente had three triples in a game, the next day he was benched. On at least two occasions, a pinch hitter was used for Clemente in the first inning!

"The idea was to make me look bad," he said later. "If I struck out, I stayed in there; if I played well, I was benched. Most of the season they used me as a pinch hitter or in second games of doubleheaders."

Predictably, Clemente's statistics were unimpressive that year, but the Dodgers' strategy failed. They couldn't hide him. A wise old scout named Clyde Sukeforth saw Clemente.

The Pirates were on their way that year to finishing last for the second straight year, which meant they would have the first pick in the draft of minor league players. Rickey sent Sukeforth to Montreal to scout Joe Black, the once-great Dodgers' relief pitcher who was attempting a comeback; Black would be eligible for the draft.

Sukeforth had seen Clemente bat a few times in early season games; so he had an appreciation for his offensive talents. On this particular July day, in Richmond, Virginia, Sukeforth arrived early enough to watch outfield practice. "He forgot all about old Joe Black," Black himself noted wryly.

"I saw Clemente throwing in the outfield . . . I couldn't take my eyes off him," said Sukeforth. Clemente didn't even play in the game that day, but it didn't matter. Sukeforth had seen enough. "Take care of our boy," he told Macon after the game, and the Pirates drafted Clemente that December.

Clemente did not burn up the league as a rookie with the Pirates. He hit only .255, but it didn't matter. In his second year, he settled into a groove, hitting .311. Clemente was a star from then on. On the day he died he was the team career leader in five categories and in the top three in six others, a considerable accomplishment for a team that has had players like Honus Wagner, Paul and Lloyd Waner, Pie Traynor, Ralph Kiner and Willie Stargell.

Nobody watching Clemente bat for the first time could have suspected he would be that kind of hitter. His form was terrible. When he swung, one part of his torso seemed to go in one direction, another part of him in the other. He almost always took the first pitch, but after that, he would swing at anything. Asked once what kind of pitch Clemente hit, Don Drysdale said, "Ball four."

But there are a lot of batters with perfect form who make outs with regularity. Many great hitters have been unorthodox, and Clemente's form worked for him.

One reason it did was that Clemente was a smart hitter, smarter than most people realized. When he first came up to the Pirates, he took a long look at spacious Forbes Field and decided that it would be folly to try to hit home runs there. From then on, he was a line drive hitter, though he hit a respectable 240 home runs during his career.

Much of hitting is mental, a psychological contest between hitter and pitcher, and Clemente realized that. When he first came to the club, teammates would snicker to see Roberto stretched out on a trainer's table before a game, seemingly asleep. In fact, he was going over in his mind what he was likely to see from the pitcher in the upcoming game, and how he would deal with it. Sometimes, long before a game, he would take his place in the batter's box, think about the pitches he expected to get and take imaginary swings.

Though he was not an authentic home run hitter, he would go for the long ball when the Pirates needed it. In 1966, when he won the Most Valuable Player award he felt he should have received years earlier, he was told by Pirate manager Harry Walker that the club needed more home runs from him. Clemente hit 29 that season, his career high, and knocked in 119 runs, also a career high.

But most of the time, he rapped a succession of line drives to all fields. There was literally no good way to pitch to Clemente because he hit every kind of pitch; and because he hit to all fields, no overshifted defense could be used against him.

Clemente made himself into a good fielder. He lacked the natural instincts of Willie Mays, but he compensated with long hours of practice. He had teammates throw the ball off the right field wall so he could practice grabbing it with his bare right hand.

He studied the hitters and his own pitchers. He would vary his position in the field depending on the hitter and what pitch was coming next. More often than not, then, he was in the right position to make the play, but if the batter managed to hit the ball to an unexpected spot, Clemente would chase the ball recklessly and dive for it if he had to. He always played that way—in a World Series game or a meaningless spring exhibition.

His arm was legendary. All around the league, baseball people talked of one of Clemente's throws as the best they had ever seen. No right fielder in league history had Clemente's combination of strength and accuracy. Runners never went from first to third on a single to right when Clemente was there, and he was so good at throwing behind runners who had taken too big a turn at first base that he once cut down even Willie Mays that way.

One Clemente play that everyone remembers came in a 1964 game against Houston, when Clemente beecame probably the first outfielder to field a bunt.

Houston had runners at first and second. Both the first and third basemen for the Pirates charged the plate, hoping to field the expected bunt. The shortstop covered third, the second baseman first.

But the bunt was popped into the air in the direction of second base, which had been vacated by the Pittsburgh infielders. Anticipating the bunt, Clemente had charged in and he grabbed the bouncing ball while it was still in the infield and threw to third to force the startled Houston base runner, Walter Bonds.

For all his greatness, Clemente felt that he did not get the attention he deserved, a complaint often echoed by his contemporary, Hank Aaron. In fact, Clemente got reams of adulation from the Pittsburgh media, but he got less than he deserved from the national media for two reasons: (1) The Pirates won only two pennants, widely spaced, during his career. (2) He did not play for New York or Los Angeles.

By the end of his career, though, Clemente was receiving all the attention he deserved. In 1971, he had an outstanding World Series, hitting .414 with two home runs (and another drive that hit perhaps two inches foul in the right-field seats in Pittsburgh). He also made two outstanding catches. If any proof were still needed that he was a great and unique player, he had supplied it.

In 1972, he reported to spring training only 118 hits away from the coveted 3,000-hit plateau. Though he was approaching his 38th birthday, it seemed the mark was within easy reach.

Publicly, Clemente downplayed the drive for number 3,000. "It means nothing," he said one day. "I am playing this season not because I have a chance at 3,000 hits. I am playing because I feel good."

With friends, he was more candid. He expressed fears that he might not play beyond 1972. When a Pirate charter plane nearly collided in midair with another plane, he told teammate Manny Sanguillen, "I have to get that hit this year. I might die."

The 3,000th hit did not come easily. Injuries and illness restricted Clemente to 102 games. At one point, his weight was down to 170, and he had to borrow Rennie Stennett's smaller uniform pants.

But, as always, he rose to the occasion. Finally healthy, he came roaring down the stretch, finishing with a .312 batting average. Hit number 2,999 came in Philadelphia, off Steve Carlton. It was the Pirates' last road game of

MEMBERS OF THE 3000 HIT CLUB:

ROBERTO CLEMENTE
TY COBB   STAN MUSIAL
IS SPEAKER   HONUS WAGNER   HANK AARON
DIE COLLINS   NAP LAJOIE   WILLIE MAYS
PAUL WANER   CAP ANSON

The Pittsburgh scoreboard announces Roberto Clemente's 3,000th hit. It would be his last. *(Pittsburgh Pirates photo)*

the season. He was then immediately removed from the lineup so the biggest hit of all could come at home.

Clemente went hitless against the Mets the first night home. The next night, Jon Matlack hung a curve ball, and Clemente knocked it into left center. Cheers from the 13,117 fans reverberated through the stands as Clemente stood at second base, doffing his cap in acknowledgment.

The Mets' Dave Schneck threw the ball in, and umpire Doug Harvey gave it to Clemente, who gave it to first-base coach Don Leppert to keep for him. The scoreboard named those who had 3,000 hits, with Clemente's name on top. His 3,000th was his last hit.

●

Roberto Clemente was more than just a great baseball player, and it is a measure of the man that he was killed because he was deeply committed to a cause.

Clemente had been named honorary chairman of a Puerto Rican committee to help the earthquake victims of Nicaragua in December 1972. He was not content with the title. He worked day and night to get supplies to the stricken country. Then, he got a distressing call from Anastasio Somoza, chief of state of Nicaragua. The city of Managua had no water, no electricity, and it was littered with corpses. Supplies were not being properly distributed, Clemente was told. He decided he would go to Managua to distribute the supplies himself.

The plane he was flying in to Nicaragua was an old DC-7 that had not been test-flown since new props had been installed on the inboard engines. It was overloaded by two tons.

Vera Clemente begged her husband not to go, but Roberto—who always feared air travel—was a fatalist. "When your time comes, it comes; if you are going to die, you will die," he said.

His time came that New Year's Eve. At 9:22 P.M., pilot Jerry Hill revved his four engines to the maximum, shoved the throttles up, and took off. One engine exploded almost as soon as the plane was airborne.

"I'm turning back," Hill radioed the San Juan control tower, but he never made it. There were three more explosions, and the plane fell into the Atlantic Ocean. There were no survivors.

A few days after Clemente's death, Joe Heiling, president of the Baseball Writers Association of America, called a meeting of several prominent writers to discuss the waiving of the five-year retirement period for election to the Hall of Fame. After the discussion, he sent out ballots to BBWAA members.

On March 20, at a dinner in New York, it was officially announced that Roberto Clemente had received 393 votes and would be enshrined in the Hall of Fame in August. Only 29 writers had voted against Clemente, because they feared a precedent was being set. Nobody denied that he belonged.

"He was a very special guy," said one of the electors. "It is not the Hall of Fame which will honor him; he will honor it."

31. Baaad Henry

On March 13, 1954, the Milwaukee Braves and New York Yankees were playing an exhibition game at the Yankees' spring home in St. Petersburg, Florida. Braves' outfielder Bobby Thomson hit a line drive into right-center, rounded first, and slid hard into second for a double. As he did, he broke his leg.

The break hurt the Braves almost as much as it did Thomson. In the off-season, Milwaukee had traded a young left-handed pitcher, Johnny Antonelli, to the New York Giants for Thomson. It was a calculated risk because Antonelli, who had been a big bonus baby for the Braves when he graduated from high school in 1948, seemed on the verge of becoming one of the league's top pitchers. But the Braves felt that Thomson, a good fielder and strong hitter who had averaged better than 25 home runs and 100 RBIs for the previous five seasons, would give them the extra power they needed to win the pennant.

When Thomson broke his leg, the Braves' pennant chances were gone. Milwaukee eventually finished third that year, and New York—with Antonelli winning 21 games—won the pennant. But that dark cloud held a tremendous silver lining for the Braves: Thomson's injury made room in the lineup for a young outfielder named Henry ("Hank") Aaron.

Nobody in the Milwaukee organization at the time doubted that Aaron would eventually find a place in the Braves' starting lineup. In about a season and a half in the minor leagues, he had already shown that he was a remarkable hitter, batting .336 in 87 games for Eau Claire of the Northern League in 1952 and .362, with 22 home runs and 125 RBIs, in 137 games for Jacksonville of the Sally League the following year.

But Aaron had played the infield in both towns, shortstop the first year, second base the second, and the Braves had seen enough of his play at those positions to know that he didn't have sufficient major leaguer defensive skills to play the infield. The plan was to convert Aaron to an outfielder in the Braves' spring training camp, and then give him a year of training at Toledo in the American Association. By 1955, he should be ready.

Thomson's injury changed that well-conceived plan. Aaron, who had been hitting over .400 in spring training, was put into the starting lineup and he stayed there for 23 seasons.

Aaron had a good rookie season but not a great one, hitting .280 with 13 home runs. That wasn't good enough to win Rookie of the Year honors; the award went to Wally Moon, who hit .304 for the Cardinals that year. But the next season, Aaron batted .314 with 27 home runs, giving the first indication of the kind of hitter he would be.

An even better indication was that baseball people were starting to make comparisons between Aaron and great National League hitters of the past.

Charley Grimm, Aaron's first manager with the Braves, laughed about Hank's free-swinging style. "Hank's strike zone is from the tip of his cap to the tops of his shoes," said Grimm. "I haven't seen the likes of him as a bad-ball hitter since Joe Medwick was in his prime."

Aaron himself said, "I make up my mind to swing at a pitch, I swing. I admit I ain't up there looking for no walks."

Fred Haney, who replaced Grimm as the Milwaukee manager early in the 1956 season, was not a man given to superlatives. He contented himself with saying that Aaron "is as good a natural hitter as I've seen."

But in 1957, even Haney was overcome. Aaron, winning the only Most Valuable Player award of his career, had the first of a series of remarkable years, leading the league in home runs (44), runs (118) and RBIs (132) and batting .322 as the Braves won their first pennant in Milwaukee.

"In the next couple of years they'll be talking about Hank the way they do about Rogers Hornsby," said Haney. "Hornsby's best power was to right center field. This kid's got just as much there and more to the other fields. He's one of those things that come along once in a lifetime for a manager."

Eventually, though, Aaron was to do some things that even the great Hornsby couldn't. Hornsby had better individual seasons, certainly, but nobody in National League history has ever maintained such a high level of hitting for as long a period of time as Aaron did.

Year after year, Henry Aaron was there, hitting home runs, knocking in runs, and usually hitting for average, too. He broke his leg in September of his rookie year (ironically, the same injury that Thomson had suffered in spring training), but he suffered no serious injuries for the rest of his career. Starting in 1955, he played in at least 140 games for 16 straight years, and in his 23-year career, he played in fewer than 120 games only twice.

His consistency was amazing. He had 20 straight years in which he hit at least 20 home runs, 18 straight in which he hit at least 20 doubles. In one 16-year period, he scored more than 100 runs 14 times, batted in more than 100 runs 11 times. In one 11-year period, he hit over .300 10 times, and he finished with a lifetime mark of .305. Three times he got more than 200 hits in a season, four more times, better than 190.

When his career finally ended, Henry Aaron held the major league records for home runs (755), total bases (6,856), RBIs (2,297), games (3,298), and at bats (12,364), as well as National League records for hits (3,771) and runs (2,174).

There was more to Aaron, of course, than just his hitting skills. He developed into a fine defensive outfielder, especially when he was moved to right field. He had deceptive speed and he was always a fine base runner. When the Braves decided to let him run more, he became an excellent base stealer. He had six seasons in which he stole at least 21 bases, and he reached his peak in 1963 when he became one of only three men in league history (Willie Mays and Bobby Bonds are the others) to steal at least 30 bases and hit at least 30 home runs in the same season; Hank's figures were 31 and 44.

Still, when people talk about Aaron, it is inevitably his hitting that dominates the discussion. One of his secrets was the way Aaron approached hitting. Pitchers often described Aaron's style as if he knew what pitch was coming. There was a reason for that.

"Suppose a pitcher has three good pitches—a fast ball, a curve, and a slider," he said. "What I do, after a lot of consideration and analyzing and studying, is to eliminate two of those pitches, since it's impossible against a good pitcher to keep all three possibilities on my mind at the plate."

When the pitch that Aaron was waiting for came, he was ready. It didn't always come on the first pitch or the second, but it usually came at least once during Aaron's time at bat.

Looking for a pitch and hitting it, of course, are two different matters. Aaron knew what to do with the pitch when it arrived. He would snap his bat and, usually, blast a line drive somewhere. Unlike most home run hitters, Aaron seldom hit long towering drives. Even his home runs were line drives. Players often said Hank's hits seemed to go just over the shortstop's glove and then kept rising until they went into the stands.

Aaron could do that because he had strong, supple wrists. Typically, he held back on his swing until the final moment.

And he did that right to the end of his career. Don Gullett told George Plimpton, researching his book, *One For the Record,* that, "When the batter gets older, his reflexes are supposed to slow down. Throw it by them! I could do that with Willie Mays when he was finishing. But Aaron . . . even if you think you have it by him, those great wrists of his flick it out of the catcher's mitt."

Gullett, it should be noted, had a fastball timed at 96 mph.

Besides his wrists, the one component of Aaron's style that always caused comment was his ability to relax. He could sleep anywhere at any time; even standing up, he joked. He strolled to the batting box with a style so foot-heavy that teammates nicknamed him "Snowshoes" when he first came to the Braves. Robin Roberts once cracked that it was impossible to fool Aaron because he fell asleep between pitches.

Hank's ability to relax and the seeming nonchalance made many people believe that Aaron was oblivious to what was happening around him, and that he wasn't very bright. There was a certain amount of racism involved in those opinions, too, because Aaron's rookie year was only seven years removed from the time Jackie Robinson broke the major league color line.

All sorts of stories sprang up around Aaron to support the uncomplimentary myth. When he hit a home run off Roberts in spring training, Hank was supposed to have been unaware that it was Roberts who was on the mound. When he was fined $50 by commissioner Ford Frick for reporting early in 1955, he supposedly said, "Who's Ford Frick?"

The truth is quite different. Aaron had been following baseball and dreaming of playing in the big leagues since he was 12; and he was well aware of Robin Roberts, the premier pitcher of the day. And not only did he know who Ford Frick was, he got the Braves to pay the fine for him, since they were the ones who had ordered him to report early.

When he first came up to the Braves, Aaron was only 20 and no doubt awed by his surroundings. Shy around reporters, he gave short answers to most questions. But shyness is not stupidity, and anyone who talked to Aaron later in his career knew that he is an intelligent man, aware of who he is and where he is going. By 1974, he was going directly after Babe Ruth's career home run record of 714.

That home run record was one of two career marks that seemed out of reach of modern players. (The other, Ty Cobb's mark of 892 stolen bases, was also finally broken by a National Leaguer, Lou Brock.)

Of the two records, Ruth's was easily the most revered because the home run is baseball's ultimate weapon and home run hitters are the game's biggest celebrities. "Home run hitters drive Cadillacs; singles hitters drive Fords," said Ralph Kiner, who hit very few singles.

The Babe's record was thought not only unreachable, it was thought

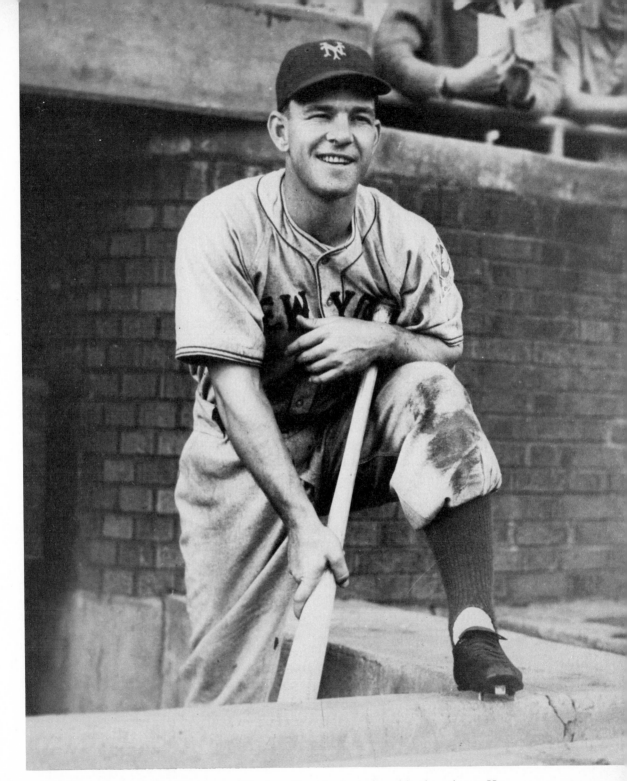

Mel Ott came up to the Giants as a 16-year-old and never played in the minors. He went on to set a National League home run record, since broken, and later managed the Giants. *(George Brace photo)*

unapproachable. Until the great black players came along in the National League, Mel Ott held the senior circuit record of 511, more than 200 under Ruth's magic total. In the American League, Jimmie Foxx was second to Ruth, 180 homers behind.

It seemed impossible that a hitter could ever match Ruth's combination of power and consistency. Some outstanding power hitters surfaced in the National League, but they couldn't sustain their efforts. Hack Wilson hit a league record 56 home runs in 1930 but had only 244 in his career. Kiner hit 54 and 51, but quit after only ten seasons with 369. Johnny Mize hit 51—the same year Kiner did, 1947—but finished with only 359.

Eddie Mathews, a teammate of Aaron's for many years, started strong with 47 home runs in his second year, when he was not yet 22. Mathews seemed young enough and powerful enough, especially when he surpassed 40 home runs in four of his first eight seasons, to have a chance at Ruth, but he finished with 512. Duke Snider had more than 40 home runs for five straight seasons in the fifties, but then the Dodgers moved to Los Angeles and a much less hospitable stadium, and Snider retired with 407 homers.

The first hint that Ruth's record was approachable came in 1969, when Willie Mays became only the second man in history to reach 600 home runs. But Mays was 38 and slowing down; he hit only 13 that year. His once extraordinary reflexes were not what they once were, and it was obvious that Willie would not challenge Ruth. Four years later, he retired with 660 home runs.

By that time, Aaron had caught Mays and passed him. Aaron's 600th homer came off Gaylord Perry of the Giants on April 27, 1971. His 700th came on July 21, 1973, off Ken Brett of Philadelphia. And, with a high sense of drama, he ended that season with his 713th on September 29 against Jerry Reuss of Houston. The baseball world would have the whole off-season, six months, to think about where and how Aaron would get numbers 714 and 715.

For sure, Aaron's 714th home run was going to get far more attention than Ruth's 714. Ruth's home run hitting had been so prodigious that it had stunned the baseball world. The career homer record was only 136, by Roger Connors, when Ruth passed it, in 1921. When he hit number 700, only two others had even passed 300!

Ruth's 714th was one of three hit in Pittsburgh in a game in May 1935, only two weeks before he retired. It was a fitting climax to his career. The Babe's was the first fair ball hit over the right field roof at Forbes Field, but few had been at the game to see it. That would not happen with Aaron.

Tickets were moving at a lively clip for the Braves' first three 1974 games in Cincinnati and their subsequent home stand.

Before the season even started, in mid-February, the Braves' management announced that Aaron would be kept out of the three games in Cincinnati so that he could hit his historic home runs before the home fans in Atlanta. The Braves spoke of history, but the gate receipts were a possible factor, too.

Eddie Mathews, by this time manager of the Braves, didn't rule out Aaron's participation in the three-game Cincinnati series. If the occasion merited, he said, he would use Aaron as a pinch hitter. "I think one thing that a lot of people have overlooked," said Mathews, "is that Hank sitting on the bench (as a possible pinch hitter) stops managers from making moves they might want to make."

This didn't satisfy others, who felt that the Braves should present their best lineup against the Reds. Cincinnati, they felt, shouldn't be given an unnatural advantage in the pennant race.

Typical of much of the press reaction was a column written by the respected Dave Anderson of the *New York Times*. Anderson, it should be noted, is not a writer who indulges in controversy for its own sake. He criticizes only that which he thinks truly deserves criticism, but he left no doubt about his feelings in this matter.

"In brazen defiance of baseball's integrity," wrote Anderson, "the Atlanta Braves have decreed that they will not fulfill their 162-game commitment to the National League schedule this year. Instead, the Braves will play 159 games. The other three, their opening series in Cincinnati, have emerged as exhibitions now that Henry Aaron won't be in the starting lineup."

Commissioner Bowie Kuhn, not usually the most forceful of men, ruled that Aaron should play in Cincinnati, a ruling that aroused as much controversy as the Braves' original announcement.

"I have had a number of discussions with [Atlanta owner] Bill Bartholomay about his February announcement regarding Henry Aaron," Kuhn said. "Although he has advanced some substantial arguments, he has not been able to persuade me that the procedure he wishes to follow is good for baseball.

"As a result, I have advised him that I am disapproving the announcement and that, barring disability, I will expect the Braves to use him in the opening series in Cincinnati."

Club executives around the league generally felt that the Braves' decision had been a correct one. That included Cincinnati's Bob Howsam. "The Cincinnati fans are interested in how the Reds play the game," said

Howsam. "Sure, they would enjoy seeing Aaron break the record, but there is no guarantee he will do it in the first game of the season. Or the tenth."

Perhaps the most pointed remark was that made by Bud Harrelson of the New York Mets, referring to the fact that the Braves had moved from Milwaukee to Atlanta during Aaron's career; "If they want Hank Aaron to hit those home runs for the fans, why don't they let him go back to Milwaukee and do it?"

As always, Aaron took a practical view of the matter. "No matter what I do, I'll get criticism," Hank said. "I'd rather get criticism in New York than in my home town (Atlanta). I can take it in New York. We don't go there but a couple of times a year."

Aaron had another practical reason for preferring to sit out the opening series: If he wanted in the future to show his family and friends where he had hit his most historic home runs, it would be much easier for him to get to the Atlanta stadium than Cincinnati's.

Nonetheless, Henry Aaron was always a man who gave full measure, through 23 National League seasons. When he was told to play, he played— and held nothing back. On his first swing of the 1974 season, he hit the 714th home run of his career.

Cincinnati pitcher Jack Billingham had thrown two balls and then a strike, which Aaron took. Billingham then threw another ball to bring the count to 3–1. The next pitch was a fastball that was supposed to sink but didn't. Aaron whipped his bat around once again with those magnificent wrists and the ball didn't come down until it had cleared the left-field fence.

"It wasn't a bad pitch," said Billingham, "but it wasn't good enough against Hank Aaron."

The game was stopped while the ball was retrieved and Aaron thanked the fans over the loudspeaker system. Billingham, whose first reaction was not that he had given up a historic home run but that he was down 3–0 in the first inning, continued warming up during the ceremonies and then retired the side.

Only when he had walked to his dugout and sat down did Billingham comprehend what had really happened. "I didn't waste any time, did I?" he said to fellow pitcher Clay Kirby.

The Braves couldn't hold the lead and lost in the 11th inning, 7–6; Aaron was subdued after the game. "I thought tying the record would mean a great deal to me," he said, "but it seemed like just another homer. I guess if we had won, I would have felt like drinking champagne."

Hank Aaron breaks the best-known record in baseball as he hits his 715th career home run on April 8, 1974, in Atlanta Stadium. *(Atlanta Braves photo)*

As it was, he told the Braves to put the Moet et Chandon champagne back on ice, to await number 715 and, hopefully, a Braves' win.

The controversy was not over. Mathews announced that he would not play Aaron in the second and third games of the series, and Aaron sat out the Saturday game. Commissioner Kuhn then ordered Mathews to put Aaron back in the lineup for the Sunday game.

As it happened, Kuhn's second edict neither helped the Braves nor affected history. Aaron had a bad game Sunday, striking out twice and grounding out weakly the third time. He looked so bad, in fact, that some suggested he was trying to save number 715 for Atlanta, a gross libel against a man who had never dogged it. "I never went on the field and failed to give anything but my best," said the hurt Aaron. "I don't know how to play the game any other way."

The Braves' opponents in the first game in Atlanta were the Los Angeles Dodgers, and the pitcher was Al Downing, a gentlemanly left-hander who had been pitching in the major leagues since 1961. When he first came up with the New York Yankees, Downing had an excellent fastball, but a sore arm took that from him. By 1974 he was relying chiefly on guile.

Downing was resigned to his role in the situation, neither pleased nor displeased. "Look," he told Plimpton, "if I throw 715 I'm not going to run and hide. There's no disgrace in that. On the other hand, I'm not going to run into the plate and congratulate him."

Downing walked Aaron on his first at bat. In the fourth inning, Aaron came to the plate again. Downing threw him a fastball and Aaron swung. It was a typical Aaron hit, the ball rising as it went toward the left center alley. Left fielder Bill Buckner went to the fence and stopped, and the ball soared over at the 385-foot mark. Braves' pitcher Tom House caught it in the bull pen and brought it in to Aaron. Hank would blast 40 more home runs before retiring, but none would match this one.

"715" flashed on the Atlanta scoreboard, and then the message: "You were there. You fans here at Atlanta Stadium have just witnessed the great, if not the greatest, moment in recorded sports history." In case they didn't know.

"Thank God it's over," said Aaron, "and thank God I hit it in Atlanta."

One final footnote: A capacity crowd watched Aaron hit his historic home run, but commissioner Kuhn was not among them. He had intentionally stayed away and was at dinner in Cleveland when the home run was hit.

32. The Big Red Machine

For the most part, the National League has been well-balanced. No National League team has ever approached the long-term dominance that the New York Yankees had in the American League from the early 1920s through the mid-sixties.

Still, over shorter periods of time, there have been dominating teams. The Baltimore Orioles just before the turn of the century, for instance; the Chicago Cubs, 1906–10; the New York Giants of the early twenties; the St. Louis Cardinals, 1942–46; the Brooklyn Dodgers, 1947–56.

And the Big Red Machine, known more prosaically as the Cincinnati Reds, 1970–76.

The Reds of that period were a magnificent team, winning five Western Division championships, four National League pennants, and two World Series.

Six times in that stretch, individual Reds won Most Valuable Player awards. George Foster became only the fifth man in National League history to hit more than 50 home runs in a season. Johnny Bench set league records for home runs by a catcher in a season and career. Pete Rose became only the eighth player in league history to get 3,000 hits and, in 1978, tied Willie Keeler's consecutive game hitting record.

At home and away, the fans poured out to see the Big Red Machine. Seasonal attendance of more than two million became the norm at Cincinnati's Riverfront Stadium, and, in 1977, the Reds became only the second team in league history (the 1966 San Francisco Giants were the first) to play before more than two million fans on the road.

Though their nickname made them an easy butt for jokes—when the Reds lost the 1970 and '72 World Series, somebody quipped that the Big Red Machine came equipped with an automatic choke—there has probably never been a team that more deserved its nickname. The Reds were indeed a machine, rolling over their competitors for most of that stretch.

No one is sure who invented that nickname—it is claimed by both Pete Rose and Bob Hunter, a baseball writer for the *Los Angeles Herald-Examiner.*

Rose maintains that he originated the machine nickname even before the team became so good, in the late sixties, when the Reds were still playing in antiquated Crosley Field. "At that time," said Rose, "I had this red '34 Ford. That, I said, was the Little Red Machine and the team was the Big Red Machine."

Hunter was unquestionably the first writer to use the nickname, and he remembers exactly how it happened. "The Reds had just finished winning a game, 19–17," he said, "from the Philadelphia Phillies. I thought about the color of the uniforms and the power they had. They were like a machine, big and red."

When the Reds came to Los Angeles for a series after that, Hunter referred to the invasion of the Big Red Machine. Dave Bristol, then manager of the Reds, told Hunter he liked the nickname, and it soon stuck.

As usual, the success of the organization started in the front office. Bob Howsam was named general manager of the Reds in 1967 and president in 1973. Howsam has not hesitated to make the risky trade, such as the one that brought Joe Morgan to the club in 1972, or the unpopular one, as in 1977, when he traded Tony Perez to make room for Dan Driessen at first base.

Howsam also made a courageous move in 1970 when he named the unknown Sparky Anderson as manager. Only 36, Anderson had no major league managing experience and had spent only one year as a major league coach, with San Diego in 1969.

Since then, Anderson has vindicated Howsam's judgment by becoming the winningest manager in Cincinnati history. In 1978, he also tied Bill McKechnie's record for longevity with the Reds, nine years—though he was fired after the season ended.

In many ways, the Big Red Machine resembled the great Dodger teams of two decades earlier. Like the Dodgers, the Reds had awesome hitting and superb fielding, and their weakness was pitching. In their great seven-year stretch, the Reds had only one 20-game winner, Jim Merritt in 1970. To make up for the weakness in starting pitchers, Anderson went often to his bullpen; it earned him the nickname "Captain Hook."

Like the Dodgers, the Reds had continuity in their star players. Bench, Rose, Perez and Dave Concepcion were starters in each of the seven glory years, 1970–76. Morgan and Cesar Geronimo both came to the club in 1972. That was a strong nucleus, and the team became even stronger when George Foster and Ken Griffey became full-timers in 1975.

There was not a weak spot in the Cincinnati starting lineup in 1975–76, when they became only the third team in National League history to win

George Foster set a Cincinnati club record with 52 home runs en route to the Most Valuable Player award in 1977. *(Copyright Cincinnati Reds, Inc., 1977)*

back-to-back World Series (and the first in more than five decades). The key men throughout the glory years were Morgan, Bench and Rose. Bench and Rose are certain to make the Hall of Fame when they become eligible, and Morgan has a good chance.

Many long time baseball experts say there has never been a better defensive catcher than Bench. For the first ten years of his career he won a Gold Glove. Throughout the league, he was the standard of excellence; whenever a manager wanted to praise his catcher, he would make remarks like "He's almost as good as Bench," or "His arm is nearly as good as Bench's." When he first came to the Reds, Bench used to cut down would-be base stealers with great regularity. As word of his arm spread through the league, base runners became cautious and seldom tested him.

The strength of his arm is no surprise because Bench was a pitcher in high school in Oklahoma. He was a good one; his record was 75–3. He was also All-State as a basketball player, which attests to his natural ability.

Surprisingly, in view of his later success, Bench was not picked in the first round of the free agent draft in 1965, the first year of that draft. The Reds picked him on the second round, after selecting outfielder Bernie Carbo on the first round.

Despite his high school pitching success, the Reds wanted Bench as a catcher. They had him practice behind the plate before a game in high school; he then went out and pitched (and won) the game. But even the Reds couldn't have known how good Bench would become.

Bench played only 255 games in the minor leagues, before coming up to the Reds to stay at the end of the 1967 season. In 1968, when he hit 15 home runs and batted .275, Bench was the National League Rookie of the Year, and he was not yet 21.

There are two starting positions, catcher and shortstop, at which defense is so important that managers will play weak hitters who can do the job defensively. Bench was so good as a defensive catcher, cat-quick in handling bunts and pop flies and with that cannonlike arm, that the Reds would have played him if he had been no more than a .200 hitter. As it turned out, he was considerably more.

In 1970, when everything came together for the Reds, Bench had an incredible year, hitting 45 home runs, knocking in 148 runs, scoring another 97, and hitting .293. He played in 158 games, 140 of them behind the plate, and became the youngest player ever to win the league's Most Valuable Player award.

It was perhaps the best offensive year a National League catcher ever had.

Johnny Bench quickly won recognition as one of the finest catchers–if not THE finest–in league history. *(Cincinnati Reds Photo)*

Only two other catchers have had comparable seasons. In 1953, Roy Campanella batted .312 with 41 homers, 142 RBIs, and 103 runs scored. In 1930, Gabby Hartnett batted .339 with 37 home runs, 122 RBIs, and 84 runs scored.

In 1972, Bench had another year almost as good, with 40 home runs and 125 RBIs, though his average fell off to .270. And the Reds won another pennant. It was becoming obvious that Bench was the key to the club's success.

It is not surprising that Bench has not come back to quite that level of hitting since. Most catchers have their best offensive years early in their careers, before the accumulation of injuries that are part of the job slows them down. And Bench has had more than his share of problems. In 1972, immediately after the World Series, he had an operation on his lung; doctors feared cancer, but the growth was benign.

In April 1975, San Francisco outfielder Gary Matthews dove into Bench's left shoulder trying to score, and Bench played in pain throughout the season. He was operated on after the season and cartilage was removed. Dr. Donald O'Donoghue said the cartilage looked as if it had been hit by a hammer. The same year, he was hit in the ankle by a pitch. When X rays were taken, three previous breaks showed up. Bench had played on all three while they healed!

Those injuries make Bench's offensive statistics all the more remarkable. In his first ten years, he had eight seasons in which he hit at least 20 home runs, four years in which he hit at least 30, two in which he belted 40 or more. He had six seasons when he had at least 100 RBIs, and he is one of only five NL players to lead the league in RBIs in three years.

He is already the leading home run hitter among catchers in National League history, for both a season and career, and he is closing in on Hartnett's career RBI mark of 1,179; Bench went over the 1,000 plateau, at 1,038, with the '77 season.

Like all great athletes, Bench is often at his best in the most important games. He was the MVP of the '76 World Series, for instance, when he hit .533 and banged two homers in the deciding game. And perhaps the most impressive statistic of his career is this: In 42 World Series and championship series games, Bench caught every inning and had only two bases stolen against him, by Matty Alou of the Oakland A's in 1972 and Mickey Rivers of the New York Yankees in 1976.

If Bench was the heart of the Big Red Machine, Rose was its spirit, an indomitable player who was a throwback to the great players of another era in his zest for the game.

Rose's nickname is "Charlie Hustle." It was first applied sarcastically when Rose was a rookie, by players who felt he was showboating when he ran to first after getting a base on balls. But in time, the nickname implied respect, as Rose showed what hustle could mean to a player.

Pete Rose made himself a star. He does not have the arm of a Bench, the speed of a Morgan, the power of a Foster, the fielding grace of a Concepcion. But nobody has ever worked harder. He has played wherever he could do the most good for the team—at second base, left field, and third base. He made himself into a switch-hitter, getting an extra edge. He knew he had to do it.

"The whole secret is not trying to be something you're not," he says. "I couldn't become the best home run hitter or RBI man, but I could become the best switch-hitter." He has more hits and more home runs than any NL switch-hitter in history.

"I'm proud of that," he says. "Not many guys in baseball or any other sport become the all-time best at what they do."

The key to Rose's game is consistency. He never lets up, from at bat to at bat, from game to game, from year to year. Every year, he's right around .300 and with 200 hits.

Early in the 1978 season Rose reached the 3,000 hit plateau. The magnitude of that achievement is measured not only by those who preceded Rose to the mark in the National League—Hank Aaron, Stan Musial, Honus Wagner, Willie Mays, Paul Waner, Cap Anson and Roberto Clemente—but by those who didn't.

Some great hitters never made it. Willie Keeler stopped at 2,955, for instance, Rogers Hornsby at 2,930, Frankie Frisch at 2,880, Mel Ott at 2,876.

But at 37, Rose appeared finally to be slowing down. On June 14, he was locked in one of the deepest slumps of his career, hitting only .267, lower than he had hit in any of his 15 major league seasons. He was having special problems against left-handers, hitting only .229 against them.

Then he made some minor adjustments. He began choking up more on the bat and spread his stance. He also hit one of those mysterious periods that athletes welcome, when the game suddenly seems easier. For Rose, the difference was that he started picking up the ball faster when it left the pitcher's hand. "That little white rat looks like a big white rat," he said.

That day, June 14, he got two hits against the Cubs, after getting only five hits in his previous 44 at bats. He thought of that only as a slump-breaker at the time, but it turned out that he was beginning a historic hitting streak.

Game after game, the hits kept falling in, and he kept passing record-holders. In game 27, he tied the club hitting streak, held jointly by Edd Roush (1920 and '24) and Vada Pinson (1965). The next day, he tied the switch-hitters' record held by Red Schoendienst.

The next mark was the modern National League record of 37, set by Tommy Holmes of the Boston Braves in 1945. As it happened, in one of those interesting twists of fate, Rose's try for number 37 (and then number 38) came in New York against the Mets, for whom Holmes was working in the community relations department. Naturally, Holmes was watching Rose's efforts.

The first three times up, against former teammate Pat Zachry, Rose flied out twice and hit into a fielder's choice. When he came up for the fourth time in the seventh—and what would probably be his last at bat—he bunted the first pitch foul and then took a ball. On the next pitch, a change-up, Rose swung and lined the ball to left field to tie Holmes's record.

The next day, Rose appeared more relaxed, though he was determined to break Holmes's record. "You don't really accomplish anything if you just tie somebody," he said.

This time, he left no doubt. He went out the first time but then got three straight hits, the first one in the third inning, off Craig Swan.

The 61-year-old Holmes greeted Rose after that hit, trotting from the stands to first base to shake Pete's hand and pose for pictures.

"I had the record for a third of a century," said Holmes. "Let him have it. It's in the hands of a better man. It's in the hands of a Hall of Famer.

"I've had chills up and down my spine ever since it happened . . . Pete's put me back in the news for a couple of days. It's been great."

Typically, Rose gave Holmes every chance to talk when they were together on the field, a fact that Holmes noted and appreciated. Rose also made another promise, but Holmes didn't hold him to it. "He told me if he got the hit he would give me the baseball," said Holmes, "but when he gave it to me on the field, I gave it back. It's his honor and his moment."

The pressure only increased for Rose after that, because he was now chasing Keeler's before-1900 record of 44 straight and the media attention was fearsome. At least 100 newsmen gathered around him before each game, and he was interviewed constantly on television.

That didn't bother Rose. "I like pressure situations," he said. "They're fun. When people are urging me on, I can do things that are impossible sometimes."

On and on he went. On July 28, he hit safely in games 40 and 41 against Philadelpia, getting one hit in each game. In the opener, he lashed a double to center that Garry Maddox nearly caught, the ball just skidding off his glove after a long run.

In the second game, facing Steve Carlton, against whom he was 0-for-13 for the season, he tried the unusual strategy of bunting as a right-handed hitter. The bunt caught Philadelphia third baseman Mike Schmidt by surprise—though Rose had done the same thing against the Phillies and Schmidt in game number 32—and Rose legged out the hit to keep the streak alive.

Rose hit in game number 42 against the Phillies, a first-inning single against Jim Lonborg, and then in number 43. This time, his bunts in previous games worked in reverse fashion. Schmidt was moving in to prevent another bunt when Rose lined a shot past him. Now, he was only one away from Keeler's record.

There was considerable debate whether Keeler's record should even be considered a legitimate goal. Keeler had had some advantages that Rose lacked. For one thing, the plate was only 12 inches wide in Keeler's day, compared to 17 now. Foul balls were not counted as strikes.

But Rose did not join the argument. "I'm a National Leaguer and so was Keeler," he said. "What difference does it make that he played before 1900 or after 1900?"

In his first two at bats against knuckleballer Phil Niekro of the Braves in Atlanta, Rose walked and lined out to short. But in the sixth, he led off with a single to right to keep the streak alive.

"I wanted to get a hit early because the umpires told me there was a threat of a downpour," he said. "I was looking for a fastball because he had me 2–0 in a 1–1 game and I knew he didn't want to walk me. He has the best knuckleball in the National League, but he doesn't like to throw fastballs."

The streak ended the next night, though, and Rose indulged himself in a rare display of pettiness. Atlanta routed the Reds, 16–4, and relief pitcher Gene Garber struck out Rose for the final out, after Rose had walked, lined out twice, and grounded out in four previous trips.

Rose was upset because Garber threw him a change-up for the final strike. "If I'd had any guts, I would have bunted that last change-up," he said. He thought Garber should have thrown him a fastball. "I had one pitch to swing at that was a strike.

"I thought he won the World Series. Did you see him jump up? . . . Most pitchers in baseball just challenge a guy in that situation (referring to the big Atlanta lead). He was just trying to in-and-out, up-and-down you."

But Rose probably realized when he had time to reflect on the situation, that the record would have been tainted if Garber had pitched less than his best.

At any rate, Rose's streak was a remarkable achievement. He neither got any help from friendly scorers—there was not a questionable hit during the streak—nor from any extra at bats in extra inning games. Six times he got hits in his last at bat to keep his streak going, and four times his only hit was a bunt.

Schmidt, victimized twice at bunts, praised Rose lavishly. "He'd never bunted on me before, and then he laid down two perfect ones that I couldn't come up with. I've really got to respect him. He brought our game into focus for people who never appreciated it before."

And in contrast to his somewhat churlish comments about Garber in the immediate wake of the ending of his streak, Rose showed what kind of person he really is a few hours later, at 2 A.M. in an Atlanta all-night restaurant.

With perhaps half a dozen people around him, all strangers, Rose stood up and began showing how Atlanta starter Larry McWilliams had speared his line drive and how Garber had struck him out.

That's Pete Rose.

There was a final, ironic note to Rose's career in 1978. Failing to reach terms on a new contract with Cincinnati, he played out his option and signed a four-year, $3.2 million contract with Philadelphia in December. The man who was the very symbol of Cincinnati and the spirit of the Big Red Machine, was now a Phillie. Nothing was certain any more.

The combination of
Mike Schmidt and
Greg Luzinski was a
big factor in the
Phillies' success
in the seventies.
(Paul Roedig photos)

Harvey Haddix pitched a perfect game for 12 innings for the Pirates in 1959—yet lost the game to Milwaukee in the 13th. *(George Brace photo)*

Historical Moments

1845   First baseball game is played.

1876   National League is formed, with Morgan G. Bulkeley as president. George Washington Bradley throws first league no-hitter, for St. Louis against Hartford.

1880   John Richmond throws first perfect game, for Worcester against Cleveland.

1884   Charlie Sweeney, Providence, strikes out 19 men in nine-inning game.

1888   Tim Keefe, New York, wins 19 consecutive games.

1892   Wilbert Robinson, Baltimore, makes seven hits in nine-inning game.

1894   Bobby Lowe, Boston, becomes first player to hit four home runs in nine-inning game.

1897   Willie Keeler, Baltimore, hits in 44 consecutive games.

1900   National League reduces from 12 teams to 8.

1903   First World Series is played, with Boston of the American League beating NL champion Pittsburgh, five games to three.

1912   Rube Marquard, New York, wins 19 consecutive games.

1913   Christy Mathewson pitches 68 consecutive innings without walking a man.

1916   New York wins 26 consecutive games, but finishes fourth.

1917   Fred Toney, Cincinnati, and Hippo Vaughn, Chicago, pitch double no-hit game for nine innings. Toney pitches no-hitter for ten innings and wins when Vaughn yields hit in tenth.

1920   Boston and Brooklyn play longest game in history, a 26-inning tie.

1924   Jim Bottomley knocks in 12 runs in nine-inning game. New York Giants become first team to win four consecutive pennants.

1930   Bill Terry and Lefty O'Doul set record with 254 hits in season.

1934   Carl Hubbell strikes out five consecutive batters in All-Star game.

1935   First night game is played, at Cincinnati.

1936-37   Hubbell wins 24 consecutive games over two seasons.

1938   Johnny Vander Meer, Cincinnati, becomes first pitcher to throw consecutive no-hit games, against Boston and Brooklyn.

1946   Cardinals beat Dodgers in first play-off for pennant in league history.

1947   Jackie Robinson breaks color line. Ralph Kiner hits eight home runs in four consecutive games. Dodger manager Leo Durocher suspended for year for "conduct detrimental to baseball."

1951   Giants beat Dodgers in second NL pennant playoff, after winning 38 of last 47 games to make up 13½ game deficit.

1953   Boston becomes first National League club to move in 53 years, switching franchise to Milwaukee.

1954   Stan Musial hits five home runs in doubleheader.

1955   Dodgers win first World Series, after seven losses.

1956   The Pirates' Dale Long hits home runs in eight consecutive games.

1958   Dodgers move from Brooklyn to Los Angeles and Giants from New York to San Francisco, the first time major league clubs have been located west of the Mississippi Valley.

1959   Harvey Haddix of the Pirates pitches 12 consecutive perfect innings but loses to Braves in 13th inning. Sandy Koufax sets league record by striking out 18 Giants. Dodgers, in third pennant play-off, defeat Braves.

1961   Chicago owner Phil Wrigley appoints "College of Coaches," with Vedie Himsl, Harry Craft, Elvin Tappe and Lou Klein alternating as man in charge for Cubs. The team finishes seventh.

1962   National League expands for first time, with teams in New York and Houston. Giants beat Dodgers in fourth pennant play-off. Maury Wills steals 118 bases.

1964   Mets and Giants play seven-hour, 23-minute game, won by Giants, 8-6, in 23 innings. Jim Bunning, Philadelphia, becomes the first pitcher to throw a no-hitter in both major leagues, 6-0 over the Mets.

1965   Koufax becomes the first pitcher to throw four no-hit games, with a perfect game against the Cubs, and also sets a major league season strikeout record of 382. Houston Astrodome first indoor stadium, opens.

1968   Don Drysdale, Los Angeles, sets record with 58⅔ consecutive scoreless innings. Gaylord Perry, San Francisco, and Ray Washburn, St. Louis, become first pitchers to throw back-to-back no-hitters.

1969   Steve Carlton, St. Louis, sets major league record with 19 strikeouts in nine-inning game.

1970   Henry Aaron, Atlanta, and Willie Mays, San Francisco, join 3,000-hit club. Curt Flood challenges reserve clause in suit against baseball. Billy Williams, Chicago, ends consecutive game streak at 1,117, a league record.

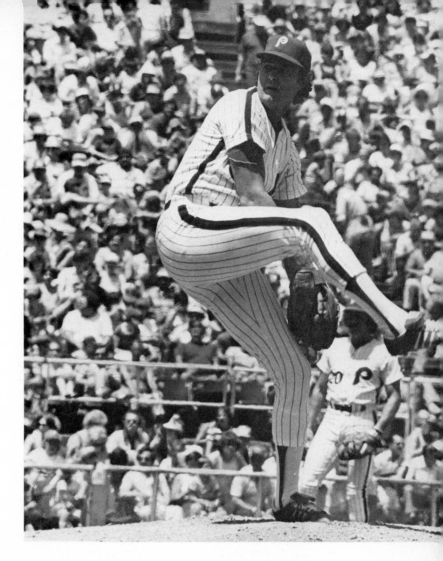

Steve Carlton became the first pitcher to strike out 19 batters in a nine-inning game in 1969.
(Paul Roedig photo)

1971 Mays sets National League runs-scored record with 1,950th. Ron Hunt, Montreal, is hit by a pitch for 50th time, a major league record.

1972 Roberto Clemente, Pittsburgh, gets 3,000th hit. Jim Barr, San Francisco, sets major league record by retiring 41 batters in a row over two games. Nate Colbert, San Diego, gets five home runs in a doubleheader.

1974 Henry Aaron, Atlanta, breaks Babe Ruth's career record with 715th home run on April 8 in Atlanta. Lou Brock, St. Louis, sets season record with 118 stolen bases.

1977 Brock sets career stolen base record, finishing season with 900.

1978 Pete Rose, Cincinnati, ties league hitting record with 44 consecutive game streak.

League Statistics

National League Team Standings: Year-By-Year

(* play-off to break tie)

1876

TEAM	W	L	PCT	MGR
CHI	52	14	.788	Spalding
ST.L	45	19	.703	Graffen
HAR	47	21	.691	Ferguson
BOS	39	31	.557	Wright, W.
LOU	30	36	.456	Fulmer
MUT	21	35	.375	Cammeyer
ATH	14	45	.237	Wright, A.
CIN	9	56	.135	Gould

1877

TEAM	W	L	PCT	MGR
BOS	42	18	.700	Wright
LOU	35	25	.583	Chapman
HAR	31	27	.534	Ferguson
ST.L	28	32	.467	Lucas
				McManus
CHI	26	33	.441	Spalding
CIN	15	42	.263	Pike
				Addy

1878

TEAM	W	L	PCT	MGR
BOS	41	19	.683	Wright
CIN	37	23	.617	McVey
PRO	33	27	.550	Ware
CHI	30	30	.500	Ferguson
IND	24	36	.400	Clapp
MIL	15	45	.250	Chapman

1879

TEAM	W	L	PCT	MGR
PRO	55	23	.705	Wright, G.
BOS	49	29	.628	Wright, W.
BUF	44	32	.579	McGunnigle
CHI	44	32	.579	Anson
CIN	38	36	.514	White, J. L.
				McVey
SYR	15	27	.357	Smith
CLE	24	53	.312	McCormick
TRO	19	56	.253	Ferguson

1880

TEAM	W	L	PCT	MGR
CHI	67	17	.798	Anson
PRO	52	32	.619	Bullock
CLE	47	37	.559	McCormick
TRO	41	42	.494	Ferguson
WOR	40	43	.482	Bancroft
				Brown
BOS	40	44	.476	Wright, W.
BUF	24	58	.293	McGunnigle
				Crane
CIN	21	59	.263	Clapp

1881

TEAM	W	L	PCT	MGR
CHI	56	28	.667	Anson
PRO	47	37	.559	Bullock
				Morrow
BUF	45	38	.542	O'Rourke
DET	41	43	.488	Bancroft
TRO	39	45	.464	Ferguson
BOS	38	45	.458	Wright, W.
CLE	36	48	.429	McCormick
WOR	32	50	.390	Brown

1882

TEAM	W	L	PCT	MGR
CHI	55	29	.655	Anson
PRO	52	32	.619	Wright, W.
BOS	45	39	.536	Morrill
BUF	45	39	.536	O'Rourke
CLE	42	40	.512	Evans
DET	42	41	.506	Bancroft
TRO	35	48	.422	Ferguson
WOR	18	66	.214	Brown
				Bond
				Chapman

1883

TEAM	W	L	PCT	MGR
BOS	63	35	.643	Burdock
				Morrill
CHI	59	39	.602	Anson
PRO	58	40	.592	Wright, W.
CLE	55	42	.567	Bancroft
BUF	52	45	.536	O'Rourke
N Y	46	50	.479	Clapp
DET	40	58	.408	Chapman
PHI	17	81	.173	Ferguson

1884

TEAM	W	L	PCT	MGR
PRO	84	28	.750	Bancroft
BOS	73	38	.658	Morrill
BUF	64	47	.577	O'Rourke
CHI	62	50	.554	Anson
N Y	62	50	.554	Price
PHI	39	73	.348	Wright, W.
CLE	35	77	.313	Hackett
DET	28	84	.250	Chapman

1885

TEAM	W	L	PCT	MGR
CHI	87	25	.776	Anson
N Y	85	27	.758	Mutrie
PHI	56	54	.509	Wright, W.
PRO	53	57	.481	Bancroft
BOS	46	66	.410	Morrill
DET	41	67	.379	Morton
				Watkins
BUF	38	74	.339	Chapman
				Hughson
				Galvin
ST.L	36	72	.333	Dunlap
				Fine
				Lucas

1886

TEAM	W	L	PCT	MGR
CHI	90	34	.725	Anson
DET	87	35	.707	Watkins
N Y	75	44	.630	Mutrie
PHI	71	43	.622	Wright, W.
BOS	56	61	.478	Morrill
ST.L	43	79	.352	Schmelz
K C	30	91	.247	Rowe
WAS	28	92	.233	Scanlon
				Gaffney

1887

TEAM	W	L	PCT	MGR
DET	79	45	.637	Watkins
PHI	75	48	.610	Wright, W.
CHI	71	50	.587	Anson
N Y	68	55	.553	Mutrie
BOS	61	60	.504	Morrill
PIT	55	69	.444	Phillips
WAS	46	76	.377	Gaffney
				Dennis
IND	37	89	.294	Fogel
				Burnham
				Thomas

1888

TEAM	W	L	PCT	MGR
N Y	84	47	.641	Mutrie
CHI	77	58	.578	Anson
PHI	69	61	.531	Wright, W.
BOS	70	64	.522	Morrill
DET	68	63	.519	Watkins
				Leadley
PIT	66	68	.493	Phillips
IND	50	85	.370	Spence
WAS	48	86	.358	Hewitt
				Sullivan
				Whitney

1889

TEAM	W	L	PCT	MGR
N Y	83	43	.659	Mutrie
BOS	83	45	.648	Hart
CHI	67	65	.508	Anson
PHI	63	64	.496	Wright, W.
PIT	61	71	.462	Phillips
				Dunlap
				Hanlon
CLE	61	72	.459	Loftus
IND	59	75	.440	Bancroft
				Glasscock
WAS	41	83	.331	Morrill
				Irwin

1890

TEAM	W	L	PCT	MGR
BRO	86	43	.667	McGunnigle
CHI	83	53	.610	Anson
PHI	78	53	.595	Wright, W.
CIN	78	55	.586	Loftus
BOS	76	57	.571	Selee
N Y	63	68	.481	Mutrie
CLE	44	88	.333	Schmelz
				Leadley
PIT	23	114	.168	Hecker

1891

TEAM	W	L	PCT	MGR
BOS	87	51	.630	Selee
CHI	82	53	.607	Anson
N Y	71	61	.538	Mutrie
PHI	68	69	.496	Wright, W.
CLE	65	74	.468	Leadley
				Tebeau
BRO	61	76	.445	Ward
CIN	56	81	.409	Loftus
PIT	55	80	.407	Hanlon
				McGunnigle

1892

TEAM	W	L	PCT	MGR
BOS	102	48	.680	Selee
CLE	93	56	.624	Tebeau
BRO	95	59	.617	Ward
PHI	87	66	.569	Wright, W.
CIN	82	68	.547	Comiskey
PIT	80	73	.523	Burns
				Bucken-
				berger
CHI	70	76	.479	Anson
N Y	71	80	.470	Powers
LOU	63	89	.414	Pfeffer
				Chapman
WAS	58	93	.384	Barnie
				Irwin
				Richardson
				Wagner
ST.L	56	94	.373	Von der Ahe
BAL	46	101	.313	Van Haltren
				Waltz
				Hanlon

1893

TEAM	W	L	PCT	MGR
BOS	86	44	.662	Selee
PIT	81	48	.628	Bucken-
				berger
CLE	73	55	.570	Tebeau
PHI	72	57	.558	Wright, W.
N Y	68	64	.515	Ward
BRO	65	63	.508	Foutz
CIN	65	63	.508	Comiskey
BAL	60	70	.462	Hanlon
CHI	57	71	.445	Anson
ST.L	57	75	.432	Watkins
LOU	50	75	.400	Barnie
WAS	40	89	.310	Wagner
				O'Rourke

1894

TEAM	W	L	PCT	MGR
BAL	89	39	.695	Hanlon
N Y	88	44	.667	Ward
BOS	83	49	.629	Selee
PHI	71	56	.559	Irwin
BRO	70	61	.534	Foutz
CLE	68	61	.527	Tebeau
PIT	65	65	.500	Bucken-
				berger
				Mack
CHI	57	75	.432	Anson
ST.L	58	76	.424	Miller
CIN	54	75	.419	Comiskey
WAS	45	87	.341	Schmelz
LOU	38	94	.277	Barnie

1895

TEAM	W	L	PCT	MGR
BAL	87	43	.689	Hanlon
CLE	84	45	.646	Tebeau
PHI	78	53	.595	Irwin
CHI	72	58	.554	Anson
BOS	71	60	.542	Selee
BRO	71	60	.542	Foutz
PIT	71	61	.538	Mack
CIN	68	64	.508	Ewing
N Y	86	85	.504	Davis
				Doyle
				Watkins
WAS	43	85	.338	Schmelz
ST.L	39	92	.298	Bucken-
				berger
				Quinn
				Phelan
				Von der Ahe
LOU	35	96	.267	McCloskey

1896

TEAM	W	L	PCT	MGR
BAL	90	39	.698	Hanlon
CLE	80	48	.625	Tebeau
CIN	77	50	.606	Ewing
BOS	74	57	.565	Selee
CHI	71	57	.555	Anson
PIT	66	63	.512	Mack
N Y	64	67	.489	Irwin / Joyce
PHI	62	68	.477	Nash
BRO	58	73	.443	Foutz
WAS	58	73	.443	Smelz
ST.L	40	90	.308	Diddlebock / Latham / Conner / Dowd
LOU	38	93	.290	McCloskey / McGunnigle

1897

TEAM	W	L	PCT	MGR
BOS	93	39	.705	Selee
BAL	90	40	.693	Hanlon
N Y	83	48	.634	Joyce
CIN	76	56	.576	Ewing
CLE	69	62	.527	Tebeau
BRO	61	71	.462	Barnie
WAS	61	71	.462	Schmelz / Brown
PIT	60	71	.458	Donovan
CHI	59	73	.447	Anson
PHI	55	77	.417	Stallings
LOU	52	78	.400	Rogers / Clarke
ST.L	29	102	.221	Dowd / Nicol / Hallman / Von der Ahe

1898

TEAM	W	L	PCT	MGR
BOS	102	47	.685	Selee
BAL	96	53	.644	Hanlon
CIN	92	60	.605	Ewing
CHI	85	65	.567	Burns
CLE	81	68	.544	Tebeau
PHI	78	71	.523	Stallings / Shettaline
N Y	77	73	.513	Joyce / Anson
PIT	72	76	.486	Watkins
LOU	70	81	.464	Clarke
BRO	54	91	.372	Barnie / Griffin / Ebbets
WAS	51	101	.336	Brown / Doyle / McGuire / Irwin
ST.L	39	111	.260	Hurst

1899

TEAM	W	L	PCT	MGR
BRO	88	42	.677	Hanlon
BOS	95	57	.625	Selee
PHI	94	58	.618	Shettaline
BAL	84	58	.592	McGraw
ST.L	83	66	.557	Tebeau
CIN	83	67	.553	Ewing
PIT	76	73	.510	Watkins / Donovan
CHI	75	73	.507	Burns
LOU	75	77	.493	Clarke
N Y	60	86	.411	Day / Hoey / Irwin
WAS	53	95	.358	Cross
CLE	20	134	.129	Quinn

1900

TEAM	W	L	PCT	MGR
BRO	82	54	.603	Hanlon
PIT	79	60	.568	Clarke
PHI	75	63	.543	Shettaline
BOS	66	72	.478	Selee
CHI	65	75	.484	Loftus
ST.L	65	75	.484	Tebeau / Heilbroner
CIN	62	77	.446	Allen
N Y	60	73	.435	Ewing / Davis

1901

TEAM	W	L	PCT	MGR
PIT	90	49	.647	Clarke
PHI	83	57	.593	Shettaline
BRO	79	57	.581	Hanlon
ST.L	76	64	.543	Donovan
BOS	69	69	.500	Selee
CHI	53	86	.381	Loftus
N Y	52	85	.380	Davis
CIN	52	87	.374	McPhee

1902

TEAM	W	L	PCT	MGR
PIT	103	36	.741	Clarke
BRO	75	63	.543	Hanlon
BOS	73	64	.533	Buckenberger
CIN	70	70	.500	McPhee / Bancroft / Kelley
CHI	68	69	.496	Selee
ST.L	56	78	.418	Donovan
PHI	56	81	.409	Shettaline
N Y	48	88	.353	Fogel / Smith / McGraw

1903

TEAM	W	L	PCT	MGR
PIT	91	49	.650	Clarke
N Y	84	55	.604	McGraw
CHI	82	56	.594	Selee
CIN	74	65	.532	Kelley
BRO	70	68	.515	Hanlon
BOS	58	80	.420	Buckenberger
PHI	49	86	.363	Zimmer
ST.L	43	94	.314	Donovan

1904

TEAM	W	L	PCT	MGR
N Y	106	47	.693	McGraw
CHI	93	60	.608	Selee
CIN	88	65	.575	Kelley
PIT	87	68	.569	Clarke
ST.L	75	79	.487	Nichols
BRO	56	97	.386	Hanlon
BOS	55	98	.360	Buckenberger
PHI	52	100	.342	Duffy

1905

TEAM	W	L	PCT	MGR
N Y	105	48	.688	McGraw
PIT	96	57	.627	Clarke
CHI	92	61	.601	Selee / Chance
PHI	83	69	.546	Duffy
CIN	79	74	.516	Kelley
ST.L	58	96	.377	Nichols / Burke / Robison
BOS	51	103	.331	Tenney
BRO	48	104	.316	Hanlon

1906

TEAM	W	L	PCT	MGR
CHI	116	38	.763	Chance
N Y	96	56	.632	McGraw
PIT	93	60	.608	Clarke
PHI	71	82	.464	Duffy
BRO	66	86	.434	Donovan
CIN	64	87	.424	Hanlon
ST.L	52	98	.347	McCloskey
BOS	49	102	.324	Tenney

1907

TEAM	W	L	PCT	MGR
CHI	107	45	.704	Chance
PIT	91	63	.591	Clarke
PHI	83	64	.566	Murray
N Y	82	71	.536	McGraw
BRO	65	83	.439	Donovan
CIN	66	87	.431	Hanlon
BOS	58	90	.392	Tenney
ST.L	52	101	.340	McCloskey

1908

TEAM	W	I	PCT	MGR
CHI	99	55	.643	Chance
N Y	98	56	.636	McGraw
PIT	98	56	.636	Clarke
PHI	83	71	.539	Murray
CIN	73	81	.474	Ganzel
BOS	83	91	.409	Kelley
BRO	53	101	.344	Donovan
ST.L	49	105	.318	McCloskey

1909

TEAM	W	I	PCT	MGR
PIT	110	42	.724	Clarke
CHI	104	49	.680	Chance
N Y	92	61	.601	McGraw
CIN	77	76	.504	Griffith
PHI	74	79	.484	Murray
BRO	55	98	.359	Lumley
ST.L	54	98	.355	Bresnahan
BOS	45	108	.294	Bowerman
				Smith

1910

TEAM	W	I	PCT	MGR
CHI	104	50	.676	Chance
N Y	91	63	.591	McGraw
PIT	86	67	.562	Clarke
PHI	78	75	.510	Dooin
CIN	75	79	.487	Griffith
BRO	64	90	.416	Dahlen
ST.L	63	90	.412	Bresnahan
BOS	53	100	.346	Lake

1911

TEAM	W	I	PCT	MGR
N Y	99	54	.647	McGraw
CHI	92	62	.597	Chance
PIT	85	69	.552	Clarke
PHI	79	73	.520	Dooin
ST.L	75	74	.503	Bresnahan
CIN	70	83	.458	Griffith
BRO	64	86	.427	Dahlen
BOS	44	107	.291	Tenney

1912

TEAM	W	I	PCT	MGR
N Y	103	48	.682	McGraw
PIT	93	58	.616	Clarke
CHI	91	59	.607	Chance
CIN	75	78	.490	O'Day
PHI	73	79	.480	Dooin
ST.L	63	90	.412	Bresnahan
BRO	58	95	.379	Dahlen
BOS	52	101	.340	Kling

1913

TEAM	W	L	PCT	MGR
N Y	101	51	.664	McGraw
PHI	88	63	.583	Dooin
CHI	88	65	.575	Evers
PIT	78	71	.523	Clarke
BOS	69	82	.457	Stallings
BRO	65	84	.436	Dahlen
CIN	64	89	.418	Tinker
ST.L	51	99	.340	Huggins

1914

TEAM	W	L	PCT	MGR
BOS	94	59	.614	Stallings
N Y	84	70	.545	McGraw
ST.L	81	72	.529	Huggins
CHI	78	76	.506	O'Day
BRO	75	79	.487	Robinson
PHI	74	80	.481	Dooin
PIT	69	85	.448	Clarke
CIN	60	94	.390	Herzog

1915

TEAM	W	L	PCT	MGR
PHI	90	62	.592	Moran
BOS	83	69	.546	Stallings
BRO	80	72	.527	Robinson
CHI	73	80	.477	Bresnahan
PIT	73	81	.474	Clarke
ST.L	72	81	.471	Huggins
CIN	71	83	.461	Herzog
N Y	69	83	.454	McGraw

1916

TEAM	W	L	PCT	MGR
BRO	94	60	.610	Robinson
PHI	91	62	.595	Moran
BOS	89	63	.586	Stallings
N Y	86	66	.566	McGraw
CHI	67	86	.438	Tinker
PIT	65	89	.422	Callahan
CIN	60	93	.392	Herzog
				Wingo
				Mathewson
ST.L	60	93	.392	Huggins

1917

TEAM	W	L	PCT	MGR
N Y	98	56	.636	McGraw
PHI	87	65	.572	Moran
ST.L	82	70	.539	Huggins
CIN	78	76	.506	Mathewson
CHI	74	80	.481	Mitchell
BOS	72	81	.471	Stallings
BRO	70	81	.484	Robinson
PIT	51	103	.331	Callahan
				Wagner
				Bezdek

1918

TEAM	W	I	PCT	MGR
CHI	84	45	.651	Mitchell
N Y	71	53	.573	McGraw
CIN	68	60	.531	Mathewson
				Groh
PIT	65	60	.520	Bezdek
BRO	57	69	.452	Robinson
PHI	55	68	.447	Moran
BOS	53	71	.427	Stallings
ST.L	51	78	.395	Hendricks

1919

TEAM	W	L	PCT	MGR
CIN	96	44	.686	Moran
N Y	87	53	.621	McGraw
CHI	75	65	.536	Mitchell
PIT	71	68	.511	Bezdek
BRO	69	71	.493	Robinson
BOS	57	82	.410	Stallings
ST.L	54	83	.394	Rickey
PHI	47	90	.343	Coombs
				Cravath

1920

TEAM	W	L	PCT	MGR
BRO	93	61	.604	Robinson
N Y	86	68	.558	McGraw
CIN	82	71	.536	Moran
PIT	79	75	.513	Gibson
CHI	75	79	.487	Mitchell
ST.L	75	79	.487	Rickey
BOS	62	90	.408	Stallings
PHI	62	91	.405	Cravath

1921

TEAM	W	L	PCT	MGR
N Y	94	59	.614	McGraw
PIT	90	63	.588	Gibson
ST.L	87	66	.569	Rickey
BOS	79	74	.516	Mitchell
BRO	77	75	.507	Robinson
CIN	70	83	.458	Moran
CHI	64	89	.418	Evers
				Killefer
PHI	51	103	.331	Donovan
				Wilhelm

1922

TEAM	W	I	PCT	MGR
N Y	93	61	.604	McGraw
CIN	86	68	.558	Moran
PIT	85	69	.552	Gibson
				McKechnie
ST.L	85	69	.552	Rickey
CHI	80	74	.520	Killefer
BRO	76	78	.494	Robinson
PHI	57	96	.373	Wilhelm
BOS	53	100	.346	Mitchell

1923

TEAM	W	L	PCT	MGR
N Y	95	58	.621	McGraw
CIN	91	63	.591	Moran
PIT	87	67	.565	McKechnie
CHI	83	71	.539	Killefer
ST.L	79	74	.516	Rickey
BRO	76	78	.494	Robinson
BOS	54	100	.351	Mitchell
PHI	50	104	.325	Fletcher

1924

TEAM	W	L	PCT	MGR
N Y	93	60	.608	McGraw
BRO	92	62	.597	Robinson
PIT	90	63	.588	McKechnie
CIN	83	70	.542	Hendricks
CHI	81	72	.530	Killefer
ST.L	65	89	.422	Rickey
PHI	55	96	.364	Fletcher
BOS	53	100	.346	Bancroft

1925

TEAM	W	L	PCT	MGR
PIT	95	58	.621	McKechnie
N Y	86	66	.566	McGraw
CIN	80	73	.523	Hendricks
ST.L	77	76	.503	Rickey / Hornsby
BOS	70	83	.458	Bancroft
BRO	68	85	.444	Robinson
PHI	68	85	.444	Fletcher
CHI	68	86	.442	Killefer / Maranville / Gibson

1926

TEAM	W	L	PCT	MGR
ST.L	89	65	.578	Hornsby
CIN	87	67	.565	Hendricks
PIT	84	69	.549	McKechnie
CHI	82	72	.532	McCarthy
N Y	74	77	.490	McGraw
BRO	71	82	.464	Robinson
BOS	66	86	.434	Bancroft
PHI	58	93	.384	Fletcher

1927

TEAM	W	L	PCT	MGR
PIT	94	60	.610	Bush
ST.L	92	61	.601	O'Farrell
N Y	92	62	.597	McGraw
CHI	85	68	.556	McCarthy
CIN	75	78	.490	Hendricks
BRO	65	88	.425	Robinson
BOS	60	94	.390	Bancroft
PHI	51	103	.331	McInnis

1928

TEAM	W	L	PCT	MGR
ST.L	95	59	.617	McKechnie
N Y	93	61	.604	McGraw
CHI	91	63	.591	McCarthy
PIT	85	67	.559	Bush
CIN	78	74	.513	Hendricks
BRO	77	76	.503	Robinson
BOS	50	103	.327	Slattery / Hornsby
PHI	43	109	.283	Shotton

1929

TEAM	W	L	PCT	MGR
CHI	98	54	.645	McCarthy
PIT	88	65	.575	Bush / Ens
N Y	84	67	.556	McGraw
ST.L	78	74	.513	McKechnie / Southworth
PHI	71	82	.464	Shotton
BRO	70	83	.458	Robinson
CIN	66	88	.429	Hendricks
BOS	56	98	.384	Fuchs / Evers

1930

TEAM	W	L	PCT	MGR
ST.L	92	62	.597	Street
CHI	90	54	.584	McCarthy / Hornsby
N Y	87	57	.565	McGraw
BRO	88	68	.558	Robinson
PIT	80	74	.519	Ens
BOS	70	84	.455	McKechnie
CIN	59	95	.383	Howley
PHI	52	102	.333	Shotton

1931

TEAM	W	L	PCT	MGR
ST.L	101	53	.656	Street
N Y	87	65	.572	McGraw
CHI	84	70	.545	Hornsby
BRO	79	73	.520	Robinson
PIT	75	79	.487	Ens
PHI	66	88	.429	Shotton
BOS	64	90	.416	McKechnie
CIN	58	96	.377	Howley

1932

TEAM	W	L	PCT	MGR
CHI	90	64	.584	Hornsby / Grimm
PIT	86	68	.558	Gibson
BRO	81	73	.526	Carey
PHI	78	76	.506	Shotton
BOS	77	77	.500	McKechnie
N Y	72	82	.468	McGraw / Terry
ST.L	72	82	.468	Street
CIN	60	94	.390	Howley

1933

TEAM	W	L	PCT	MGR
N Y	91	61	.599	Terry
PIT	87	67	.565	Gibson
CHI	86	68	.558	Grimm
BOS	83	71	.539	McKechnie
ST.L	82	71	.536	Street / Frisch
BRO	65	88	.425	Carey
PHI	60	92	.395	Shotton
CIN	58	94	.382	Bush

1934

TEAM	W	L	PCT	MGR
ST.L	95	58	.621	Frisch
N Y	93	60	.608	Terry
CHI	86	65	.570	Grimm
BOS	78	73	.517	McKechnie
PIT	74	76	.493	Gibson / Traynor
BRO	71	81	.467	Stengel
PHI	56	93	.376	Wilson
CIN	52	99	.344	O'Farrell / Shotton / Dressen

1935

TEAM	W	L	PCT	MGR
CHI	100	54	.649	Grimm
ST.L	96	58	.623	Frisch
N Y	91	62	.595	Terry
PIT	86	67	.562	Traynor
BRO	70	83	.458	Stengel
CIN	68	85	.444	Dressen
PHI	64	89	.418	Wilson
BOS	38	115	.248	McKechnie

1936

TEAM	W	L	PCT	MGR
N Y	92	62	.597	Terry
CHI	87	67	.565	Grimm
ST.L	87	67	.565	Frisch
PIT	84	70	.545	Traynor
CIN	74	80	.431	Dressen
BOS	71	83	.461	McKechnie
BRO	67	87	.435	Stengel
PHI	54	100	.351	Wilson

1937

TEAM	W	L	PCT	MGR
N Y	95	57	.625	Terry
CHI	93	61	.604	Grimm
PIT	86	68	.558	Traynor
ST.L	81	73	.526	Frisch
BOS	79	73	.520	McKechnie
BRO	62	91	.405	Grimes
PHI	61	92	.399	Wilson
CIN	56	98	.364	Dressen / Wallace

1938

TEAM	W	L	PCT	MGR
CHI	89	63	.586	Grimm
				Hartnett
PIT	86	64	.573	Traynor
N Y	83	67	.553	Terry
CIN	82	68	.547	McKechnie
BOS	77	75	.507	Stengel
ST.L	71	80	.470	Frisch
				Gonzales
BRO	69	80	.463	Grimes
PHI	45	105	.300	Wilson
				Lobert

1939

TEAM	W	L	PCT	MGR
CIN	97	57	.630	McKechnie
ST.L	92	61	.601	Blades
BRO	84	69	.549	Durocher
CHI	84	70	.545	Hartnett
N Y	77	74	.510	Terry
PIT	68	85	.444	Traynor
BOS	63	88	.417	Stengel
PHI	45	106	.298	Prothro

1940

TEAM	W	L	PCT	MGR
CIN	100	53	.654	McKechnie
BRO	88	65	.575	Durocher
ST.L	84	69	.549	Blades
				Gonzales
				Southworth
PIT	78	78	.506	Frisch
CHI	75	79	.487	Hartnett
N Y	72	80	.474	Terry
BOS	65	87	.428	Stengel
PHI	50	103	.327	Prothro

1941

TEAM	W	L	PCT	MGR
BRO	100	54	.649	Durocher
ST.L	97	56	.634	Southworth
CIN	88	66	.571	McKechnie
PIT	81	73	.526	Frisch
N Y	74	79	.484	Terry
CHI	70	84	.455	Wilson
BOS	62	92	.403	Stengel
PHI	43	111	.279	Prothro

1942

TEAM	W	L	PCT	MGR
ST.L	106	48	.688	Southworth
BRO	104	50	.675	Durocher
N Y	85	67	.559	Ott
CIN	76	76	.500	McKechnie
PIT	66	81	.449	Frisch
CHI	68	86	.442	Wilson
BOS	59	89	.399	Stengel
PHI	42	109	.278	Lobert

1943

TEAM	W	L	PCT	MGR
ST.L	105	49	.682	Southworth
CIN	87	67	.565	McKechnie
BRO	81	72	.529	Durocher
PIT	80	74	.519	Frisch
CHI	74	79	.484	Wilson
BOS	68	85	.444	Stengel
PHI	64	90	.416	Harris
				Fitzsimmons
N Y	55	98	.359	Ott

1944

TEAM	W	L	PCT	MGR
ST.L	105	49	.682	Southworth
PIT	90	63	.588	Frisch
CIN	89	65	.578	McKechnie
CHI	75	79	.487	Wilson
				Johnson
				Grimm
N Y	67	87	.435	Ott
BOS	65	89	.422	Coleman
BRO	63	91	.409	Durocher
PHI	61	92	.399	Fitzsimmons

1945

TEAM	W	L	PCT	MGR
CHI	98	56	.636	Grimm
ST.L	95	59	.617	Southworth
BRO	87	67	.565	Durocher
PIT	82	72	.532	Frisch
N Y	78	74	.513	Ott
BOS	67	85	.441	Coleman
				Bissonette
CIN	61	93	.396	McKechnie
PHI	46	108	.299	Fitzsimmons
				Chapman

1946

TEAM	W	L	PCT	MGR
ST.L	98*	58	.628	Dyer
BRO	96*	60	.615	Durocher
CHI	82	71	.536	Grimm
BOS	81	72	.529	Southworth
PHI	69	85	.448	Chapman
CIN	67	87	.435	McKechnie
				Gowdy
PIT	63	91	.409	Frisch
				Davis
N Y	61	93	.396	Ott

1947

TEAM	W	L	PCT	MGR
BRO	94	60	.610	Sukeforth
				Shotton
ST.L	89	65	.578	Dyer
BOS	86	68	.558	Southworth
N Y	81	73	.526	Ott
CIN	73	81	.474	Neun
CHI	69	85	.448	Grimm
PHI	62	92	.403	Chapman
PIT	62	92	.403	Herman
				Burwell

1948

TEAM	W	L	PCT	MGR
BOS	91	62	.595	Southworth
ST.L	85	69	.552	Dyer
BRO	84	70	.545	Durocher
				Shotton
PIT	83	71	.539	Meyer
N Y	78	76	.506	Ott
				Durocher
PHI	66	88	.429	Chapman
				Cooke
				Sawyer
CIN	64	89	.418	Neun
				Walters
CHI	64	90	.416	Grimm

1949

TEAM	W	L	PCT	MGR
BRO	97	57	.630	Shotton
ST.L	96	58	.623	Dyer
PHI	81	73	.526	Sawyer
BOS	75	79	.487	Southworth
				Cooney
N Y	73	81	.474	Durocher
PIT	71	83	.461	Meyer
CIN	62	92	.403	Walters
				Sewell
CHI	61	93	.396	Grimm
				Frisch

1950

TEAM	W	L	PCT	MGR
PHI	91	63	.591	Sawyer
BRO	89	65	.578	Shotton
N Y	86	68	.558	Durocher
BOS	83	71	.539	Southworth
ST.L	78	75	.510	Dyer
CIN	66	87	.431	Sewell
CHI	64	89	.418	Frisch
PIT	57	96	.373	Meyer

1951

TEAM	W	L	PCT	MGR
N Y	98*	59	.624	Durocher
BRO	97*	60	.618	Dressen
ST.L	81	73	.526	Marion
BOS	76	78	.494	Southworth
				Holmes
PHI	73	81	.474	Sawyer
CIN	68	86	.442	Sewell
PIT	64	90	.416	Meyer
CHI	62	92	.403	Frisch
				Cavarretta

1952

TEAM	W	L	PCT	MGR
BRO	96	57	.627	Dressen
N Y	92	62	.597	Durocher
ST.L	88	66	.571	Stanky
PHI	87	67	.565	Sawyer
				O'Neill
CHI	77	77	.500	Cavarretta
CIN	69	85	.448	Sewell
				Hornsby
BOS	64	89	.418	Holmes
				Grimm
PIT	42	112	.273	Meyer

1953

TEAM	W	L	PCT	MGR
BRO	105	49	.682	Dressen
MIL	92	62	.597	Grimm
PHI	83	71	.539	O'Neill
ST.L	83	71	.539	Stanky
N Y	70	84	.455	Durocher
CIN	68	86	.442	Hornsby
				Mills
CHI	65	89	.422	Cavarretta
PIT	50	104	.325	Haney

1954

TEAM	W	L	PCT	MGR
N Y	97	57	.630	Durocher
BRO	92	62	.597	Alston
MIL	89	65	.578	Grimm
PHI	75	79	.487	O'Neill
				Moore
CIN	74	80	.481	Tebbetts
ST.L	72	82	.468	Stanky
CHI	64	90	.416	Hack
PIT	53	101	.344	Haney

1955

TEAM	W	L	PCT	MGR
BRO	98	55	.641	Alston
MIL	85	69	.552	Grimm
N Y	80	74	.519	Durocher
PHI	77	77	.500	Smith
CIN	75	79	.487	Tebbetts
CHI	72	81	.471	Hack
ST.L	68	86	.442	Stanky
				Walker
PIT	60	94	.390	Haney

1956

TEAM	W	L	PCT	MGR
BRO	93	61	.604	Alston
MIL	92	62	.597	Grimm
				Haney
CIN	91	63	.591	Tebbetts
ST.L	76	78	.494	Hutchinson
PHI	71	83	.461	Smith
N Y	67	87	.435	Rigney
PIT	66	98	.429	Bragan
CHI	60	94	.390	Hack

1957

TEAM	W	L	PCT	MGR
MIL	95	59	.617	Haney
ST.L	87	67	.565	Hutchinson
BRO	84	70	.545	Alston
CIN	80	74	.519	Tebbetts
PHI	77	77	.500	Smith
N Y	69	85	.448	Rigney
CHI	62	92	.403	Scheffing
PIT	62	92	.403	Bragan
				Murtaugh

1958

TEAM	W	L	PCT	MGR
MIL	92	62	.597	Haney
PIT	84	70	.545	Murtaugh
S F	80	74	.519	Rigney
CIN	76	78	.494	Tebbetts
				Dykes
ST.L	72	82	.468	Hutchinson
				Hack
CHI	72	82	.468	Scheffing
L A	71	83	.461	Alston
PHI	69	85	.448	Smith
				Sawyer

1959

TEAM	W	L	PCT	MGR
L A	88*	68	.564	Alston
MIL	86*	70	.551	Haney
S F	83	71	.539	Rigney
PIT	78	76	.506	Murtaugh
CHI	74	80	.481	Scheffing
CIN	74	80	.481	Smith
				Hutchinson
ST.L	71	83	.461	Hemus
PHI	64	90	.416	Sawyer

1960

TEAM	W	L	PCT	MGR
PIT	95	59	.617	Murtaugh
MIL	88	66	.571	Dressen
ST.L	86	68	.558	Hemus
L A	82	72	.532	Alston
S F	79	75	.513	Rigney
				Sheehan
CIN	67	87	.435	Hutchinson
CHI	60	94	.390	Grimm
				Boudreau
PHI	59	95	.383	Sawyer
				Mauch

1961

TEAM	W	L	PCT	MGR
CIN	93	61	.604	Hutchinson
L A	89	65	.578	Alston
S F	85	69	.552	Dark
MIL	83	71	.539	Dressen
				Tebbetts
ST.L	80	74	.519	Hemus
				Keane
PIT	75	79	.487	Murtaugh
CHI	64	90	.416	Himsl
				Craft
				Tappe
				Klein
PHI	47	107	.305	Mauch

1962

TEAM	W	L	PCT	MGR
S F	103*	62	.624	Dark
L A	102*	63	.618	Alston
CIN	98	64	.605	Hutchinson
PIT	93	68	.578	Murtaugh
MIL	86	76	.531	Tebbetts
ST.L	84	78	.519	Keane
PHI	81	80	.503	Mauch
HOU	64	96	.400	Craft
CHI	59	103	.364	Tappe
				Klein
				Metro
N Y	40	120	.250	Stengel

1963

TEAM	W	L	PCT	MGR
L A	99	63	.611	Alston
ST.L	93	69	.574	Keane
S F	88	74	.543	Dark
PHI	87	75	.537	Mauch
CIN	86	76	.531	Hutchinson
MIL	84	78	.516	Bragan
CHI	82	80	.506	Kennedy
PIT	74	88	.457	Murtaugh
HOU	66	96	.407	Craft
N Y	51	111	.315	Stengel

1964

TEAM	W	L	PCT	MGR
ST.L	93	69	.574	Keane
CIN	92	70	.568	Hutchinson
PHI	92	70	.568	Mauch
S F	90	72	.556	Dark
MIL	88	74	.543	Bragan
L A	80	82	.494	Alston
PIT	80	82	.494	Murtaugh
CHI	76	86	.469	Kennedy
HOU	66	96	.407	Craft / Harris
N Y	53	109	.327	Stengel

1965

TEAM	W	L	PCT	MGR
L A	97	65	.599	Alston
S F	95	67	.586	Franks
PIT	90	72	.556	Walker
CIN	89	73	.549	Sisler
MIL	86	76	.531	Bragan
PHI	85	76	.528	Mauch
ST.L	80	81	.497	Schoendienst
CHI	72	90	.444	Kennedy / Klein
HOU	65	97	.401	Harris
N Y	50	112	.309	Stengel

1966

TEAM	W	L	PCT	MGR
L A	95	67	.586	Alston
S F	93	68	.578	Franks
PIT	92	70	.568	Walker
PHI	87	75	.537	Mauch
ATL	85	77	.525	Bragan / Hitchcock
ST.L	83	79	.512	Schoendienst
CIN	76	84	.495	Heffner / Bristol
HOU	72	90	.444	Hatton
N Y	66	95	.410	Westrum
CHI	59	103	.364	Durocher

1967

TEAM	W	L	PCT	MGR
ST.L	101	60	.627	Schoendienst
S F	91	71	.562	Franks
CHI	87	74	.540	Durocher
CIN	87	75	.537	Bristol
PHI	82	80	.506	Mauch
PIT	81	81	.500	Walker / Murtaugh
ATL	77	85	.475	Hitchcock / Silvestri
L A	73	89	.451	Alston
HOU	69	93	.426	Hatton
N Y	61	101	.377	Westrum / Parker

1968

TEAM	W	L	PCT	MGR
ST.L	97	65	.599	Schoendienst
S F	88	74	.543	Franks
CHI	84	78	.519	Durocher
CIN	83	79	.512	Bristol
ATL	81	81	.500	Harris
PIT	80	82	.494	Shepard
L A	76	86	.469	Alston
PHI	76	86	.469	Mauch / Myatt / Skinner
N Y	73	89	.451	Hodges
HOU	72	90	.444	Hatton / Walker

1969

EASTERN DIVISION

TEAM	W	L	PCT	MGR
N Y	100	62	.617	Hodges
CHI	92	70	.568	Durocher
PIT	88	74	.543	Shepard / Grammas
ST.L	87	75	.537	Schoendienst
PHI	63	99	.389	Skinner / Myatt
MON	52	110	.321	Mauch

WESTERN DIVISION

TEAM	W	L	PCT	MGR
ATL	93	69	.574	Harris
S F	90	72	.556	King
CIN	89	73	.549	Bristol
L A	85	77	.525	Alston
HOU	81	81	.500	Walker
S D	52	110	.321	Gomez

1970

EASTERN DIVISION

TEAM	W	L	PCT	MGR
PIT	89	73	.549	Murtaugh
CHI	84	78	.519	Durocher
N Y	83	79	.512	Hodges
ST.L	76	86	.469	Schoendienst
PHI	73	88	.453	Lucchesi
MON	73	89	.451	Mauch

WESTERN DIVISION

TEAM	W	L	PCT	MGR
CIN	102	60	.630	Anderson
L A	87	74	.540	Alston
S F	86	76	.531	King / Fox
HOU	79	83	.488	Walker
ATL	76	86	.469	Harris
S D	63	99	.389	Gomez

1971

EASTERN DIVISION

TEAM	W	L	PCT	MGR
PIT	97	65	.599	Murtaugh
ST.L	90	72	.556	Schoendienst
CHI	83	79	.512	Durocher
N Y	83	79	.512	Hodges
MON	71	90	.441	Mauch
PHI	67	95	.414	Lucchesi

WESTERN DIVISION

TEAM	W	L	PCT	MGR
S F	90	72	.556	Fox
L A	89	73	.549	Alston
ATL	82	80	.506	Harris
HOU	79	83	.488	Walker
CIN	79	83	.488	Anderson
S D	61	100	.379	Gomez

1972

EASTERN DIVISION

TEAM	W	L	PCT	MGR
PIT	96	59	.619	Virdon
CHI	85	70	.548	Durocher / Lockman
N Y	83	73	.532	Berra
ST.L	75	81	.481	Schoendienst
MON	70	86	.449	Mauch
PHI	59	97	.378	Lucchesi / Owens

WESTERN DIVISION

TEAM	W	L	PCT	MGR
CIN	95	59	.617	Anderson
HOU	84	69	.549	Walker
				Parker
				Durocher
L A	85	70	.548	Alston
ATL	70	84	.455	Harris
				Mathews
S F	69	86	.445	Fox
S D	58	95	.379	Gomez
				Zimmer

1973
EASTERN DIVISION

N Y	82	79	.509	Berra
ST.L	81	81	.500	Schoen-
				dienst
PIT	80	82	.494	Virdon
				Murtaugh
MON	79	83	.488	Mauch
CHI	77	84	.478	Lockman
PHI	71	91	.438	Ozark

WESTERN DIVISION

CIN	99	63	.611	Anderson
L A	95	66	.590	Alston
S F	88	74	.543	Fox
HOU	82	80	.506	Durocher
ATL	76	85	.472	Mathews
S D	60	102	.370	Zimmer

1974
EASTERN DIVISION

PIT	88	74	.543	Murtaugh
ST.L	86	75	.534	Schoen-
				dienst
PHI	80	82	.494	Ozark
MON	79	82	.491	Mauch
N Y	71	91	.438	Berra
CHI	66	96	.407	Lockman
				Marshall

WESTERN DIVISION

L A	102	60	.630	Alston
CIN	98	64	.605	Anderson
ATL	88	74	.543	Mathews
				King
HOU	81	81	.500	Gomez
S F	72	90	.444	Fox
				Westrum
S D	60	102	.370	McNamara

1975
EASTERN DIVISION

TEAM	W	L	PCT	MGR
PIT	92	69	.571	Murtaugh
PHI	86	76	.531	Ozark
N Y	82	80	.506	Berra
				McMillan
ST.L	82	80	.506	Schoen-
				dienst
CHI	75	87	.463	Marshall
MON	75	87	.463	Mauch

WESTERN DIVISION

CIN	108	54	.667	Anderson
L A	88	74	.543	Alston
S F	80	81	.497	Westrum
S D	71	91	.438	McNamara
ATL	67	94	.416	King
HOU	64	97	.398	Gomez
				Virdon

1976
EASTERN DIVISION

PHI	101	61	.623	Ozark
PIT	92	70	.568	Murtaugh
N Y	86	76	.531	Frazier
CHI	75	87	.463	Marshall
ST.L	72	90	.444	Schoen-
				dienst
MON	55	107	.340	Kuehl
				Fox

WESTERN DIVISION

CIN	102	60	.630	Anderson
L A	92	70	.568	Alston
				Lasorda
HOU	80	82	.494	Virdon
S F	74	88	.457	Rigney
S D	73	89	.451	McNamara
ATL	70	92	.432	Bristol

1977
EASTERN DIVISION

TEAM	W	L	PCT	MGR
PHI	101	61	.623	Ozark
PIT	96	66	.593	Tanner
ST.L	83	79	.512	Rapp
CHI	81	81	.500	Franks
MON	75	87	.463	Williams
N Y	64	98	.395	Torre

WESTERN DIVISION

L A	98	64	.605	LaSorda
CIN	88	74	.543	Anderson
HOU	81	81	.500	Virdon
S F	75	87	.463	Altobelli
S D	69	93	.426	McNamara
				Dark
ATL	61	101	.377	Bristol

1978
EASTERN DIVISION

PHI	90	72	.556	Ozark
PIT	88	73	.547	Tanner
CHI	78	83	.488	Franks
MON	76	86	.469	Williams
ST.L	69	93	.426	Rapp
				Boyer
N Y	66	96	.407	Torre

WESTERN DIVISION

L A	95	67	.586	Lasorda
CIN	92	69	.571	Anderson
S F	89	73	.549	Altobelli
S D	84	78	.519	Dark
				Craig
HOU	74	88	.457	Virdon
ATL	69	93	.426	Cox

CHAMPIONSHIP SERIES
1969
NY (East) 3, ATL (West) 0
1970
CIN (West) 3, PIT (East) 0
1971
PIT (East) 3, SF (West) 1
1972
CIN (West) 3, PIT (East) 2
1973
NY (East) 3, CIN (West) 2
1974
LA (West) 3, PIT (East) 0
1975
CIN (West) 3, PIT (East) 0
1976
CIN (West) 3, PHI (East) 0
1977
LA (West) 3, PHI (East) 1
1978
LA (West) 3, PHI (East) 1

World Series Results and Receipts

Year	National League	American League (or AA)	Games W-L	Attendance	Receipts	Winning Player's Share	Losing Player's Share
1882	Chicago	Cincinnati(AA)	1-1	7,200	$ 2,000.00	$ 0	$ 0
1884	* Providence	Metropolitans(AA)	3-0	3,100	850.00	100.00	0
1885	Chicago	St. Louis(AA)	3-3a	14,200	3,000.00	0	0
1886	Chicago	* St. Louis(AA)	2-4	43,000	14,000.00	855.00	0
1887	* Detroit	St. Louis(AA)	10-5	51,455	41,050.00	500.00	0
1888	* New York	St. Louis(AA)	6-4	42,270	24,362.10	450.00	0
1889	* New York	Brooklyn(AA)	6-3	47,256	24,262.10	380.15	389.29
1890	Brooklyn	Louisville(AA)	3-3a	13,910	6,000.00	100.00	100.00
1903	Pittsburgh	* Boston	3-5	100,429	55,500.00	1,316.25	1,182.00
1905	* New York	Philadelphia	4-1	91,723	68,437.00	1,142.00	833.75
1906	Chicago	* Chicago	2-4	99,845	106,550.00	1,874.63	439.50
1907	* Chicago	Detroit	4-0a	78,068	101,728.50	2,142.85	1,945.96
1908	* Chicago	Detroit	4-1	62,232	94,975.50	1,317.58	870.00
1909	* Pittsburgh	Detroit	4-3	145,295	188,302.50	1,825.22	1,274.76
1910	Chicago	* Philadelphia	1-4	124,222	173,980.00	2,062.79	1,375.16
1911	New York	* Philadelphia	2-4	179,851	342,164.50	3,654.58	2,436.39
1912	New York	* Boston	3-4a	252,037	490,449.00	4,024.68	2,566.47
1913	New York	* Philadelphia	1-4	151,000	325,980.00	3,246.36	2,164.22
1914	* Boston	Philadelphia	4-0	111,009	225,739.00	2,812.28	2,031.65
1915	Philadelphia	* Boston	1-4	143,351	320,361.50	3,780.25	2,520.17
1916	Brooklyn	* Boston	1-4	162,859	385,590.50	3,910.28	2,834.82
1917	New York	* Chicago	2-4	186,654	425,878.00	3,669.32	2,442.61
1918	Chicago	* Boston	2-4	128,483	179,619.00	1,102.51	671.09
1919	* Cincinnati	Chicago	5-3	236,928	722,414.00	5,207.01	3,254.36
1920	Brooklyn	* Cleveland	2-5	178,737	564,800.00	4,168.00	2,419.60
1921	* New York	New York	5-3	269,976	900,233.00	5,265.00	3,510.00
1922	* New York	New York	4-0a	185,947	605,475.00	4,470.00	3,225.00
1923	New York	* New York	2-4	301,430	1,063,815.00	6,143.49	4,112.89
1924	New York	* Washington	3-4	283,665	1,093,104.00	5,969.64	3,820.29
1925	* Pittsburgh	Washington	4-3	282,848	1,182,854.00	5,332.72	3,734.60
1926	* St. Louis	New York	4-3	328,051	1,207,864.00	5,584.51	3,417.75
1927	Pittsburgh	* New York	0-4	201,705	783,217.00	5,592.17	3,728.10
1928	St. Louis	* New York	0-4	199,072	777,290.00	5,531.91	4,197.37
1929	Chicago	* Philadelphia	1-4	190,490	859,494.00	5,620.57	3,782.01
1930	St. Louis	* Philadelphia	2-4	212,619	953,772.00	5,785.00	3,875.00
1931	* St. Louis	Philadelphia	4-3	231,567	1,030,723.00	4,467.59	3,032.09
1932	Chicago	* New York	0-4	191,998	713,377.00	5,231.77	4,244.60
1933	* New York	Washington	4-1	163,076	679,365.00	4,256.72	3,019.86
1934	* St. Louis	Detroit	4-3	281,510	1,031,341.00	5,389.57	3,354.57
1935	Chicago	* Detroit	2-4	286,672	1,073,794.00	6,544.76	4,198.53
1936	New York	* New York	2-4	302,924	1,204,399.00	6,430.55	4,655.58
1937	New York	* New York	1-4	238,142	985,994.00	6,471.10	4,489.05
1938	Chicago	* New York	0-4	200,833	851,166.00	5,782.76	4,674.87
1939	Cincinnati	* New York	0-4	183,849	745,329.00	5,614.26	4,282.58
1940	* Cincinnati	Detroit	4-3	281,927	1,222,328.21	5,803.62	3,531.81

World Series Results and Receipts (Continued)

Year	National League	American League (or AA)	Games W-L	Attendance	Receipts	Winning Player's Share	Losing Player's Share
1941	Brooklyn	*New York	1-4	235,773	1,007,762.00	5,943.31	4,829.40
1942	*St. Louis	New York	4-1	277,101	1,105,249.00	5,573.78	3,018.77
1943	St. Louis	*New York	1-4	277,312	1,105,784.00	6,139.46	4,321.96
1944	*St. Louis	St. Louis	4-2	206,708	906,122.00	4,626.01	2,743.79
1945	Chicago	*Detroit	3-4	333,457	1,492,454.00	6,443.34	3,930.22
1946	*St. Louis	Boston	4-3	250,071	1,052,900.00	3,742.34	2,140.89
1947	Brooklyn	*New York	3-4	389,763	1,781,348.92	5,830.03	4,081.19
1948	Boston	*Cleveland	2-4	358,362	1,633,685.56	6,772.05	4,651.51
1949	Brooklyn	*New York	1-4	236,710	1,129,627.88	5,665.54	4,272.73
1950	Philadelphia	*New York	0-4	196,009	953,669.03	5,737.95	4,081.34
1951	New York	*New York	2-4	341,977	1,633,457.47	6,446.09	4,951.03
1952	Brooklyn	*New York	3-4	340,906	1,622,753.01	5,982.65	4,200.64
1953	Brooklyn	*New York	2-4	307,350	1,779,269.44	8,280.68	6,178.42
1954	*New York	Cleveland	4-0	251,507	1,566,203.38	11,147.90	6,712.50
1955	*Brooklyn	New York	4-3	362,310	2,337,515.34	9,768.00	5,598.00
1956	Brooklyn	*New York	3-4	345,903	2,183,254.59	8,714.76	6,934.34
1957	*Milwaukee	New York	4-3	394,712	2,475,978.94	8,924.36	5,606.06
1958	Milwaukee	*New York	3-4	393,909	2,397,223.03	8,759.10	5,896.09
1959	*Los Angeles	Chicago	4-2	420,784	2,628,809.44	11,231.18	7,257.17
1960	*Pittsburgh	New York	4-3	349,813	2,230,627.88	8,417.94	5,214.64
1961	Cincinnati	*New York	1-4	223,247	1,480,059.95	7,389.13	5,356.37
1962	San Francisco	*New York	3-4	376,864	2,878,891.11	9,882.74	7,291.49
1963	*Los Angeles	New York	4-0	247,279	1,995,189.09	12,794.00	7,874.32
1964	*St. Louis	New York	4-3	321,807	2,243,187.96	8,622.19	5,309.29
1965	*Los Angeles	Minnesota	4-3	364,326	2,975,041.60	10,297.43	6,634.36
1966	Los Angeles	*Baltimore	0-4	220,791	2,047,142.46	11,683.04	8,189.36
1967	*St. Louis	Boston	4-3	304,085	2,350,607.10	8,314.81	5,115.23
1968	St. Louis	*Detroit	3-4	379,670	3,018,113.40	10,936.66	7,078.71
1969	*New York	Baltimore	4-1	272,378	2,857,782.78	18,338.18	14,904.21
1970	Cincinnati	*Baltimore	1-4	253,183	2,599,170.26	18,215.78	13,687.59
1971	*Pittsburgh	Baltimore	4-3	351,091	3,049,803.46	18,164.58	13,906.46
1972	Cincinnati	*Oakland	3-4	363,149	3,954,542.99	20,705.01	15,080.25
1973	New York	*Oakland	3-4	358,289	3,923,968.37	24,617.57	14,950.17
1974	Los Angeles	*Oakland	1-4	260,004	3,007,194.00	22,219.09	15,703.97
1975	*Cincinnati	Boston	4-3	308,272	3,380,579.61	19,060.46	13,325.87
1976	*Cincinnati	New York	4-0	223,009	2,498,416.53	26,366.68	19,935.48
1977	Los Angeles	*New York	2-4	337,708	3,978,825.33	27,758.04	20,899.05
1978	Los Angeles	*New York	2-4	337,304	4,650,164.57	31,236.99	25,483.21

Note: Player's shares for 1969 to date include League Championship Series

* indicates winning team   a indicates one game tied

National League Annual Attendance

1901 —	1,920,031	1927 —	5,309,917	1957 —	8,819,601
1902 —	1,683,012	1928 —	4,881,097	1958 —	10,164,596
1903 —	2,390,362	1929 —	4,925,713	1959 —	9,994,525
1904 —	2,664,271	1930 —	5,446,532	1960 —	10,684,963
1905 —	2,734,310	1931 —	4,583,815	1961 —	8,731,502
1906 —	2,781,213	1932 —	3,841,334	1962 —	11,360,159
1907 —	2,640,220	1933 —	3,162,821	1963 —	11,382,227
1908 —	3,512,108	1934 —	3,200,105	1964 —	12,045,190
1909 —	3,496,420	1935 —	3,657,309	1965 —	13,581,136
1910 —	3,494,544	1936 —	3,903,691	1966 —	15,015,471
1911 —	3,231,768	1937 —	4,204,228	1967 —	12,971,430
1912 —	2,735,759	1938 —	4,560,837	1968 —	11,785,358
1913 —	2,831,531	1939 —	4,707,177	1969 —	15,094,946
1914 —	1,707,397	1940 —	4,389,693	1970 —	16,662,198
1915 —	2,430,142	1941 —	4,777,647	1971 —	17,324,857
1916 —	3,051,634	1942 —	4,353,353	1972 —	15,529,730
1917 —	2,361,136	1943 —	3,769,342	1973 —	16,675,322
1918 —	1,372,127	1944 —	3,974,588	1974 —	16,978,314
1919 —	2,878,203	1945 —	5,260,703	1975 —	16,600,490
1920 —	4,036,575	1946 —	8,902,107	1976 —	16,660,529
1921 —	3,986,984	1947 —	10,388,470	1977 —	19,070,228
1922 —	3,941,820	1948 —	9,770,743	1978 —	20,106,924
1923 —	4,069,817	1949 —	9,484,718	1953 —	7,419,721
1924 —	4,340,644	1950 —	8,320,616	1954 —	8,013,519
1925 —	4,353,704	1951 —	7,244,002	1955 —	7,674,412
1926 —	4,920,399	1952 —	6,339,148	1956 —	8,649,567

National League Record Single Game Attendance

Atlanta	53,775	(vs. L.A., Apr. 8, 1974) *
Chicago	46,572	(vs. Bro., May 18, 1947)
Cincinnati	52,526	(vs. L.A., Apr. 7, 1975)
Houston	50,908	(vs. L.A., June 22, 1966) *
Los Angeles	78,672	(vs. S.F., Apr. 18, 1958)
Montreal	34,331	(vs. Phi., Sept. 15, 1973)
New York	56,738	(vs. L.A., June 23, 1968)
Philadelphia	60,492	(vs. L.A., July 5, 1976) *
Pittsburgh	51,695	(vs. St.L., Apr. 6, 1973)
St. Louis	50,548	(vs. N.Y., Sept. 14, 1975)
San Diego	49,618	(vs. Cin., July 5, 1975) *
San Francisco	56,103	(vs. L.A., May 28, 1978)

* Night Game

Stadium Dimensions
Active Stadiums

| Team | Stadium | Home Run Distances (in ft.) | | | Seating |
		LF	CF	RF	Capacity
Atlanta Braves	Atlanta Stadium	330	402	330	52,870
Chicago Cubs	Wrigley Field	355	400	353	37,741
Cincinnati Reds	Riverfront Stadium	330	404	330	51,726
Houston Astros	Astrodome	330	400	330	44,500
Los Angeles Dodgers	Dodger Stadium	330	395	330	56,000
Montreal Expos	Olympic Stadium	325	404	325	59,511
New York Mets	Shea Stadium	341	410	341	55,300
Philadelphia Phillies	Veterans Stadium	330	408	330	56,581
Pittsburgh Pirates	Three Rivers Stadium	340	410	340	50,235
St. Louis Cardinals	Busch Memorial Stadium	330	404	330	50,100
San Diego Padres	San Diego Stadium	330	410	330	47,634
San Francisco Giants	Candlestick Park	335	410	335	58,000

Former Stadiums

| Team | Stadium | Home Run Distances (in ft.) | | | Seating |
		LF	CF	RF	Capacity
Houston Colts 45	Colt Stadium	360	420	360	32,601
Brooklyn Dodgers	Ebbets Field	365	389	352	31,902
Pittsburgh Pirates	Forbes Field	365	457	300	35,000
New York Giants	Polo Grounds	279	483	257	55,000
St. Louis Cardinals	Busch Stadium	315	426	310	30,490
Cincinnati Reds	Crosley Field	328	390	366	29,488
San Francisco Giants	Seals Stadium	375	415	350	22,900
Milwaukee Braves	County Stadium	320	420	315	43,799
Montreal Expos	Jarry Park	340	417	340	30,000
Philadelphia Phillies	Connie Mack Stadium	334	410	329	43,608
Los Angeles Dodgers	Coliseum	251	420	333	94,600

National Leaguers in Baseball Hall of Fame

PLAYERS
Year selected

Cap Anson *	1939
Dave Bancroft *	1971
Ernie Banks	1977
Jake Beckley *	1971
Jim Bottomley *	1974
Roger Bresnahan *	1945
Dan Brouthers *	1945
Jesse Burkett *	1946
Roy Campanella	1969
Max Carey *	1961
Frank Chance *	1946
Fred Clarke *	1945
Roberto Clemente	1973
Roger Connor *	1976
Kiki Cuyler *	1968
Ed Delahanty *	1945
Hugh Duffy *	1945
Johnny Evers *	1946
Buck Ewing *	1946
Frank Frisch	1947
Chick Hatey *	1971
Billy Hamilton *	1961
Gabby Hartnett	1955
Billy Herman *	1975
Rogers Hornsby	1942
Hugh Jennings	1945
Willie Keeler	1939
Joe Kelley *	1971
George Kelly *	1973
Mike Kelly *	1945
Ralph Kiner	1975
Fred Lindstrom *	1976
Rabbit Maranville	1954
Willie Mays	1979
Tommy McCarthy *	1946
Joe Medwick	1968
Stan Musial	1969
Jim O'Rourke *	1945
Mel Ott	1951
Jackie Robinson	1962
Edd Roush *	1962
Bill Terry	1954
Sam Thompson *	1974

PLAYERS (con'd)
Year selected

Joe Tinker *	1946
Pie Traynor	1948
Honus Wagner	1936
Paul Waner	1952
Monte Ward *	1964
Zach Wheat *	1959
Hack Wilson *	1978
Ross Youngs *	1972

PITCHERS
Year selected

Grover Alexander	1938
Mordecai Brown *	1949
John Clarkson *	1963
Dizzy Dean	1953
Jim Galvin *	1965
Burleigh Grimes *	1964
Jesse Haines *	1970
Carl Hubbell	1947
Tim Keefe *	1964
Sandy Koufax	1971
Rube Marquard *	1971
Christy Mathewson	1936
Joe McGinnity *	1946
Kid Nichols *	1949
Charles Radbourn *	1939
Eppa Rixey *	1963
Robin Roberts	1976
Amos Rusie *	1977
Warren Spahn	1973
Dazzy Vance	1955
Mickey Welch *	1973
Cy Young	1937

MANAGERS *
Year selected

John McGraw	1937
Bill McKechnie	1962
Wilbert Robinson	1945
Harry Wright	1953
George Wright	1937

SELECTED FOR MERITORIOUS SERVICES *

Morgan G. Bulkeley (Executive)
Alexander J. Cartwright (Executive)
Henry Chadwick (Writer-Statistician)
John "Jocko" Conlan (Umpire)
William A. Cummings (Early Pitcher)
Ford C. Frick (Commissioner-Executive)
William Harridge (Executive)
William Klem (Umpire)
W. Branch Rickey (Manager-Executive)
Albert G. Spalding (Early Player)

* Special Committee Nominees

Individual Batting Records

GAMES
  Season: 165, Maury Wills, Los Angeles, 1962
  Career: 3,076, Henry Aaron, Milwaukee/Atlanta, 1954–74 *

AT BATS
  Season: 699, Dave Cash, Philadelphia, 1975.
  Career: 11,268, Henry Aaron, Milwaukee/Atlanta, 1954–74 *

HITS
  Season: 254, Bill Terry, New York, and Left O'Doul, Philadelphia, 1930
  Career: 3,630, Stan Musial, St. Louis, 1941–63

BATTING AVERAGE
  Season: (Since 1900), .424, Rogers Hornsby, St. Louis, 1924
  Career: .358, Rogers Hornsby, St. Louis/New York/Boston/Chicago, 1915–32

SLUGGING PERCENTAGE
  Season: .756, Rogers Hornsby, St. Louis, 1925
  Career: .578, Rogers Hornsby, St. Louis/New York/Boston/Chicago, 1915–32

HOME RUNS
  Season: 56, Hack Wilson, Chicago, 1930
  Career: 733, Hank Aaron, Milwaukee/Atlanta, 1954–74 *

TRIPLES
  Season: 36, J. Owen Wilson, Pittsburgh, 1912
  Career: 252, Honus Wagner, Louisville/Pittsburgh, 1897–1917

DOUBLES
  Season: 64, Joe Medwick, St. Louis, 1936
  Career: 725, Stan Musial, St. Louis, 1941–63

RBIs
  Season: 190, Hack Wilson, Chicago, 1930
  Career: 2,202, Henry Aaron, Milwaukee/Atlanta, 1954–74 *

RUNS
  Season: (Since 1900), 158, Chuck Klein, Philadelphia, 1930
          (Before 1900), 196, William Hamilton, Philadelphia, 1894
  Career: 2,107, Henry Aaron, Milwaukee/Atlanta, 1954–74 *

Rube Marquard set a major league
record that has never been
equaled. He won 19 straight games
in 1912. *(George Brace photo)*

Jim Bunning pitched no-hitters
in both leagues, and his perfect
game for the Phillies in 1964
was the first in the majors
during the regular season in 42 years.
(Roger W. Luce photo)

STOLEN BASES
>	*Season:* 118, Lou Brock, St. Louis, 1974
>	*Career:* 917, Lou Brock, St. Louis, 1961–78

Individual Pitching Records

GAMES
>	*Season:* 106, Mike Marshall, Los Angeles, 1974
>	*Career:* 846, ElRoy Face, Pittsburgh/Montreal, 1953–69

GAMES STARTED
>	*Season:* Since 1900), 48, Joe McGinnity, New York, 1903
>	(Before 1900), 74, William White, Cincinnati, 1879
>	*Career:* 665, Warren Spahn, Boston/Milwaukee/New York/San Francisco, 1942–65

COMPLETE GAMES
>	*Season:* (Since 1900), 45, Vic Willis, Boston, 1902
>	(Before 1900), 74, William White, Cincinnati, 1879
>	*Career:* (Since 1900), 437, Grover C. Alexander, Philadelphia/Chicago/St. Louis, 1911–29
>	(Before 1900), 557, James F. Galvin, Buffalo/Pittsburgh/St. Louis, 1879–92

INNINGS PITCHED
>	*Season:* (Since 1900), 434, Joe McGinnity, New York, 1093
>	(Before 1900), 683, William White, Cincinnati, 1879
>	*Career:* 5,246, Warren Spahn, Boston/Milwaukee/New York/San Francisco, 1942–65

WINS
>	*Season:* (Since 1900), 37, Christy Mathewson, New York, 1908
>	(Before 1900), 60, Charles Radbourne, Providence, 1884
>	*Career:* 373, Christy Mathewson, New York/Cincinnati, 1900–16; Grover C. Alexander, Philadelphia/Chicago/St. Louis, 1911–29

WINNING PERCENTAGE
>	*Season:* .947 (18–1), ElRoy Face, Pittsburgh, 1959
>	*Career:* .665 (373–188), Christy Mathewson, New York/Cincinnati, 1900–16

EARNED RUN AVERAGE
>	*Season:* 1.12, Bob Gibson, St. Louis, 1968
>	*Career:* 2.33, James L. Vaughn, Chicago, 1913–21

SHUTOUTS
> *Season:* 16, Grover C. Alexander, Philadelphia, 1916; George W. Bradley, St. Louis, 1876
> *Career:* 90, Grover C. Alexander, Philadelphia/Chicago/St. Louis, 1911–29

STRIKEOUTS
> *Season:* 382, Sandy Koufax, Los Angeles, 1965
> *Career:* 3,117, Bob Gibson, St. Louis, 1959–75

* N.L. totals only

Best Lifetime Marks

SEASONS MANAGED: John J. McGraw, New York Giants, 34.

PENNANTS WON: John J. McGraw, New York Giants, 10.

WORLD SERIES WON: Walter Alston, Brooklyn/Los Angeles Dodgers, 4.

HITTERS WITH THREE THOUSAND HITS:
> Hank Aaron, 3,771
> Stan Musial, 3,630
> Cap Anson, 3,516
> Honus Wagner, 3,430
> Willie Mays, 3,283
> Paul Waner, 3,152
> Pete Rose, 3,064
> Roberto Clemente, 3,000

PITCHERS WITH THREE HUNDRED WINS:
> Grover Cleveland Alexander, 373
> Christy Mathewson, 373
> Warren Spahn, 363
> Jim Galvin, 362
> Kid Nichols, 361
> Tim Keefe, 345
> John Clarkson, 327
> Mike Welch, 315
> Charles Radbourn, 306

HITTERS WITH 500 CAREER HOME RUNS:
    Hank Aaron, 733
    Willie Mays, 660
    Eddie Mathews, 512
    Ernie Banks, 512
    Mel Ott, 511
    Willie McCovey, 505

HITTERS WITH .340 LIFETIME AVERAGE OR BETTER:
    Rogers Hornsby, .358
    Lefty O'Doul, .349
    Dan Brouthers, .348
    Willie Keeler, .345
    Billy Hamilton, .344
    Bill Terry, .341

TRIPLE CROWN WINNERS (HOME RUNS, RBIs, BATTING AVERAGE)

Rogers Hornsby, St. Louis	1922
Rogers Hornsby, St. Louis	1925
Chuck Klein, Philadelphia	1933
Joe Medwick, St. Louis	1937

CONSECUTIVE GAMES PLAYED (600 or more)

Billy Williams	1,117
Stan Musial	895
Gus Suhr	822
Richie Ashburn	730
Ernie Banks	717
Pete Rose	678
Frank McCormick	652
Eddie Brown	618

GRAND-SLAM HOME RUNS

Willie McCovey	18
Hank Aaron	16
Gil Hodges	14
Ernie Banks	12
Rogers Hornsby	12
Ralph Kiner	12

Most Valuable Players

National League

1911	Frank Schulte, Chicago (OF)	1963	Sandy Koufax, Los Angeles (P)
1912	Larry Doyle, New York (2B)	1964	Ken Boyer, St. Louis (3B)
1913	Jake Daubert, Brooklyn (1B)	1965	Willie Mays, San Francisco (OF)
1914	Johnny Evers, Chicago (2B)	1966	Roberto Clemente, Pittsburgh (OF)
1922	No Selection	1967	Orlando Cepeda, St. Louis (1B)
1923	No Selection	1968	Bob Gibson, St. Louis (P)
1924	Dazzy Vance, Brooklyn (P)	1969	Willie McCovey, San Francisco (1B)
1925	Rogers Hornsby, St. Louis (2B)	1970	Johnny Bench, Cincinnati (C)
1926	Bob O'Farrell, St. Louis (C)	1971	Joe Torre, St. Louis (3B)
1927	Paul Waner, Pittsburgh (CF)	1972	Johnny Bench, Cincinnati (C)
1928	Jim Bottomley, St. Louis (1B)	1973	Pete Rose, Cincinnati (OF)
1929	Rogers Hornsby, St. Louis (2B)	1974	Steve Garvey, Los Angeles (1B)
1931 *	Frankie Frisch, St. Louis (2B)	1975	Joe Morgan, Cincinnati (2B)
1932	Chuck Klein, Philadelphia (OF)	1976	Joe Morgan, Cincinnati (2B)
1933	Carl Hubbell, New York (P)	1977	George Foster, Cincinnati (OF)
1934	Dizzy Dean, St. Louis (P)	1978	Dave Parker, Pittsburgh (OF)
1935	Gabby Hartnett, Chicago (C)		
1936	Carl Hubbell, New York (P)		
1937	Joe Medwick, St. Louis (OF)		
1938	Ernie Lombardi, Cincinnati (C)		
1939	Bucky Walters, Cincinnati (P)		**NL Rookie of the Year**
1940	Frank McCormick, Cincinnati (1B)		
1941	Dolph Camilli, Brooklyn (1B)	1947	Jackie Robinson, Brooklyn (1B)
1942	Mort Cooper, St. Louis (P)	1948	Alvin Dark, New York (SS)
1943	Stan Musial, St. Louis (OF)	1949	Don Newcombe, Brooklyn (P)
1944	Marty Marion, St. Louis (SS)	1950	Sam Jethroe, Boston (OF)
1945	Phil Cavarretta, Chicago (1B)	1951	Willie Mays, New York (OF)
1946	Stan Musial, St. Louis (1B)	1952	Joe Black, Brooklyn (P)
1947	Bob Elliott, Boston (3B)	1953	Junior Gilliam, Brooklyn (2B)
1948	Stan Musial, St. Louis (OF)	1954	Wally Moon, St. Louis (OF)
1949	Jackie Robinson, Brooklyn (2B)	1955	Bill Virdon, St. Louis (OF)
1950	Jim Konstanty, Philadelphia (P)	1956	Frank Robinson, Cincinnati (OF)
1951	Roy Campanella, Brooklyn (C)	1957	Jack Sanford, Philadelphia (P)
1952	Hank Sauer, Chicago (OF)	1958	Orlando Cepeda, San
1953	Roy Campanella, Brooklyn (C)		Francisco (1B)
1954	Willie Mays, New York (OF)	1959	Willie McCovey, San Francisco (1B)
1955	Roy Campanella, Brooklyn (C)	1960	Frank Howard, Los Angeles (OF)
1956	Don Newcombe, Brooklyn (P)	1961	Billy Williams, Chicago (OF)
1957	Henry Aaron, Milwaukee (OF)	1962	Ken Hubbs, Chicago (2B)
1958	Ernie Banks, Chicago (SS)	1963	Pete Rose, Cincinnati (2B)
1959	Ernie Banks, Chicago (SS)	1964	Richie Allen, Philadelphia (3B)
1960	Dick Groat, Pittsburgh (SS)	1965	Jim Lefebvre, Los Angeles (2B)
1961	Frank Robinson, Cincinnati (OF)	1966	Tommy Helms, Cincinnati (2B)
1962	Maury Wills, Los Angeles (SS)	1967	Tom Seaver, New York (P)

* From 1931 on, selections were made by the Baseball Writers Association of America.

1968	Johnny Bench, Cincinnati (C)
1969	Ted Sizemore, Los Angeles (2B)
1970	Carl Morton, Montreal (P)
1971	Earl Williams, Atlanta (C)
1972	Jon Matlack, New York (P)
1973	Gary Matthews, San Francisco (OF)

1974	Bake Mcbride, St. Louis (OF)
1975	John Montefusco, San Francisco (P)
1976	Pat Zachry, Cincinnati (P)
(tie)	Butch Metzger, San Diego (P)
1977	Andrew Dawson, Montreal (OF)
1978	Bob Horner, Atlanta (3B)

Cy Young Award Winners (one selection 1956–66)

1956	Don Newcombe, Brooklyn
1957	Warren Spahn, Milwaukee
1960	Vernon Law, Pittsburgh
1962	Don Drysdale, Los Angeles
1963	Sandy Koufax, Los Angeles
1965	Sandy Koufax, Los Angeles
1966	Sandy Koufax, Los Angeles
1967	Mike McCormick, San Francisco
1968	Bob Gibson, St. Louis
1969	Tom Seaver, New York

1970	Bob Gibson, St. Louis
1971	Ferguson Jenkins, Chicago
1972	Steve Carlton, Philadelphia
1973	Tom Seaver, New York
1975	Mike Marshall, Los Angeles
1975	Tom Seaver, New York
1976	Randy Jones, San Diego
1977	Steve Carlton, Philadelphia
1978	Gaylord Perry, San Diego

National League Batting Champions

1876	Roscoe Barnes, Chicago	.403
1877	James White, Boston	.385
1878	Abner Dalrymple, Milwaukee	.356
1879	Cap Anson, Chicago	.407
1880	George Gore, Chicago	.365
1881	Cap Anson, Chicago	.399
1882	Dan Brouthers, Buffalo	.367
1883	Dan Brouthers, Buffalo	.371
1884	Jim O'Rourke, Buffalo	.350
1885	Roger Connor, New York	.371
1886	Mike Kelly, Chicago	.388
1887	Cap Anson, Chicago	.421
1888	Cap Anson, Chicago	.343
1889	Dan Brouthers, Boston	.373
1890	Jack Glasscock, New York	.336
1891	Billy Hamilton, Philadelphia	.338
1892	"Cupid" Childs, Cleveland	.335
1892	Dan Brouthers, Brooklyn	.335
1893	Hugh Duffy, Boston	.378
1894	Hugh Duffy, Boston	.438
1895	Jesse Burkett, Cleveland	.423
1896	Jesse Burkett, Cleveland	.410
1897	Willie Keeler, Baltimore	.432
1898	Willie Keeler, Baltimore	.379
1899	Ed Delahanty, Philadelphia	.408
1900	Hans Wagner, Pittsburgh	.380
1901	Jesse Burkett, St. Louis	.382

1902	C.H. Beaumont, Pittsburgh	.357
1903	Hans Wagner, Pittsburgh	.355
1904	Hans Wagner, Pittsburgh	.349
1905	J. Bentley Seymour, Cincinnati	.377
1906	Hans Wagner, Pittsburgh	.339
1907	Hans Wagner, Pittsburgh	.350
1908	Hans Wagner, Pittsburgh	.354
1909	Hans Wagner, Pittsburgh	.339
1910	Sherwood Magee, Philadelphia	.331
1911	Hans Wagner, Pittsburgh	.334
1912	Heinie Zimmerman, Chicago	.372
1913	Jake Daubert, Brooklyn	.350
1914	Jake Daubert, Brooklyn	.329
1915	Larry Doyle, New York	.320
1916	Hal Chase, Cincinnati	.339
1917	Edd Roush, Cincinnati	.341
1918	Zack Wheat, Brooklyn	.335
1919	Edd Roush, Cincinnati	.321
1920	Rogers Hornsby, St. Louis	.370
1921	Rogers Hornsby, St. Louis	.397
1922	Rogers Hornsby, St. Louis	.401
1923	Rogers Hornsby, St. Louis	.384
1924	Rogers Hornsby, St. Louis	.424
1925	Rogers Hornsby, St. Louis	.403
1926	Bubbles Hargrave, Cincinnati	.353
1927	Paul Waner, Pittsburgh	.380
1928	Rogers Hornsby, Boston	.387

1929	Lefty O'Doul, Philadelphia	.398
1930	Bill Terry, New York	.401
1931	Chick Hafey, St. Louis	.349
1932	Lefty O'Doul, Brooklyn	.368
1933	Chuck Klein, Philadelphia	.368
1934	Paul Waner, Pittsburgh	.362
1935	Arky Vaughn, Pittsburgh	.385
1936	Paul Waner, Pittsburgh	.373
1937	Joe Medwick, St. Louis	.374
1938	Ernie Lombardi, Cincinnati	.342
1939	Johnny Mize, St. Louis	.349
1940	Debs Garms, Pittsburgh	.355
1941	Pete Reiser, Brooklyn	.343
1942	Ernie Lombardi, Boston	.330
1943	Stan Musial, St. Louis	.357
1944	Dixie Walker, Brooklyn	.357
1945	Phil Cavarretta, Chicago	.355
1946	Stan Musial, St. Louis	.365
1947	Harry Walker, St. Louis-Philadelphia	.363
1948	Stan Musial, St. Louis	.376
1949	Jackie Robinson, Brooklyn	.342
1950	Stan Musial, St. Louis	.346
1951	Stan Musial, St. Louis	.355
1952	Stan Musial, St. Louis	.336
1953	Carl Furillo, Brooklyn	.344
1954	Willie Mays, New York	.345
1955	Richie Ashburn, Philadelphia	.338
1956	Hank Aaron, Milwaukee	.328
1957	Stan Musial, St. Louis	.351
1958	Richie Ashburn, Philadelphia	.350
1959	Hank Aaron, Milwaukee	.355
1960	Dick Groat, Pittsburgh	.325
1961	Roberto Clemente, Pittsburgh	.351
1962	Tommy Davis, Los Angeles	.346
1963	Tommy Davis, Los Angeles	.326
1964	Roberto Clemente, Pittsburgh	.339
1965	Roberto Clemente, Pittsburgh	.329
1966	Matty Alou, Pittsburgh	.342
1967	Roberto Clemente, Pittsburgh	.357
1968	Pete Rose, Cincinnati	.335
1969	Pete Rose, Cincinnati	.348
1970	Rico Carty, Atlanta	.366
1971	Joe Torre, St. Louis	.363
1972	Billy Williams, Chicago	.333
1973	Pete Rose, Cincinnati	.338
1974	Ralph Garr, Atlanta	.353
1975	Bill Madlock, Chicago	.354
1976	Bill Madlock, Chicago	.339
1977	Dave Parker, Pittsburgh	.338
1978	Dave Parker, Pittsburgh	.334

National League Home Run Champions

1900	Herman Long, Boston	12
1901	Sam Crawford, Cincinnati	16
1902	Tom Leach, Pittsburgh	6
1903	Jim Sheckard, Brooklyn	9
1904	Harry Lumley, Brooklyn	9
1905	Fred Odwell, Cincinnati	9
1906	Tim Jordan, Brooklyn	12
1907	Dave Brain, Boston	10
1908	Tim Jordan, Brooklyn	12
1909	Jim Murray, New York	7
1910	Fred Beck, Boston	10
	Frank Schulte, Chicago	10
1911	Frank Schulte, Chicago	21
1912	Heinie Zimmerman, Chicago	14
1913	Gavvy Cravath, Philadelphia	19
1914	Gavvy Cravath, Philadelphia	19
1915	Gavvy Cravat, Philadelphia	24
1916	Dave Robertson, New York	12
	Cy Williams, Chicago	12
1917	Gavvy Cravath, Philadelphia	12
	Dave Robertson, New York	12
1918	Gavvy Cravath, Philadelphia	8
1919	Gavvy Cravath, Philadelphia	12
1920	Cy Williams, Philadelphia	15
1921	George Kelly, New York	23
1922	Rogers Hornsby, St. Louis	42
1923	Cy Williams, Philadelphia	41
1924	Jack Fournier, Brooklyn	27
1925	Rogers Hornsby, St. Louis	39
1926	Hack Wilson, Chicago	21
1927	Cy Williams, Philadelphia	30
	Hack Wilson, Chicago	30
1928	Jim Bottomley, St. Louis	31
	Hack Wilson, Chicago	31

1929	Chuck Klein, Philadelphia	43
1930	Hack Wilson, Chicago	56
1931	Chuck Klein, Philadelphia	31
1932	Chuck Klein, Philadelphia	38
	Mel Ott, New York	38
1933	Chuck Klein, Philadelphia	28
1934	Rip Collins, St. Louis	35
	Mel Ott, New York	35
1935	Wally Berger, Boston	34
1936	Mel Ott, New York	33
1937	Joe Medwick, St. Louis	31
	Mel Ott, New York	31
1938	Mel Ott, New York	36
1939	Johnny Mize, St. Louis	28
1940	Johnny Mize, St. Louis	43
1941	Adolf Camilli, Brooklyn	34
1942	Mel Ott, New York	30
1943	Bill Nicholson, Chicago	29
1944	Bill Nicholson, Chicago	33
1945	Tom Holmes, Boston	28
1946	Ralph Kiner, Pittsburgh	23
1947	Ralph Kiner, Pittsburgh	51
	Johnny Mize, New York	51
1948	Ralph Kiner, Pittsburgh	40
	Johnny Mize, New York	40
1949	Ralph Kiner, Pittsburgh	54
1950	Ralph Kiner, Pittsburgh	47
1951	Ralph Kiner, Pittsburgh	42
1952	Ralph Kiner, Pittsburgh	37
	Hank Sauer. Chicago	37
1953	Eddie Mathews, Milwaukee	47
1954	Ted Kluszewski, Cincinnati	49
1955	Willie Mays, New York	51
1956	Duke Snider, Brooklyn	43
1957	Hank Aaron, Milwaukee	44
1958	Ernie Banks, Chicago	47
1959	Eddie Mathews, Milwaukee	46
1960	Ernie Banks, Chicago	41
1961	Orlando Cepeda, San Francisco	46
1962	Willie Mays, San Francisco	49
1963	Hank Aaron, Milwaukee	44
	Willie McCovey, San Francisco	44
1964	Willie Mays, San Francisco	47
1965	Willie Mays, San Francisco	52
1966	Hank Aaron, Atlanta	44
1967	Hank Aaron, Atlanta	39
1968	Willie McCovey, San Francisco	36
1969	Willie McCovey, San Francisco	45
1970	Johnny Bench, Cincinnati	45
1971	Willie Stargell, Pittsburgh	48
1972	Johnny Bench, Cincinnati	40
1973	Willie Stargell, Pittsburgh	44
1974	Mike Schmidt, Philadelphia	36
1975	Mike Schmidt, Philadelphia	38
1976	Mike Schmidt, Philadelphia	38
1977	George Foster, Cincinnati	52
1978	George Foster, Cincinnati	40

Prior to the 1931 season a batted ball that bounced into the stands was scored as a home run; it's now a ground-rule double.

NL Runs Batted in Leaders

1920	Rogers Hornsby, St. Louis	94
	George Kelly, New York	94
1921	Rogers Hornsby, St. Louis	126
1922	Rogers Hornsby, St. Louis	155
1923	Emil Meusel, New York	125
1924	George Kelly, New York	136
1925	Rogers Hornsby, St. Louis	143
1926	Jim Bottomley, St. Louis	120
1927	Paul Waner, Pittsburgh	131
1928	Jim Bottomley, St. Louis	136
1929	Hack Wilson, Chicago	159
1930	Hack Wilson, Chicago	190
1931	Chuck Klein, Philadelphia	121
1932	Frank Hurst, Philadelphia	143
1933	Chuck Klein, Philadelphia	120
1934	Mel Ott, New York	135
1935	Wally Berger, Boston	130
1936	Joe Medwick, St. Louis	138
1937	Joe Medwick, St. Louis	154
1938	Joe Medwick, St. Louis	122
1939	Frank McCormick, Cincinnati	128
1940	Johnny Mize, St. Louis	137
1941	Adolf Camilli, Brooklyn	120
1942	Johnny Mize, New York	110

1943	Bill Nicholson, Chicago	128
1944	Bill Nicholson, Chicago	122
1945	Dixie Walker, Brooklyn	124
1946	Enos Slaughter, St. Louis	130
1947	Johnny Mize, New York	138
1948	Stan Musial, St. Louis	131
1949	Ralph Kiner, Pittsburgh	127
1950	Del Ennis, Philadelphia	126
1951	Monte Irvin, New York	121
1952	Hank Sauer, Chicago	121
1953	Roy Campanella, Brooklyn	142
1954	Ted Kluszewski, Cincinnati	141
1955	Duke Snider, Brooklyn	136
1956	Stan Musial, St. Louis	109
1957	Hank Aaron, Milwaukee	132
1958	Ernie Banks, Chicago	129
1959	Ernie Banks, Chicago	143
1960	Hank Aaron, Milwaukee	126
1961	Orlando Cepeda, San Francisco	142
1962	Tommy Davis, Los Angeles	153
1963	Hank Aaron, Milwaukee	130
1964	Ken Boyer, St. Louis	119
1965	Deron Johnson, Cincinnati	130
1966	Hank Aaron, Atlanta	127
1967	Orlando Cepeda, St. Louis	111
1968	Willie McCovey, San Francisco	105
1969	Willie McCovey, San Francisco	126
1970	Johnny Bench, Cincinnati	148
1971	Joe Torre, St. Louis	137
1972	Johnny Bench, Cincinnati	125
1973	Willie Stargell, Pittsburgh	119
1974	Johnny Bench, Cincinnati	129
1975	Greg Luzinski, Philadelphia	120
1976	George Foster, Cincinnati	121
1977	George Foster, Cincinnati	149
1978	George Foster, Cincinnati	120

NL Stolen Base Leaders

1900	Jim Barrett, Cincinnati	46
1901	Honus Wagner, Pittsburgh	48
1902	Honus Wagner, Pittsburgh	43
1903	Frank Chance, Chicago	67
	Jim Sheckard, Brooklyn	67
1904	Honus Wagner	53
1905	Art Devlin, New York	59
	Bill Maloney, Chicago	59
1906	Frank Chance, Chicago	57
1907	Honus Wagner, Pittsburgh	61
1908	Honus Wagner, Pittsburgh	53
1909	Bob Bescher, Cincinnati	54
1910	Bob Bescher, Cincinnati	70
1911	Bob Bescher, Cincinnati	80
1912	Bob Bescher, Cincinnati	67
1913	Max Carey, Pittsburgh	61
1914	George Burns, New York	62

1915	Max Carey, Pittsburgh	36	1947	Jackie Robinson, Brooklyn	29
1916	Max Carey, Pittsburgh	63	1948	Richie Ashburn, Philadelphia	32
1917	Max Carey, Pittsburgh	46	1949	Jackie Robinson, Brooklyn	37
1918	Max Carey, Pittsburgh	58	1950	Sam Jethroe, Boston	35
1919	George Burns, New York	40	1951	Sam Jethroe, Boston	35
1920	Max Carey, Pittsburgh	52	1952	Pee Wee Reese, Brooklyn	30
1921	Frank Frisch, New York	49	1953	Bill Bruton, Milwaukee	26
1922	Max Carey, Pittsburgh	51	1954	Bill Bruton, Milwaukee	34
1923	Max Carey, Pittsburgh	51	1955	Bill Bruton, Milwaukee	25
1924	Max Carey, Pittsburgh	49	1956	Willie Mays, New York	40
1925	Max Carey, Pittsburgh	46	1957	Willie Mays, New York	38
1926	Kiki Cuyler, Pittsburgh	35	1958	Willie Mays, San Francisco	31
1927	Frank Frisch, St. Louis	48	1959	Willie Mays, San Francisco	27
1928	Kiki Cuyler, Chicago	37	1960	Maury Wills, Los Angeles	50
1929	Kiki Cuyler, Chicago	43	1961	Maury Wills, Los Angeles	35
1930	Kiki Cuyler, Chicago	37	1962	Maury Wills, Los Angeles	104
1931	Frank Frisch, St. Louis	28	1963	Maury Wills, Los Angeles	40
1932	Chuck Klein, Philadelphia	20	1964	Maury Wills, Los Angeles	53
1933	Pepper Martin, St. Louis	26	1965	Maury Wills, Los Angeles	94
1934	Pepper Martin, St. Louis	23	1966	Lou Brock, St. Louis	74
1935	Augie Galan, Chicago	22	1967	Lou Brock, St. Louis	52
1936	Pepper Martin, St. Louis	23	1968	Lou Brock, St. Louis	62
1937	Augie Galan, Chicago	23	1969	Lou Brock, St. Louis	53
1938	Stan Hack, Chicago	16	1970	Bob Tolan, Cincinnati	57
1939	Stan Hack, Chicago	17	1971	Lou Brock, St. Louis	64
	Lee Handley, Pittsburgh	17	1972	Lou Brock, St. Louis	63
1940	Lonny Frey, Cincinnati	22	1973	Lou Brock, St. Louis	70
1941	Dan Murtaugh, Philadelphia	18	1974	Lou Brock, St. Louis	118
1942	Pete Reiser, Brooklyn	20	1975	Dave Lopes, Los Angeles	77
1943	Arky Vaughan, Brooklyn	20	1976	Dave Lopes, Los Angeles	63
1944	John Barrett, Pittsburgh	28	1977	Frank Taveras, Pittsburgh	70
1945	Red Schoendienst, St. Louis	26	1978	Omar Moreno, Pittsburgh	71
1946	Pete Reiser, Brooklyn	34			

35 or More Home Runs—Season

Total Homers	Player and Club	Year			
56	Hack Wilson, Chicago	1930	49	Willie Mays, San Francisco	1962
54	Ralph Kiner, Pittsburgh	1949	48	Willie Stargell, Pittsburgh	1971
52	Willie Mays, San Francisco	1965	47	Ralph Kiner, Pittsburgh	1950
52	George Foster, Cincinnati	1977	47	Ernie Banks, Chicago	1958
51	Ralph Kiner, Pittsburgh	1947	47	Willie Mays, San Francisco	1964
51	Johnny Mize, New York	1947	47	Hank Aaron, Atlanta	1971
51	Willie Mays, New York	1955	46	Ed Mathews, Milwaukee	1959
49	Ted Kluszewski, Cincinnati	1954	46	Orlando Cepeda, San Francisco	1961

45	Ernie Banks, Chicago	1959
45	Hank Aaron, Milwaukee	1962
45	Willie McCovey, San Francisco	1969
45	Johnny Bench, Cincinnati	1970
44	Hank Aaron, Milwaukee	1957, 1963
	Atlanta	1966, 1969
44	Ernie Banks, Chicago	1955
44	Willie McCovey, San Francisco	1963
44	Willie Stargell, Pittsburgh	1973
43	Chuck Klein, Philadelphia	1929
43	Johnny Mize, St. Louis	1940
43	Duke Snider, Brooklyn	1956
43	Ernie Banks, Chicago	1957
43	Dave Johnson, Atlanta	1973
42	Rogers Hornsby, St. Louis	1922
42	Mel Ott, New York	1929
42	Ralph Kiner, Pittsburgh	1951
42	Duke Snider, Brooklyn	1953, 1955
42	Gil Hodges, Brooklyn	1954
42	Billy Williams, Chicago	1970
41	Fred Williams, Philadelphia	1923
41	Roy Campanella, Brooklyn	1953
41	Willie Mays, New York	1954
41	Hank Sauer, Chicago	1954
41	Ed Mathews, Milwaukee	1955
41	Ernie Banks, Chicago	1960
41	Darrell Evans, Atlanta	1973
41	Jeff Burroughs, Atlanta	1977
40	Rogers Hornsby, Chicago	1929
40	Chuck Klein, Philadelphia	1930
40	Ralph Kiner, Pittsburgh	1948
40	Johnny Mize, New York	1948
40	Gil Hodges, Brooklyn	1951
40	Ted Kluszewski, Cincinnati	1953
40	Ed Mathews, Milwaukee	1954
40	Duke Snider, Brooklyn	1954, 1957
40	Wally Post, Cincinnati	1955
40	Hank Aaron, Milwaukee	1960
	Atlanta	1973
40	Willie Mays, San Francisco	1961
40	Richie Allen, Philadelphia	1966
40	Tony Perez, Cincinnati	1970
40	Johnny Bench, Cincinnati	1972
40	George Foster, Cincinnati	1978
39	Rogers Hornsby, St. Louis	1925
39	Hack Wilson, Chicago	1929
39	Stan Musial, St. Louis	1948

39	Hank Aaron, Milwaukee	1959
	Atlanta	1967
39	Ed Mathews, Milwaukee	1960
39	Frank Robinson, Cincinnati	1962
39	Willie McCovey, San Francisco	1965, 1970
39	Lee May, Cincinnati	1971
39	Bobby Bonds, San Francisco	1973
39	Wally Berger, Boston	1930
39	Greg Luzinski, Philadelphia	1977
38	Mel Ott, New York	1932
38	Chuck Klein, Philadelphia	1932
38	Joe Adcock, Milwaukee	1956
38	Frank Robinson, Cincinnati	1956
38	Willie Mays, San Francisco	1963
38	Lee May, Cincinnati	1969
38	Hank Aaron, Atlanta	1970
38	Nate Colbert, San Diego	1970, 1972
38	Mike Schmidt, Philadelphia	1975, '76, '77
37	Gabby Hartnett, Chicago	1930
37	Ralph Kiner, Pittsburgh	1952
37	Hank Sauer, Chicago	1952
37	Ed Mathews, Milwaukee	1956
37	Frank Robinson, Cincinnati	1961
37	Ernie Banks, Chicago	1962
37	Willie Mays, San Francisco	1966
37	Jim Wynn, Houston	1967
37	Tony Perez, Cincinnati	1969
37	Billy Williams, Chicago	1972
37	Dave Kingman, New York	1976
36	Mel Ott, New York	1938
36	Willard Marshall, New York	1947
36	Stan Musial, St. Louis	1949
36	Andy Pafko, Chicago	1950
36	Willie Mays, New York	1956
36	Wally Post, Cincinnati	1956
36	Frank Robinson, Cincinnati	1959
36	Willie McCovey, San Francisco	1966, 1968
36	Joe Torre, Atlanta	1966
36	Mike Schmidt, Philadelphia	1974
36	Dave Kingman, New York	1975
35	Babe Herman, Brooklyn	1930
35	Rip Collins, St. Louis	1934
35	Mel Ott, New York	1934
35	Walker Cooper, New York	1947

35	Hank Sauer, Cincinnati	1948	35	Frank Thomas, Pittsburgh	1958
35	Ralph Kiner, Pittsburgh-Chicago	1953	35	Joe Adcock, Milwaukee	1961
35	Stan Musial, St. Louis	1954	35	Dick Stuart, Pittsburgh	1961
35	Ted Kluszewski, Cincinnati	1956	35	Orlando Cepeda, San Francisco	1962
35	Willie Mays, New York	1957			

The Dodgers boasted the first quartet of 30-homer hitters in 1977 with Dusty Baker (30), left, seated; Roy Cey (30), right, seated; Steve Garvey (33), left, standing; and Reggie Smith (32), right, standing. *(Los Angeles Dodgers photo)*

20 Game Winners (Since 1901)

1901	
Bill Donovan, Dodgers	25-15
Deacon Phillippe, Pirates	22-12
Noodles Hahn, Reds	22-19
Jack Chesbro, Pirates	21- 9
John Powell, Cards	21-20
Charles Harper, Cards	20-12
Al Orth, Phillies	20-12
Frank Donahue, Phillies	20-13
Charles Nichols, Braves	20-14
Christy Mathewson, Giants	20-17

1902	
Jack Chesbro, Pirates	28- 6
Charles Pittinger, Braves	27-14
Vic Willis, Braves	27-19
Noodles Hahn, Reds	22-12
Jack Taylor, Cubs	22-10
* Joe McGinnity, Balt.-Giants	21-18
Jess Tannehill, Pirates	20- 6
Deacon Phillippe, Pirates	20- 9

1903	
Joe McGinnity, Giants	31-20
Christy Mathewson, Giants	30-13
Sam Leever, Pirates	25- 7
Deacon Phillippe, Pirates	25- 9
Noodles Hahn, Reds	22-12
Henry Schmidt, Dodgers	22-13
Jack Taylor, Cubs	21-14
Jake Weimer, Cubs	20- 8
Bob Wicker, Cubs	20- 9

1904	
Joe McGinnity, Giants	35- 8
Christy Mathewson, Giants	33-12
Charles Harper, Reds	23- 9
Charles Nichols, Cards	21-13
Luther Taylor, Giants	21-15
Jake Weimer, Cubs	20-14
Jack Taylor, Cards	20-19

1905	
Christy Mathewson, Giants	31- 9
Charles Pittinger, Phillies	23-14
Leon Ames, Giants	22- 8
Joe McGinnity, Giants	21-15
Sam Leever, Pirates	20- 5
Bob Ewing, Reds	20-11
Deacon Phillippe, Pirates	20-13
Irving Young, Braves	20-21

1906	
Joe McGinnity, Giants	27-12
Mordecai Brown, Cubs	26- 6
Vic Willis, Pirates	23-13
Sam Leever, Pirates	22- 7
Christy Mathewson, Giants	22-12
John Pfiester, Cubs	20- 8
Jack Taylor, Cards-Cubs	20-12
Jake Weimer, Reds	20-14

1907	
Christy Mathewson, Giants	24-12
Orval Overall, Cubs	23- 8
Frank Sparks, Phillies	22- 8
Vic Willis, Pirates	21-11
Mordecai Brown, Cubs	20- 6
Al Leifield, Pirates	20-16

1908	
Christy Mathewson, Giants	37-11
Mordecai Brown, Cubs	29- 9
Ed Reulbach, Cubs	24- 7
Nick Maddox, Pirates	23- 8
Vic Willis, Pirates	23-11
George Wiltse, Giants	23-14
George McQuillan, Phillies	23-17

1909	
Mordecai Brown, Cubs	27- 9
Christy Mathewson, Giants	25- 6
Howard Camnitz, Pirates	25- 6
Vic Willis, Pirates	22-11
Orval Overall, Cubs	20-11
George Wiltse, Giants	20-11

1910	
Christy Mathewson, Giants	27- 9
Mordecai Brown, Cubs	25-14
Earl Moore, Phillies	22-15
Leonard Cole, Cubs	20- 4
George Suggs, Reds	20-12

1911

Grover Alexander, Phillies	28-13
Christy Mathewson, Giants	26-13
Rube Marquard, Giants	24- 7
Bob Harmon, Cards	23-16
Babe Adams, Pirates	22-12
Nap Rucker, Dodgers	22-18
Mordecai Brown, Cubs	21-11
Howard Camnitz, Pirates	20-15

1912

Larry Cheney, Cubs	26-10
Rube Marquard, Giants	26-11
Claude Hendrix, Pirates	24- 9
Christy Mathewson, Giants	23-12
Howard Camnitz, Pirates	22-12

1913

Tom Seaton, Phillies	27-12
Christy Mathewson, Giants	25-11
Rube Marquard, Giants	23-10
Grover Alexander, Phillies	22- 8
Jeff Tesreau, Giants	22-13
Babe Adams, Pirates	21-10
Larry Cheney, Cubs	21-14

1914

Dick Rudolph, Braves	27-10
Grover Alexander, Phillies	27-15
Bill James, Braves	26- 7
Jeff Tesreau, Giants	26-10
Christy Mathewson, Giants	24-13
Ed Pfeffer, Dodgers	23-12
Jim Vaughn, Cubs	21-13
Erskine Mayer, Phillies	21-19
Larry Cheney, Cubs	20-18

1915

Grover Alexander, Phillies	31-10
Dick Rudolph, Braves	22-19
Al Mamaux, Pirates	21- 8
Erskine Mayer, Phillies	21-15
Jim Vaughn, Cubs	20-12

1916

Grover Alexander, Phillies	33-12
Ed Pfeffer, Dodgers	25-11
Eppa Rixey, Phillies	22-10
Al Mamaux, Pirates	21-15

1917

Grover Alexander, Phillies	30-13
Fred Toney, Reds	24-16
Jim Vaughn, Cubs	23-13
Ferdie Schupp, Giants	21- 7
Pete Schneider, Reds	20-19

1918

Jim Vaughn, Cubs	22-10
Claude Hendrix, Cubs	20- 7

1919

Jess Barnes, Giants	25- 9
Slim Sallee, Reds	21- 7
Jim Vaughn, Cubs	21-14

1920

Grover Alexander, Cubs	27-14
Wilbur Cooper, Pirates	24-15
Burleigh Grimes, Dodgers	23-11
Fred Toney, Giants	21-11
Art Nehf, Giants	21-12
Jess Barnes, Giants	20-15
Bill Doak, Cards	20-12

1921

Burleigh Grimes, Dodgers	22-13
Wilbur Cooper, Pirates	22-14
Art Nehf, Giants	20-10
Joe Oeschger, Braves	20-14

1922

Eppa Rixey, Reds	25-13
Wilbur Cooper, Pirates	23-14
Dutch Ruether, Dodgers	21-12

1923

Adolfo Luque, Reds	27- 8
John Morrison, Pirates	25-13
Grover Alexander, Cubs	22-12
Pete Donohue, Reds	21-15
Burleigh Grimes, Dodgers	21-18
Jesse Haines, Cards	20-13
Eppa Rixey, Reds	20-15

1924

Dazzy Vance, Dodgers	28- 6
Burleigh Grimes, Dodgers	22-13
Carl Mays, Reds	20- 9
Wilbur Cooper, Pirates	20-14

1925	
Dazzy Vance, Dodgers	22- 9
Eppa Rixey, Reds	21-11
Pete Donohue, Reds	21-14

1926	
Remy Kremer, Pirates	20- 6
Flint Rhem, Cards	20- 7
Lee Meadows, Pirates	20- 9
Pete Donohue, Reds	20-14

1927	
Charles Root, Cubs	26-15
Jesse Haines, Cards	24-10
Carmen Hill, Pirates	22-11
Grover Alexander, Cards	21-10

1928	
Larry Benton, Giants	25- 9
Burleigh Grimes, Pirates	25-14
Dazzy Vance, Dodgers	22-10
Bill Sherdel, Cards	21-10
Jesse Haines, Cards	20- 8
Fred Fitzsimmons, Giants	20- 9

1929	
Pat Malone, Cubs	22-10

1930	
Pat Malone, Cubs	20- 9
Remy Kremer, Pirates	20-12

1931	
—None	

1932	
Lon Warneke, Cubs	22- 6
Watson Clark, Dodgers	20-12

1933	
Carl Hubbell, Giants	23-12
Guy Bush, Cubs	20-12
Ben Cantwell, Braves	20-10
Dizzy Dean, Cards	20-18

1934	
Dizzy Dean, Cards	30- 7
Hal Schumacher, Giants	23-10
Lon Warneke, Cubs	22-10
Carl Hubbell, Giants	21-12

1935	
Dizzy Dean, Cards	28-12
Carl Hubbell, Giants	23-12
Paul Derringer, Reds	22-13
Bill Lee, Cubs	20- 6
Lon Warneke, Cubs	20-13

1936	
Carl Hubbell, Giants	26- 6
Dizzy Dean, Cards	24-13

1937	
Carl Hubbell, Giants	22- 8
Cliff Melton, Giants	20- 9
Lou Fette, Braves	20-10
Jim Turner, Braves	20-11

1938	
Bill Lee, Cubs	22- 9
Paul Derringer, Reds	21-14

1939	
Bucky Walters, Reds	27-11
Paul Derringer, Reds	25- 7
Curt Davis, Cards	22-16
Luke Hamlin, Dodgers	20-13

1940	
Bucky Walters, Reds	22-10
Paul Derringer, Reds	20-12
Claude Passeau, Cubs	20-13

1941	
J. Whitlow Wyatt, Dodgers	22-10
Kirby Higbe, Dodgers	22- 9

1942	
Mort Cooper, Cards	22- 7
John Beazley, Cards	21- 6

1943	
Mort Cooper, Cards	21- 8
Truett Sewell, Pirates	21- 9
Elmer Riddle, Reds	21-11

1944	
Bucky Walters, Reds	23- 8
Mort Cooper, Cards	22- 7
Truett Sewell, Pirates	21-12
Bill Voiselle, Giants	21-16

1945	
Chas. Barrett, Braves-Cards	23-12
Hank Wyse, Cubs	22-10
† Hank Borowy, Yanks-Cubs	21- 7

1946	
** Howard Pollet, Cards	21-10
Johnny Sain, Braves	20-14

1947	
Ewell Blackwell, Reds	22- 8
Larry Jansen, Giants	21- 5
Warren Spahn, Braves	21-10
Johnny Sain, Braves	21-12
Ralph Branca, Dodgers	21-12

1948	
Johnny Sain, Braves	24-15
Harry Brecheen, Cards	20- 7

1949	
Warren Spahn, Braves	21-14
Howard Pollett, Cards	20- 9

1950	
Warren Spahn, Braves	21-17
Robin Roberts, Phillies	20-11
Johnny Sain, Braves	20-13

1951	
Sal Maglie, Giants	23- 6
** Larry Jansen, Giants	23-11
Preacher Roe, Dodgers	22- 3
Warren Spahn, Braves	22-14
Robin Roberts, Phillies	21-15
Don Newcombe, Dodgers	20- 9
Murry Dickson, Pirates	20-16

1952	
Robin Roberts, Phillies	28- 7

1953	
Warren Spahn, Braves	23- 7
Robin Roberts, Phillies	23-16
Carl Erskine, Dodgers	20- 6
Harvey Haddix, Cards	20- 9

1954	
Robin Roberts, Phillies	23-15
John Antonelli, Giants	21- 7
Warren Spahn, Braves	21-12

1955	
Robin Roberts, Phillies	23-14
Don Newcombe, Dodgers	20- 5

1956	
Don Newcombe, Dodgers	27- 7
Warren Spahn, Braves	20-11
John Antonelli, Giants	20-13

1957	
Warren Spahn, Braves	21-11

1958	
Warren Spahn, Braves	22-11
Bob Friend, Pirates	22-14
Lou Burdette, Braves	20-10

1959	
Lou Burdette, Braves	21-15
Sam Jones, Giants	21-15
Warren Spahn, Braves	21-15

1960	
Ernie Broglio, Cardinals	21- 9
Warren Spahn, Braves	21-10
Vernon Law, Pirates	20- 9

1961	
Joey Jay, Reds	21-10
Warren Spahn, Braves	21-13

1962	
Don Drysdale, Dodgers	25- 9
Jack Sanford, Giants	24- 7
Bob Purkey, Reds	23- 5
Joey Jay, Reds	21-14

1963	
Sandy Koufax, Dodgers	25- 5
Juan Marichal, Giants	25- 8
Warren Spahn, Braves	23- 7
Jim Maloney, Reds	23- 7
Dick Ellsworth, Cubs	22-10

1964	
Larry Jackson, Cubs	24-11
Juan Marichal, Giants	21- 8
Ray Sadecki, Cards	20-11

1965	
Sandy Koufax, Dodgers	26- 8
Tony Cloninger, Braves	24-11
Don Drysdale, Dodgers	23-12
Sammy Ellis, Reds	22-10
Juan Marichal, Giants	22-13
Jim Maloney, Reds	20- 9
Bob Gibson, Cards	20-12

1966	
Sandy Koufax, Dodgers	27- 9
Juan Marichal, Giants	25- 6
Gaylord Perry, Giants	21- 8
Bob Gibson, Cards	21-12
Chris Short, Phillies	20-10

1967	
Mike McCormick, Giants	22-10
Fergie Jenkins, Cubs	20-13

1968	
Juan Marichal, Giants	26- 9
Bob Gibson, Cards	22- 9
Fergie Jenkins, Cubs	20-15

1969	
Tom Seaver, Mets	25- 7
Phil Niekro, Braves	23-13
Juan Marichal, Giants	21-11
Fergie Jenkins, Cubs	21-15
Bill Singer, Dodgers	20-12
Bob Gibson, Cards	20-13
Larry Dierker, Astros	20-13
Bill Hands, Cubs	20-14
Claude Osteen, Dodgers	20-15

1970	
Bob Gibson, Cards	23- 7
Gaylord Perry, Giants	23-13
Fergie Jenkins, Cubs	22-16
Jim Merritt, Reds	20-12

1971	
Fergie Jenkins, Cubs	24-13
Steve Carlton, Cards	20- 9
Al Downing, Dodgers	20- 9
Tom Seaver, Mets	20-10

1972	
Steve Carlton, Phillies	27-10
Tom Seaver, Mets	21-12
Claude Osteen, Dodgers	20-11
Fergie Jenkins, Cubs	20-12

1973	
Ron Bryant, Giants	24-12

1974	
Andy Messersmith, Dodgers	20- 6
Phil Niekro, Braves	20-13

1975	
Tom Seaver, Mets	22- 9
Randy Jones, Padres	20-12

1976	
Randy Jones, Padres	22-14
Jerry Koosman, Mets	21-10
Don Sutton, Dodgers	21-10
Steve Carlton, Phillies	20- 7
J.R. Richard, Astros	20-15

1977	
Steve Carlton, Phillies	23-10
Tom Seaver, Mets-Reds	21- 6
John Candelaria, Pirates	20- 5
Bob Forsch, Cardinals	20- 7
Tommy John, Dodgers	20- 7
Rick Reuschel, Cubs	20-10

1978	
Gaylord Perry, Padres	21- 6
Ross Grimsley, Expos	20-11

* Won 13 in A.L., 8 in N.L. (1902)   ** Includes playoff victory (1946, 1951)   † Won 10 in A.L., 11 in N.L. (1945)

Won and Lost Percentage (15 or More Decisions)

1901	Sam Leever, Pittsburgh	14-5	.774		1941	Elmer Riddle, Cincinnati	19-4	.826
1902	Jack Chesbro, Pittsburgh	28-6	.824		1942	Howie Krist, St. Louis	13-3	.813
1903	Sam Leever, Pittsburgh	25-7	.781		1943	Clyde Shoun, Cincinnati	14-5	.737
1904	Joe McGinnity, New York	35-8	.814			Whit Wyatt, Brooklyn	14-5	.737
1905	Sam Leever, Pittsburgh	20-5	.800		1944	Ted Wilks, St. Louis	17-4	.810
1906	Ed Ruelbach, Chicago	19-4	.826		1945	Harry Brecheen, St. Louis	15-4	.789
1907	Ed Ruelbach, Chicago	17-4	.810		1946	Schoolboy Rowe, Philadelphia	11-4	.733
1908	Ed Ruelbach, Chicago	24-7	.774		1947	Larry Jansen, New York	21-5	.808
1909	Howie Camnitz, Pittsburgh	25-6	.806		1948	Rip Sewell, Pittsburgh	13-3	.813
	Christy Mathewson, New York	25-6	.806		1949	Ralph Branca, Brooklyn	13-5	.722
1910	Deacon Phillippe, Pittsburgh	14-2	.875		1950	Sal Maglie, New York	18-4	.818
1911	Rube Marquard, New York	24-7	.774		1951	Preacher Roe, Brooklyn	22-3	.880
1912	Claude Hendrix, Pittsburgh	24-9	.727		1952	Hoyt Wilhelm, New York	15-3	.833
1913	Bert Humphries, Chicago	16-4	.800		1953	Carl Erskine, Brooklyn	20-6	.769
1914	Bill James, Boston	26-7	.788		1954	John Antonelli, New York	21-7	.750
1915	Grover Alexander, Philadelphia	31-10	.756			Hoyt Wilhelm, New York	12-4	.750
1916	Tom Hughes, Boston	16-3	.842		1955	Don Newcombe, Brooklyn	20-5	.800
1917	Ferdie Schupp, New York	21-7	.750		1956	Don Newcombe, Brooklyn	27-7	.794
1918	Claude Hendrix, Chicago	20-7	.741		1957	Bob Buhl, Milwaukee	18-7	.720
1919	Dutch Ruether, Cincinnati	19-6	.760		1958	Warren Spahn, Milwaukee	20-10	.667
1920	Burleigh Grimes, Brooklyn	23-11	.676			Lew Burdette, Milwaukee	20-10	.667
1921	Babe Adams, Pittsburgh	14-5	.737		1959	ElRoy Face, Pittsburgh	18-1	.947
	Whitey Glazner, Pittsburgh	14-5	.737		1960	Lindy McDaniel, St. Louis	12-4	.750
1922	Phil Douglas, New York	11-4	.733		1961	John Podres, Los Angeles	18-5	.783
1923	Dolf Luque, Cincinnati	27-8	.771		1962	Bob Purkey, Cincinnati	23-5	.821
1924	Emil Yde, Pittsburgh	16-3	.842		1963	Ron Perranoski, Los Angeles	16-3	.842
1925	Bill Sherdel, St. Louis	15-6	.714		1964	Sandy Koufax, Los Angeles	19-5	.792
1926	Ray Kremer, Pittsburgh	20-6	.769		1965	Sandy Koufax, Los Angeles	26-8	.765
1927	Larry Benton, New York	17-7	.708		1966	Phil Regan, Los Angeles	14-1	.933
1928	Larry Benton, New York	25-9	.735		1967	Nelson Briles, St. Louis	14-5	.737
1929	Charlie Root, Chicago	19-6	.760		1968	Steve Blass, Pittsburgh	18-6	.750
1930	Freddie Fitzsimmons, New York	19-7	.731		1969	Bob Moose, Pittsburgh	14-3	.824
1931	Jesse Haines, St. Louis	12-3	.800		1970	Wayne Simpson, Cincinnati	14-3	.824
1932	Lon Warneke, Chicago	22-6	.786		1971	Tug McGraw, New York	11-4	.733
1933	Bud Tinning, Chicago	13-6	.684		1972	Gary Nolan, Cincinnati	15-5	.750
1934	Dizzy Dean, St. Louis	30-7	.811		1973	George Stone, New York	12-3	.800
1935	Bill Lee, Chicago	20-6	.769		1974	Tommy John, Los Angeles	13-3	.813
1936	Carl Hubbell, New York	26-6	.813		1975	Al Hrabosky, St. Louis	13-3	.813
1937	Carl Hubbell, New York	22-8	.733		1976	Rick Rhoden, Los Angeles	12-3	.800
1938	Bill Lee, Chicago	22-9	.710		1977	John Candelaria, Pittsburgh	20-5	.800
1939	Paul Derringer, Cincinnati	25-7	.781		1978	Gaylord Perry, San Diego	21-6	.778
1940	Freddie Fitzsimmons, Brooklyn	16-2	.889					

Bibliography

Allen, Lee. *The National League Story.* New York: Hill and Wang, 1961.

Allen, Lee, and Meany, Tom. *Kings of the Diamond.* New York: Putnam, 1965.

Angell, Roger. *Five Seasons.* New York: Simon and Schuster, 1977.

Appel, Martin, and Goldblatt, Burt. *Baseball's Best.* New York: McGraw-Hill, 1976.

Barber, Red, and Creamer, Bob. *Rhubarb in the Catbird Seat.* New York: Double-day & Co., Inc., 1968.

A Baseball Century. New York: Rutledge Books, Macmillan Publishing Co., Inc., 1976.

The Baseball Encyclopedia. New York: Macmillan Publishing Co., Inc., 1976.

Book of Baseball Records. Edited and published by Seymour Siwoff, 1978.

Creamer, Robert. *Babe.* New York: Simon and Schuster, 1974.

Cohen, Richard M.; Deutsch, Jordan A.; Johnson, Roland T.; and Neft, David S. *The Sports Encyclopedia: Baseball.* New York: Grosset and Dunlap, 1974.

Dickey, Glenn. *The Great No-Hitters.* Radnor, Pa.: Chilton Book Co., 1976.

Durocher, Leo, and Linn, Ed. *Nice Guys Finish Last.* New York: Simon and Schuster, 1975.

Enright, Jim. *The Chicago Cubs.* New York: Rutledge Books, Macmillan Publishing Co., Inc., 1975.

Flood, Curt, and Carter, Richard. *The Way It Is.* New York: Trident Press, 1971.

Hertzel, Bob. *The Big Red Machine.* Englewood Cliffs, N.J.: Prentice-Hall, 1976.

Holmes, Tommy. *The Dodgers.* New York: Rutledge Books, Macmillan Publishing Co., Inc., 1975.

Hood, Robert. *The Gashouse Gang.* New York: William Morrow Co., Inc., 1975.

Kahn, Roger. *A Season in the Sun.* New York: Harper & Row, 1977.

Kahn, Roger. *The Boys of Summer.* New York: Harper & Row, 1973.

Koufax, Sandy, and Linn, Ed. *Koufax.* New York: Viking Press, 1966.

Mathewson, Christy. *Pitching in a Pinch.* New York: Stein and Day Publishers, 1977.

Meany, Tom. *Baseball's Greatest Teams.* Cranbury, N.J.: A. S. Barnes & Co., Inc., 1951.

Meany, Tom. *Baseball's Greatest Pitchers.* Cranbury, N.J.: A. S. Barnes & Co., Inc., 1951.

Musick, Phil. *Who Was Roberto: A Bibliography of Roberto Clemente.* New York: Doubleday & Co., Inc., 1974.

Parrott, Harold. *The Lords of Baseball.* New York: Praeger Publishers, Inc., 1976.

Plimpton, George. *One for the Record: The Inside Story of Hank Aaron's Chase for the Home-Run Record.* New York: Harper & Row, 1974.

Reichler, Joe, ed. *The Game and the Glory.* Englewood Cliffs, N.J.: Prentice-Hall, 1976.

Reidenbaugh, Lowell. 100 Years of National League Baseball. *The Sporting News.* 1976.

Ritter, Lawrence S. *The Glory of their Times.* New York: Macmillan Publishing Co., Inc., 1971.

Robinson, Jackie, and Duckett, Alfred. *Breakthrough to the Big League: The Story of Jackie Robinson.* New York: Harper & Row, 1965.

Roseboro, John, and Libby, Bill. *Glory Days with the Dodgers: And Other Days with Others.* New York: Atheneum Publishers, 1978.

Rust, Art. Jr. *Get That Nigger Off the Field.* New York: Delacorte Press, Dell Publishing Co., Inc., 1976.

Shapiro, Milton. *The Hank Aaron Story.* New York: Julian Messner, 1961.

Smith, Robert. *Baseball.* New York: Simon and Schuster, 1970.

Index